Lecture Notes in Computer Science 8356

Commenced Publication in 1973
Founding and Former Series Editors:
Gerhard Goos, Juris Hartmanis, and Jan van Leeuwen

T0212824

Stephen Poole   Oscar Hernandez
Pavel Shamis (Eds.)

OpenSHMEM and Related Technologies

Experiences, Implementations, and Tools

First Workshop, OpenSHMEM 2014
Annapolis, MD, USA, March 4-6, 2014
Proceedings

 Springer

Volume Editors

Stephen Poole
Oscar Hernandez
Pavel Shamis
Oak Ridge National Laboratory
One Bethel Valley Road
P.O. Box 2008, MS-6164
Oak Ridge, TN 37831-6164, USA
E-mail: {spoole,oscar,shamisp}@ornl.gov

ISSN 0302-9743   e-ISSN 1611-3349
ISBN 978-3-319-05214-4   e-ISBN 978-3-319-05215-1
DOI 10.1007/978-3-319-05215-1
Springer Cham Heidelberg New York Dordrecht London

Library of Congress Control Number: 2014931857

CR Subject Classification (1998): D.2, C.2, F.3, D.4, H.4, F.2

LNCS Sublibrary: SL 2 – Programming and Software Engineering

Typesetting: Camera-ready by author, data conversion by Scientific Publishing Services, Chennai, India

Printed on acid-free paper

Springer is part of Springer Science+Business Media (www.springer.com)

Preface

OpenSHMEM is a modern derivative of the SGI SHMEM API, originally developed by Cray Research, Inc., for efficient programming of large-scale systems. Because of its strong following among users, the Extreme Scale Systems Center at Oak Ridge National Laboratory, together with the University of Houston, led the effort to standardize the API with the input from the vendors and user community. In 2012, version 1.0 was released and opened for comments or further revisions. The goal of OpenSHMEM is to make sure that OpenSHMEM applications are portable across OpenSHMEM implementations provided by multiple vendors, including SGI, Cray, IBM, Hewlett-Packard, Intel, and Mellanox Technologies.

OpenSHMEMis a communication library following the partitioned global address space (PGAS) programing model and providing one-sided communication semantics that enables decoupling of the data transfer from the synchronization of the communication source and target. Irregular communication patterns with small/medium-sized data transfers, in which data source and data target are not previously known, often benefit from a one-sided communication library such as OpenSHMEM because of its low-latency operations.

This first OpenSHMEM workshop that was open to the community, which will be part of a series of annual events, was dedicated to the promotion and advancement of parallel programming with the OpenSHMEM programming interface and to helping shape its future direction. The workshop is the premier venue for discussing and presenting the latest developments, implementation technology, tools, trends, recent research ideas, and results related to OpenSHMEM and its use in applications. As we move to Exascale, there are several areas in OpenSHMEM that we need to address to ensure that OpenSHMEM will work on future systems, including better scalability, resilience, I/O, multi-threading support, power and energy efficiency, locality, etc.

This year's workshop website at http://www.csm.ornl.gov/workshops/openshmem2013 contains information about the agenda. The program consisted of a keynote speaker, several invited talks and technical paper presentations from industry, academia, and national laboratories, as well as a panel session. These talks discussed the current state of OpenSHMEM, tools, and ideas for future extensions for OpenSHMEM based on future software and hardware trends. In addition, we held four tutorials: one on the OpenSHMEM API, one on accelerator programming with OpenACC/OpenMP and OpenSHMEM, one on OpenSHMEM tools and one on InfiniBand/Verbs programming. On the last day of the workshop we held a panel session where we summarized the results of the workshop and proposed roadmap for OpenSHMEM, with input from the community. This book contains 12 technical papers, and two short position papers that were presented at the OpenSHMEM workshop. All the papers were peered reviewed by three different members of the Program Committee.

March 2014   Steve Poole
                                                              Oscar Hernandez
                                                                Pavel Shamis

Organization

Program and Co-chairs

Oscar Hernandez
Pavel Shamis
Steve Poole

Tutorials Chair

Manjunath Venkata

Workshop Organizer

Jennifer Goodpasture

Program Committee

Barbara Chapman	University of Houston, USA
Steve Poole	Oak Ridge National Laboratory, USA
Tony Curtis	University of Houston, USA
Barney Maccabe	Oak Ridge National Laboratory, USA
Nick Park	Department of Defense, USA
Duncan Poole	NVIDIA, USA
Stephane Chauveau	CAPS Enterprise, France
Sameer Shende	University of Oregon, USA
Wolfang Nagel	TU-Dresden, Germany
Duncan Roweth	Cray Inc., USA
Gary Grider	Los Alamos National Laboratory, USA
Manjunath Venkata	Oak Ridge National Laboratory, USA
Gilad Shainer	Mellanox Technologies, USA
Matt Baker	Oak Ridge National Laboratory, USA
Laura Carrington	San Diego Supercomputing Center, USA
Monika ten Bruggencate	Cray, USA
George Bosilca	University of Tennessee, USA
Gregory Koenig	Oak Ridge National Laboratory, USA
Josh Lothian	Oak Ridge National Laboratory, USA
Chung-Hsing Hsu	Oak Ridge National Laboratory, USA

Table of Contents

OpenSHMEM Extensions and Future Directions

Designing a High Performance OpenSHMEM Implementation Using Universal Common Communication Substrate as a Communication Middleware

Pavel Shamis[1], Manjunath Gorentla Venkata[1], Stephen Poole[1], Aaron Welch[2], and Tony Curtis[2]

[1] Extreme Scale Systems Center (ESSC)
Oak Ridge National Laboratory (ORNL)
{shamisp,manjugv,spoole}@ornl.gov
[2] Computer Science Department
University of Houston (UH)
{dawelch,arcurtis}@uh.edu

Abstract. OpenSHMEM is an effort to standardize the well-known SHMEM parallel programming library. The project aims to produce an open-source and portable SHMEM API and is led by ORNL and UH. In this paper, we optimize the current OpenSHMEM reference implementation, based on GASNet, to achieve higher performance characteristics. To achieve these desired performance characteristics, we have redesigned an important component of the OpenSHMEM implementation, the network layer, to leverage a low-level communication library designed for implementing parallel programming models called UCCS. In particular, UCCS provides an interface and semantics such as native atomic operations and remote memory operations to better support PGAS programming models, including OpenSHMEM. Through the use of microbenchmarks, we evaluate this new OpenSHMEM implementation on various network metrics, including the latency of point-to-point and collective operations. Furthermore, we compare the performance of our OpenSHMEM implementation with the state-of-the-art SGI SHMEM. Our results show that the atomic operations of our OpenSHMEM implementation outperform SGI's SHMEM implementation by 3%. Its RMA operations outperform both SGI's SHMEM and the original OpenSHMEM reference implementation by as much as 18% and 12% for gets, and as much as 83% and 53% for puts.

1 Introduction

OpenSHMEM [1] [2] is an effort towards creating an open standard for the well-known SHMEM library, and is a starting point to accommodate future extensions to the SHMEM API. SHMEM is a Partitioned Global Address Space (PGAS) based parallel programming model. OpenSHMEM 1.0 is a SHMEM

S. Poole, O. Hernandez, and P. Shamis (Eds.): OpenSHMEM 2014, LNCS 8356, pp. 1–13, 2014.

specification based on SGI's SHMEM API, which predominantly supports one-sided communication semantics as well as providing collective communication operations, atomic operations, and synchronization operations. Currently, there are many production-grade proprietary implementations of the SHMEM API. OpenSHMEM 1.0 is an effort to create an open, unified standard and a reference implementation [3] of the SHMEM API, led by ORNL's ESSC and UH.

The current reference implementation, which supports various network interfaces in an effort to be portable to spur adoption, is based on the GASNet communication middleware [4]. Though proprietary SHMEM implementations have outstanding performance characteristics on their native hardware, the current reference implementation of OpenSHMEM has several performance drawbacks. For example, atomic operations in the current implementation have a latency that is at least 27% slower than that of the native low-level drivers. In this paper, in order to arrive at the desired performance characteristics, we redesign the network layer of the OpenSHMEM reference implementation to leverage the Universal Common Communication Substrate (UCCS) communication library [5] [6], a low-level network library for implementing parallel programming models. For the rest of the paper, the current reference implementation will be called *OpenSHMEM-GASNet* and the new reference implementation using UCCS will be referred to as *OpenSHMEM-UCCS*.

The rest of the paper is organized as follows: Section 2 provides a brief overview of the UCCS communication middleware and OpenSHMEM specification. Section 3 discusses related works in the area of OpenSHMEM implementations. Section 4.1 details the network layer of OpenSHMEM, and the way it was designed to be independent of underlying network infrastructure. Section 4.2 provides details of UCCS interfaces, data structures, and semantics of operations, and Section 4.3 provides the details of its integration with OpenSHMEM. Section 5 provides an evaluation of the *OpenSHMEM-UCCS* implementation by comparing it to *OpenSHMEM-GASNet* and SGI's SHMEM, and we present concluding remarks in Section 6.

2   Background

This section provides a brief background for the OpenSHMEM specification and UCCS communication middleware.

2.1   OpenSHMEM

Despite the fact that the original SHMEM library was designed by Cray Research, which later was merged with Silicon Graphics (SGI), there are multiple variants of the SHMEM API that have been introduced by different system and hardware vendors. The SGI SHMEM library, which is a part of SGI's Message Passing Toolkit (MPT), provides the original SHMEM interface developed by Cray Research and SGI. Cray provides a SHMEM library implementation for the SeaStar, Aries, and Gemini interconnects. HP supports SHMEM concepts with the HP SHMEM library, which is based on the Quadrics SHMEM library and is available on HP systems. Despite the broad availability of SHMEM implementations, the SHMEM API has not been standardized. As a result, application developers have to handle incompatibilities of different SHMEM implementations at the application level. The OpenSHMEM specification was borne out of the desire to standardize the many similar yet incompatible SHMEM communication libraries into a single API. The OpenSHMEM reference implementation is an open-source implementation of this specification.

2.2 UCCS

UCCS is a communication middleware that aims to provide a high performing low-level communication interface for implementing parallel programming models. UCCS aims to deliver a broad range of communication semantics such as active messages, collective operations, puts, gets, and atomic operations. This enables implementation of one-sided and two-sided communication semantics to efficiently support both PGAS and MPI-style programming models. The interface is designed to minimize software overheads, and provide direct access to network hardware capabilities without sacrificing productivity. This was accomplished by forming and adhering to the following goals:

– Provide a universal network abstraction with an API that addresses the needs of parallel programming languages and libraries.
– Provide a high-performance communication middleware by minimizing software overheads and taking full advantage of modern network technologies with communication-offloading capabilities.
– Enable network infrastructure for upcoming parallel programming models and network technologies.

In order to evaluate the OpenSHMEM reference implementation with UCCS instead of GASNet, the reference implementation was extended to integrate with the UCCS network substrate.

3 Related Work

The OpenSHMEM reference implementation is the first open-source implementation of the OpenSHMEM specification, which was developed in conjunction with the specification by the University of Houston and Oak Ridge National Laboratory. Since the OpenSHMEM specification is based on SGI's SHMEM API, SGI SHMEM was the first commercial implementation of the specification.

The HPC community and system vendors embraced the specification and released various implementations of the specification. The University of Florida is developing the GSHMEM [7] project which is an OpenSHMEM implementation based solely on the GASNet runtime. Ohio State University (OSU) distributes the MVAPICH-X runtime environment [8], which is focused on enabling MVAPICH InfiniBand and iWARP support for OpenSHMEM and UPC in addition to MPI. Sandia National Laboratory provides an open source implementation of the specification for the Portals [9] network stack. In addition to the above implementations, there are SHMEM implementations that are tightly coupled to particular network technologies developed by network and system vendors. Mellanox ScalableSHMEM [10] provides support for a family of Mellanox interconnects and is based on proprietary software accelerators [11]. Cray and HP SHMEM provide proprietary SHMEM implementations for platforms developed by these vendors, both of which have been making steps toward supporting the OpenSHMEM specification. Tilera Many-Core processors are supported within TSHMEM [12].

The OpenSHMEM reference implementation differentiates itself as an open-source and explorable community platform for development and extension of the OpenSHMEM Specification. Using high-performance UCCS middleware, the UCCS reference implementation aims to deliver performance that is as good or better than the state-of-the-art commercial implementations.

4   Design

The design section discusses the OpenSHMEM communication layer, the UCCS API, and the integration of UCCS as a communication layer in OpenSHMEM.

4.1   OpenSHMEM Communication Layer

The OpenSHMEM reference implementation consists of the core API and a separate communication layer that can have multiple implementations for handling low-level networking hardware, designed in a way that allows them to be easily swapped out for one another. This separation between layers was done in a way that was as minimalistic as reasonably possible, yet still would be generic enough so as to be able to fully accommodate any potential communication infrastructure cleanly. This allows for the maximum amount of common functionality to be reused across communication layer implementations, but requires careful construction.

Moving in this direction, the first task involved dividing all communication primitives such as puts, gets, and atomics between network-agnostic and network-specific sections. Additionally, any particular functions that multiple network layers may share were also taken out and implemented in the upper layers of the library. These functions include a handful of basic procedures that also do not include any assumptions or code specific to a particular communication infrastructure, but may still be needed during use, such as range checking for processing element (PE) numbers, symmetric addressing, memory allocation and deallocation, and state information querying.

Other communication calls that could be implemented using the previously described primitives were done so in the upper layers of the library as well, removing additional strain on the requirements for generating and maintaining communication layers. Most notably, these include collective calls such as barrier, broadcast, and reduction operations. Finally, any functions that do not require any communication at all were implemented solely in the upper layer, such as shmem_wait().

4.2 UCCS API

The UCCS API is a generic and network hardware agnostic interface that defines abstract concepts, which isolate programmers from hardware specific details. To accomplish this, it first defines a few key concepts: communication contexts, resources, and endpoints. Communication contexts are a method of providing communication scope and isolation to multiple instances of user or system code, and are represented in application code as opaque handles. These handles contain all information about the associated communication context, including resources, endpoints, and memory, and are at the topmost layer of the communication abstraction. Resources represent a particular communication channel available for a network, for which there may be several for a given network in cases such as multi-rail architectures. Similar to communication contexts, resources are also represented by opaque handles, and all the descriptors for the available resources of a particular transport type or list of types in a given communication context are initialized at once.

In order to complete a communication call, a specific endpoint must be selected to communicate with using a specific resource. These endpoints represent the ultimate destination for a communication operation, and are also represented by opaque handles. To obtain a set of valid endpoints, a connectivity map must be generated for a resource and be queried to discover if a particular execution context is reachable via the resource for which it was generated. Endpoints in UCCS are defined in relation to resources, such that any one endpoint descriptor is only associated with one particular resource descriptor. Figure 1 describes the relationship between UCCS context, resources, and endpoints.

The interface for UCCS is divided between the core API and its run-time environment (RTE) (Figure 2). The RTE API is an interface providing run-time services such as process startup, out-of-band communication, and a key storage and retrieval system, as well as other run-time services. UCCS does not implement run-time services, but relies on external libraries such as ORTE [13], SLURM [14], STCI [15], and other third party runtime libraries. Such an approach allows it to decouple the core communication API from the run-time environment, in a way that enables easy porting to different run-time libraries.

The core API features consist of initialization, remote memory access, atomic memory operations, active messages, and collectives. Aside from the functions required for creating descriptors for communication contexts, resources, and endpoints, UCCS also provides methods for querying network capabilities and registering, deregistering, and exporting memory segments for use in future calls. Remote Memory Access (RMA) operations consist of functions for one-sided puts and gets optimized for either short, medium, or large message sizes, as well as functions for non-contiguous data. Atomic Memory Operation (AMO) functions include atomic add, fetch-and-add, increment, fetch-and-increment, swap, and

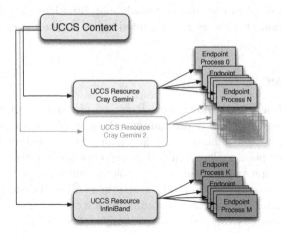

Fig. 1. A relation between the UCCS communication context, resource, and endpoints

conditional swap for both 32 and 64 bit data sizes. The Active Message (AM) interface can be used to support remote execution and two-sided communication operations. This is performed by first registering a callback handler, then sending the data itself in a manner similar to the RMA put operations. Group communication can also be performed using the provided collective operation functions.

All communication calls in UCCS are inherently non-blocking, so their completion must be checked by waiting on a request handle created for tracking an operation's progress. To aid in the management of outstanding operations, UCCS provides functions to test or wait on these handles in whichever way best suits the given situation. The user may test or wait either on a specific handle, all handles in a provided list, or any of the handles in a provided list. These management functions result in a returned status that indicates whether the operation completed successfully, an error occurred, or some other status as appropriate. In addition to the test and wait functions for remote completion, it is also possible to ensure local completion of all outstanding operations by flushing all communication intended for a particular set of endpoints from the local execution context calling the function.

4.3   UCCS and OpenSHMEM Integration

The UCCS and RTE APIs provide an interface that enables simple yet efficient implementation of the OpenSHMEM API (Figure 3). The integration process can be divided into two primary phases: UCCS library initialization and communication semantics implementation.

4.3.1   Initialization
The initialization of the RTE starts up all the PEs in the system, after which the number of participating PEs and each individual caller's index (PE number) can then be queried.

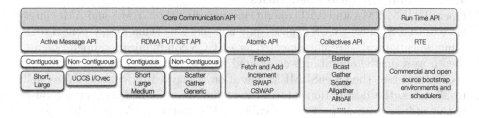

Fig. 2. UCCS API Layout

Once the RTE has been initialized, system data can then be exchanged between PEs without the need for the full communication framework to be online. For a high performance implementation of OpenSHMEM, this can be especially important for two reasons:

1. There is no requirement that the symmetric heaps on the PEs must exist in memory at exactly the same address, so all PEs must be able to broadcast the starting address of their own symmetric heap to all other PEs to allow address translation.
2. Some network technologies such as InfiniBand may require some form of memory registration information before being able to access remote devices, which would also have to be communicated first before any communication operations from client code may be called at all.

To communicate this data, the RTE layer's Storage Retrieval System (SRS) was used, which allows for the easy broadcasting of key-value pairs throughout the system. The starting addresses for the symmetric heaps as well as data on memory segments and associated registration information are individually published to the SRS session, which automatically handles distribution of the data to other PEs subscribed to the session in the system. To keep proper track of this, all information collected about a particular PE is wrapped in a container, such that the full view of the system is an array of these containers indexed by PE id. After the initial bootstrapping is complete, the UCCS context may be created, and resources discovered for it. After creating the descriptors for the resources, those resources are then queried to discover what their network capabilities are. These capabilities include the list of supported operations as well threshold values for the maximum size for small and medium messages supported by the network resource. This information is then stored so as to make the best choices for what operations and message sizes to use in future communication. When all this information is obtained and exchanged, the endpoints may then be set up. During the PE initialization process, each PE will query UCCS endpoints to determine the reachability of every other PE. Finally, a barrier is performed based on the exchanged information, which will establish successful completion of UCCS initialization upon return.

4.3.2   Communication Semantics

OpenSHMEM RMA and AMO operations map directly to RMA and AMO interfaces in UCCS. Since UCCS exposes only non-blocking semantics, OpenSHMEM communication calls are implemented as a UCCS communication operation and then a wait on the operation's associated request handle. Once the handle has been completed, the OpenSHMEM operation is marked for completion as well. In all cases, the destination address must first be modified so that the offset of the address with respect to the calling PE's symmetric heap is the same as the offset for the new address with respect to the destination PE's heap. For puts and gets on arbitrary sizes of data, the size of the message is first checked against the threshold values discovered in intialization for the maximum allowed for short or medium messages. The destination endpoint is then looked up using the address translation table built during initialization, and the put or get for the appropriate size is invoked on it for the requested values. Atomics are similar, but don't have the requirement to check for message size, merely needing to have the appropriate UCCS call invoked and waited for to satisfy OpenSHMEM's completion policy. Since all other communication operations are built off of these, all that is left is to ensure that upon exit all associated memory is freed, and call the RTE's own finalize function.

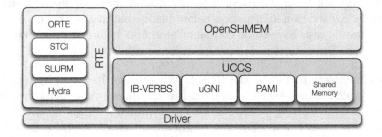

Fig. 3. OpenSHMEM and UCCS software layers

5   Results

The evaluation of this implementation was conducted on an SGI Altix XE1300 system located at the Oak Ridge National Laboratory's Extreme Scale System Center. The system consists of 12 compute nodes, each with two Intel Xeon X5660 CPUs for a total of 12 CPU cores and 24 threads. Compute nodes are interconnected with Mellanox's ConnectX-2 QDR HCA with one port. This particular system was selected due to the availability of SGI MPT version 2.03 that comes with a state-of-the-art SHMEM implementation for InfiniBand interconnects. In addition, we installed the newly updated OpenSHMEM 1.0 implementation, GASNet version 1.20.2, and pre-production UCCS version 0.4. This version of the UCCS library provides high-performance communication services for InfiniBand interconnects only. Evaluation of intra-node communication support and other interconnects is out of the scope of this paper. All tests were run with both the OpenSHMEM implementation's GASNet and UCCS communication layers, as well as SGI's SHMEM and, when appropriate, are compared to results obtained using InfiniBand verbs (IB-verbs) library. We were not able to evalute the Mellanox ScalableSHMEM implementation, since the pre-production version of the library did not run on our platform.

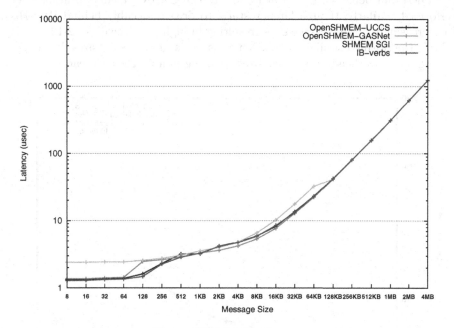

Fig. 4. SHMEM Put Latency

The first test measures the latency for put operations, by using a ping-pong approach. The first PE puts to a location on the second PE, which is simply waiting for the value at that location to fully update. Upon noticing the update, it then puts to a location on the first PE that it likewise is waiting on, upon receipt of which the ping-pong operation is complete. The time for the complete exchange is halved to determine the latency for a single put operation, in order to achieve a result similar to what the IB-verbs Perftest benchmark produces. This test found median latencies for increasingly large message sizes ranging from 8 bytes to 4 megabytes (based on powers of two). The results of this test are compared to that of IB-verbs, as seen in Figure 4. These results show performance close to IB-verbs for message sizes larger than 512 bytes, with *OpenSHMEM-UCCS* performing the closest to IB-verbs, the largest difference being only 3%. For small messages, *OpenSHMEM-UCCS* had the best performance, ranging from 2-11% slower than IB-verbs. In contrast, *OpenSHMEM-GASNet* was 1-67% slower, and SGI's implementation completed in 7-88% more time compared to IB-verbs.

The second test measures the latency for messages of varying sizes using gets. The median latency for a get of a particular size is recorded for all message sizes based on a power of two, starting from eight bytes and continually doubling up to four megabytes. The results are compared to those obtained using IB-verbs in Figure 5. It can be seen that the performance seen with IB-verbs can be closely matched in all implementations for all message sizes, with the UCCS version consistently performing the closest to IB-verbs with negligible overhead at its best and being 4% slower at its worst. The GASNet communication layer performed similarly, though latency starts to drag noticeably behind IB-verbs for increasingly large message sizes, resulting in higher overheads of 2-12%. SGI SHMEM performed similar to GASNet runs for larger message sizes, but experienced more overhead for smaller sizes resulting in a 6-22% overhead.

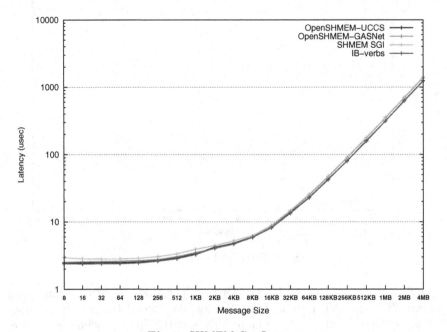

Fig. 5. SHMEM Get Latency

The third test measures the latency for atomics by using long long fetch-and-add operations. This test was the most straightforward one, simply finding the median time elapsed to perform one such operation and comparing the results to IB-verbs. The fourth test measures the time it takes to perform a barrier operation on all PEs. This test was performed using two, four, eight, and twelve PEs, with the median time recorded for only *OpenSHMEM-GASNet*, *OpenSHMEM-UCCS*, and SGI, as there is no equivalent test for IB-verbs. For the runs done using both of the OpenSHMEM implementations, a recursive doubling algorithm was used for the barrier itself. The results for the fetch-and-add tests are shown in Figure 6(a) and the barrier results are in Figure 6(b). When executing atomics, the UCCS communication layer consistently performed better than SGI's implementation, which in turn performed better than the GASNet layer. *OpenSHMEM-UCCS* took 5% more time to execute compared to IB-verbs, while

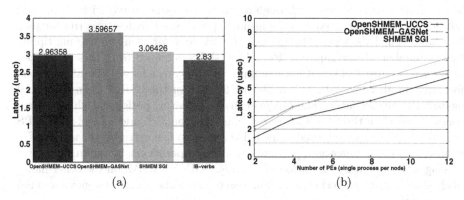

(a) (b)

Fig. 6. SHMEM Long Long Fetch-and-Add (a) and Barrier All (b)

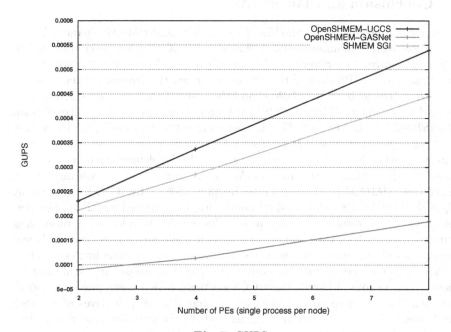

Fig. 7. GUPS

SGI took 8% more and *OpenSHMEM-GASNet* took 27% more time. On barriers, *OpenSHMEM-UCCS* again performed the best, with *OpenSHMEM-GASNet* performing 9-58% slower, and SGI performing 25-36% slower.

The final test is based on the RandomAccess benchmark from the High Performance Computing Challenge (HPCC) [16], used to measure the performance of the memory architecture of a system in terms of Giga UPdates per Second (GUPS). This is determined by the number of random memory locations that can be updated in one second, which can be used to give an idea of peak performance of the system with respect to random memory access. For each random location, a value is retrieved through a get, a new value stored with a put, and another value incremented with an atomic operation. This test was run for two, four, and eight PEs, where the amount of work done for each run was multiplied by the number of participating PEs. The GUPS achieved from these tests can be seen in Figure 7. The UCCS communication layer achieved the highest performance in all runs, with SGI achieving 82-92% of the GUPS when compared agaisnt the UCCS layer. The GASNet layer, however, performed almost three times slower than the UCCS layer, reaching between 35% and 39% of the GUPS that the UCCS layer achieved. This is likely due to the extra overhead GASNet incurs on its communication, particularly atomic operations, by relying on active messages for successful execution of its calls. SGI's SHMEM, on the other hand, likely saw its relative performance difference due to the greater latency for small put operations.

6   Conclusion and Future Work

This paper presented *OpenSHMEM-UCCS*, an OpenSHMEM reference implementation whose communication is based on UCCS, a low-level communication middleware. An evaluation with microbenchmarks and the RandomAccess benchmark for GUPS showed that it outperformed the current reference implementation (*OpenSHMEM-GASNet*) and the state-of-the-art SGI SHMEM. Particularly, the *OpenSHMEM-UCCS* RMA and atomic operations outperformed *OpenSHMEM-GASNet* and SGI's implementation. For example, for the widely used put operation, *OpenSHMEM-UCCS* outperformed the current reference implementation by as much as 53%, and SGI's implementation by as much as 83%. When running the RandomAccess benchmark for measuring GUPS, using *OpenSHMEM-GASNet* resulted in only 35-39% the GUPS achieved by *OpenSHMEM-UCCS*, while SGI's implementation achieved 82-92% of the performance. These results were able to be achieved due to a focus on minimizing software overheads in the communication path while focusing on the needs and capabilities of the underlying network hardware. The previous implementation with GASNet relied heavily on active messages for atomic and some remote memory operations, whereas the UCCS communication layer provides semantics that directly map to low-level atomic and RDMA primitives of network hardware. This allows for a much tighter and streamlined flow that can achieve results much closer to what the network hardware supports.

Moving forward with UCCS and its integration with OpenSHMEM, we plan to extend the UCCS library to support intra-node communication as well as additional transport layers such as such Cray uGNI and IBM PAMI. Moreover, we plan to extend the UCCS InfiniBand transport layer to support InfiniBand Dynamically Connected Transport, extended AMOs, and on demand memory registration.

Acknowledgments. This work is supported by the United States Department of Defense and used resources of the Extreme Scale Systems Center located at the Oak Ridge National Laboratory.

References

1. Chapman, B., Curtis, T., Pophale, S., Poole, S., Kuehn, J., Koelbel, C., Smith, L.: Introducing OpenSHMEM: SHMEM for the PGAS community. In: Proceedings of the Fourth Conference on Partitioned Global Address Space Programming Model, PGAS 2010, New York, NY, USA (2010)
2. Poole, S.W., Hernandez, O., Kuehn, J.A., Shipman, G.M., Curtis, A., Feind, K.: OpenSHMEM - Toward a Unified RMA Model. In: Encyclopedia of Parallel Computing, pp. 1379–1391 (2011)
3. Pophale, S.S.: SRC: OpenSHMEM library development. In: Lowenthal, D.K., de Supinski, B.R., McKee, S.A. (eds.) ICS, p. 374. ACM (2011)
4. Bonachea, D.: GASNet Specification, v1.1. Technical report, Berkeley, CA, USA (2002)
5. Shamis, P., Venkata, M.G., Kuehn, J.A., Poole, S.W., Graham, R.L.: Universal Common Communication Substrate (UCCS) Specification. Version 0.1. Tech Report ORNL/TM-2012/339, Oak Ridge National Laboratory, ORNL (2012)
6. Graham, R.L., Shamis, P., Kuehn, J.A., Poole, S.W.: Communication Middleware Overview. Tech Report ORNL/TM-2012/120, Oak Ridge National Laboratory, ORNL (2012)
7. Yoon, C., Aggarwal, V., Hajare, V., George, A.D., Billingsley III, M. GSHMEM: A Portable Library for Lightweight, Shared-Memory, Parallel Programming. In: Partitioned Global Address Space, Galveston, Texas (2011)
8. Jose, J., Kandalla, K., Luo, M., Panda, D.K.: Supporting Hybrid MPI and Open-SHMEM over InfiniBand: Design and Performance Evaluation. In: Proceedings of the 2012 41st International Conference on Parallel Processing, ICPP 2012, pp. 219–228. IEEE Computer Society, Washington, DC (2012)
9. Brightwell, R., Hudson, T., Pedretti, K., Riesen, R., Underwood, K.D.: (Portals 3.3 on the Sandia/Cray Red Storm System)
10. Mellanox Technologies LTD.: Mellanox ScalableSHMEM: Support the Open-SHMEM Parallel Programming Language over InfiniBand (2012), http://www.mellanox.com/related-docs/prod_software/PB_ScalableSHMEM.pdf
11. Mellanox Technologies LTD.: Mellanox Messaging (MXM): Message Accelerations over InfiniBand for MPI and PGAS libraries (2012), http://www.mellanox.com/related-docs/prod_software/PB_MXM.pdf
12. Ho Lam, B.C., George, A.D., Lam, H.: TSHMEM: Shared-Memory Parallel Computing on Tilera Many-Core Processors. In: 2013 IEEE 27th International Symposium on Parallel and Distributed Processing Workshops and PhD Forum, pp. 325–334 (2013), http://www.odysci.com/article/1010113019802138
13. Castain, R.H., Woodall, T.S., Daniel, D.J., Squyres, J.M., Barrett, B., Fagg, G.E.: The Open Run-Time Environment (OpenRTE): A Transparent Multi-Cluster Environment for High-Performance Computing. In: Di Martino, B., Kranzlmüller, D., Dongarra, J. (eds.) EuroPVM/MPI 2005. LNCS, vol. 3666, pp. 225–232. Springer, Heidelberg (2005)
14. Yoo, A.B., Jette, M.A., Grondona, M.: SLURM: Simple linux utility for resource management. In: Feitelson, D.G., Rudolph, L., Schwiegelshohn, U. (eds.) JSSPP 2003. LNCS, vol. 2862, pp. 44–60. Springer, Heidelberg (2003)
15. Buntinas, D., Bosilica, G., Graham, R.L., Vallée, G., Watson, G.R.: A Scalable Tools Communication Infrastructure. In: Proceedings of the 22nd International High Performance Computing Symposium, HPCS 2008 (2008)
16. HPCC: RandomAccess Bechmark (2013), http://icl.cs.utk.edu/hpcc/index.html

A Comprehensive Performance Evaluation of OpenSHMEM Libraries on InfiniBand Clusters*

Jithin Jose, Jie Zhang, Akshay Venkatesh,
Sreeram Potluri, and Dhabaleswar K. (DK) Panda

Department of Computer Science and Engineering, The Ohio State University
{jose,zhanjie,akshay,potluri,panda}@cse.ohio-state.edu

Abstract. OpenSHMEM is an open standard that brings together several long-standing, vendor-specific SHMEM implementations that allows applications to use SHMEM in a platform-independent fashion. Several implementations of OpenSHMEM have become available on clusters interconnected by InfiniBand networks, which has gradually become the de facto high performance network interconnect standard. In this paper, we present a detailed comparison and analysis of the performance of different OpenSHMEM implementations, using micro-benchmarks and application kernels. This study, done on TACC Stampede system using up to 4,096 cores, provides a useful guide for application developers to understand and contrast various implementations and to select the one that works best for their applications.

Keywords: OpenSHMEM, Clusters, InfiniBand, Performance Evaluation.

1 Introduction and Motivation

Data-driven applications often pose challenges associated with load balancing and often exhibit irregular communication patterns. These issues are harder to address with a traditional message-passing programming paradigm. The Partitioned Global Address Space (PGAS) programming models present an alternative approach compared to message passing and are believed to improve programmability of such applications. PGAS languages like Unified Parallel C (UPC) [15] and Co-array Fortran (CAF) [1] have been undergoing standardization for over a decade now. More recently, there has been the OpenSHMEM effort to standardize API for the different vendor specific implementations of SHMEM, a library-based PGAS model. The OpenSHMEM standard is gaining attention as it allows existing codes that were written using vendor-specific SHMEM API to be made platform-independent with minimal effort. It is also seen as an alternative to PGAS languages for designing new applications.

* This research is supported in part by National Science Foundation grants #OCI-0926691, #OCI-1148371 and #CCF-1213084.

S. Poole, O. Hernandez, and P. Shamis (Eds.): OpenSHMEM 2014, LNCS 8356, pp. 14–28, 2014.

Multi-core processors and high-performance interconnects have been driving the growth of modern high-end supercomputing systems. Earlier work has shown different alternatives to designing OpenSHMEM communication and synchronization operations on multi-core nodes [2,11]. InfiniBand (IB) has emerged as the most popular interconnect on these systems. Around 41% of the most recent Top 500 list of supercomputers use IB. Several designs have also been presented for implementing OpenSHMEM operations on InfiniBand clusters [5]. Several full-fledged implementations of OpenSHMEM are available for modern InfiniBand clusters. The performance of each of these implementations can differ based on the design choices they make. It is important for application developers to understand the performance of the various implementations to choose the one that is right for their application and system. Lack of a systematic performance comparison and an analysis of the different implementations makes it harder for application developers to make this choice.

In this paper, we address this by providing a detailed comparison and analysis of the performance of different publicly available OpenSHMEM implementations using micro-benchmarks and application kernels. We analyze the scalability of the implementations in terms of performance and memory footprint. The study is conducted on TACC Stampede system using up to 4,096 cores.

To summarize, the following contributions are made in this paper:

1. We present a detailed comparison of the performance of different OpenSH-MEM implementations using pt-to-pt and collective micro-benchmarks.
2. We provide a detailed analysis of the performance trends observed in different implementations.
3. We analyze the performance of application kernels showing how users can draw a correlation between the micro-benchmark results and application performance.

The rest of the paper is organized as follows: Section 2 provides an overview of OpenSHMEM communication routines and introduces different OpenSHMEM implementations over InfiniBand. In Section 3, we present our evaluation methodology and we present our evaluation results in Section 4. We discuss our performance results in Section 5, and finally conclude in Section 6.

2 Background

2.1 PGAS Models and OpenSHMEM

In Partitioned Global Address Space (PGAS) programming models, each Processing Element (PE) has access to its own private local memory and a global shared memory space. The locality of the global shared memory is well defined. Such a model allows for better programmability through a simple shared memory abstraction while ensuring performance by exposing data and thread locality. SHMEM (SHared MEMory) [13] is a library-based approach to realize the PGAS model and offers one-sided point-to-point communication operations, along with collective and synchronization primitives. SHMEM also offers primitives for atomic operations, managing memory, and locks. There are several implementations of the SHMEM model that are customized for different platforms. However, these implementations are not portable due to minor variations in the API and semantics. OpenSHMEM [9] aims to create a new, open specification to standardize the SHMEM model to achieve performance, programmability, and portability.

2.2   OpenSHMEM Communication Operations

The OpenSHMEM Specification v1.0 [9] defines several types of communication operations — data transfer, atomics, and collective communication operations. We provide a brief overview of these operations in this section.

Data Transfer Operations: The data transfer operations defined in OpenSH-MEM consist of `shmem_put` and `shmem_get`, and their variants. The source/ destination address of data transfer operations can either be in symmetric heap or symmetric static memory, as defined in the OpenSHMEM specification. `shmem_put` writes the local data to the corresponding data objects at target process. `shmem_get` fetches the data from a remote process and stores it in the local data object.

Atomic Operations: These routines allow operations on a symmetric object guaranteeing that another process will not update the target between the time of the fetch and the update. In OpenSHMEM specification, six atomics routines are defined. `shmem_swap` performs an atomic swap operation. `shmem_cswap` conditionally updates a target data object on an arbitrary processing element (PE) and returns the prior contents of the data object in one atomic operation. `shmem_fadd` and `shmem_finc` perform atomic fetch-and-add and atomic fetch-and-increment operations, respectively. Similarly, `shmem_add` and `shmem_inc` operations do atomic add and atomic increment operations.

Collective Operations: The collective operations defined in OpenSHMEM specification consist of `shmem_broadcast`, `shmem_collect`, `shmem_reduce`, and `shmem_barrier`. The broadcast operation copies a block of data from one PE to one or more target PEs. Collect operation concatenates elements from the source array to a target array over the specified PEs. Reduction operation performs an associative binary operation over the specified PEs. Barrier operation provides collective synchronization in which no PE may leave the barrier prior to all PEs entering the barrier.

2.3   Overview of OpenSHMEM Libraries for InfiniBand Clusters

There are several implementations of OpenSHMEM libraries that support one-sided OpenSHMEM semantics for clusters interconnected by InfiniBand (IB) networks. The OpenSHMEM group from University of Houston introduced the reference OpenSHMEM implementation [9] that first conformed to the then standardized, one-sided semantics. The reference implementation is based on data transfers over InfiniBand networks that leveraged on its RDMA capabilities for one-sided operations. This reference implementation uses GASNet [3] as the underlying communication runtime. In this paper, we denote this reference implementation as 'UH-SHMEM'.

ScalableSHMEM [6] is another OpenSHMEM implementation that supports the standard's point-to-point and collective routines over InfiniBand networks that utilize custom advanced features [12]. *OpenMPI*[8], likewise, also provides an implementation of OpenSHMEM semantics over IB and leverages on many of Mellanox's IB features. These stacks are represented as 'Scalable-SHMEM' and 'OMPI-SHMEM', respectively in this paper.

MVAPICH2-X [7] provides a unified high-performance runtime that supports both MPI and PGAS programming models on InfiniBand clusters. The unified runtime also delivers superior performance compared to using separate MPI and PGAS libraries by optimizing the use of network and memory resources. MVAPICH2-X supports two PGAS models: Unified Parallel C (UPC) and Open-SHMEM. The MVAPICH2-X OpenSHMEM is denoted as 'MV2X-SHMEM' in this paper.

We consider all four of the above-mentioned implementations (UH-SHMEM, Scalable-SHMEM, OMPI-SHMEM, and MV2X-SHMEM) in our performance evaluation.

3   Evaluation Methodology

We follow a five-pronged approach to evaluate the different OpenSH-MEM implementations available for InfiniBand clusters, as shown in Figure 1. We start with a comparison of the performance of different OpenSH-MEM API including put/get operations, atomics, and collectives. We use micro-benchmarks to evaluate each of these operations separately. We then compare the memory scalability of the implementations by measuring their memory footprint as they scale to an increasing number of cores. We finally use several application kernels to com-

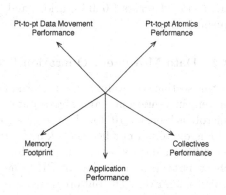

Fig. 1. Evaluation Methodology

pare the performance of different implementations. We draw a correlation between the performance of OpenSHMEM implementations using application kernels to that we see in micro-benchmarks. We summarize the performance results along these five dimensions in Section 5. This methodology helps application developers to select an implementation that is best for their use case.

4   Experimental Evaluation

In this section, we describe our experimental test-bed and discuss our evaluations. We study the performance characteristics of point-to-point and collective operations, application-level performance, and scalability characteristics for the different OpenSHMEM libraries. In the experimental evaluations, we use the following acronyms to denote the different OpenSHMEM libraries — UH-SHMEM (University of Houston - OpenSHMEM), MV2X-SHMEM (MVAPICH2X-Open-SHMEM), OMPI-SHMEM (OpenMPI OpenSHMEM), and Scalable-SHMEM (Mellanox ScalableSHMEM).

4.1   Experiment Setup

We use TACC Stampede [14] for our performance studies. This cluster is equipped with compute nodes composed of Intel Sandybridge series of processors using Xeon dual eight-core sockets, operating at 2.70 GHz with 32 GB RAM. Each node is equipped with MT4099 FDR ConnectX HCAs (54 Gbps data rate) with PCI-Ex Gen3 interfaces. The operating system used is CentOS release 6.3, with kernel version 2.6.32-279.el6, and OpenFabrics version 1.5.4.1.

For UH-SHMEM, we use version 1.d in combination with GASNet version 1.20.2. We configure GASNet with `--enable-segment-fast` option. The MV2X-SHMEM is based on MVAPICH2-X v2.0a. The OpenMPI OpenSHMEM is from the public repository `https://bitbucket.org/jladd_math/mlnx-oshmem.git`. We use "`--mca btl openib,self --mca btl_openib_if_include mlx4_0`" as runtime parameters for OMPI-SHMEM. We use Scalable-SHMEM version 2.2 in our experiments. For all microbenchmark evaluations, we report results that are averaged across 1,000 iterations and three different runs to eliminate experimental errors.

4.2   Data Movement Operation Performance

In this section, we evaluate the performance of OpenSHMEM point-to-point data movement (`shmem_put` and `shmem_get`) operations. We use OSU OpenSHMEM microbenchmarks [10] for these evaluations.

The `osu_oshm_put` benchmark measures latency of a `shmem_putmem` operation for different data sizes. In this benchmark, processing element (PE) '0' issues `shmem_putmem` to write data at PE 1 and then calls `shmem_quiet`. PE 1 waits on a `shmem_barrier`. The put operation is repeated for a fixed number of iterations, depending on the data size. The average latency per iteration is reported. A few warm-up iterations are run without timing to ignore any start-up overheads. Both PEs call `shmem_barrier_all` after the test for each message size. Similarly, `osu_oshm_get` benchmark measures the `shmem_get` operation. In this benchmark, PE 0 does a `shmem_getmem` operation to read data from PE 1 in each iteration. The average latency per iteration is reported.

The latency results of `shmem_put` and `shmem_get` are presented in Figure 2 and 3, respectively. For clarity, the results are presented in two graphs — for small messages and large messages. The graphs also present the InfiniBand verbs level latencies for RDMA write and read operations, which are denoted as 'IB-Verbs'. There exists slight difference in performance for different OpenSHMEM libraries. For a 4 byte `shmem_put` operation, the latencies reported are 1.92, 1.47, 1.41, and 1.83 μs for UH-SHMEM, MV2X-SHMEM, Scalable-SHMEM, and OMPI-SHMEM respectively. However, the verbs level RDMA write latency is 0.84 μs. The higher latency observed at OpenSHMEM layer is because of the extra synchronization operation (`shmem_quiet`). For a 64 KB `shmem_put` operation, the latencies reported are 14.83, 13.24, 17.85, and 18.54 μs for UH-SHMEM, MV2X-SHMEM, Scalable-SHMEM, and OMPI-SHMEM, respectively. The verbs level latency reported for 64 KB message size is 12.78 μs.

The performance results for the `shmem_get` operation are similar. For a 4 byte `shmem_get` operation, the latencies reported are 2.07, 1.79, 2.31, and 1.79 μs for UH-SHMEM, MV2X-SHMEM, Scalable-SHMEM, and OMPI-SHMEM, respectively. The verbs level RDMA read latency reported is about 1.79 μs, which is similar to the numbers observed at OpenSHMEM layer. Unlike the `osu_oshm_put` benchmark, there is no extra synchronization operation for `osu_oshm_get` benchmark. For a 64 KB `shmem_put` operation, the latencies reported are 15.2, 12.88, 16.84, and 13.14 μs for UH-SHMEM, MV2X-SHMEM, Scalable-SHMEM, and OMPI-SHMEM, respectively. The verbs level latency observed for 64 KB message size is 12.83 μs. For all the different message sizes, MV2X-SHMEM consistently performs the best for both `shmem_put` and `shmem_get` operations.

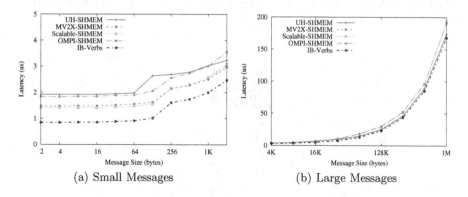

(a) Small Messages   (b) Large Messages

Fig. 2. Put Performance Results (Inter-node)

4.3 Atomic Operation Performance

The OpenSHMEM atomic operation performance is presented in Figure 4. We use the OSU benchmark for this evaluation also. The `osu_oshm_atomics` benchmark measures the performance of atomic fetch-and-operate and atomic operate routines for 64-bit data types. In this benchmark, the first PE in each pair issues back-to-back atomic operations of a type to its peer PE. The average latency per atomic operation and the aggregate operation rate are reported. This is

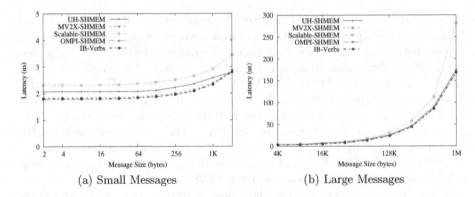

(a) Small Messages   (b) Large Messages

Fig. 3. Get Performance Results (Inter-node)

repeated for each of the atomic operations — Fetch and Add (shmem_fadd), Fetch and Increment (shmem_finc), Add (shmem_add), Increment (shmem_inc), Compare and Swap (shmem_cswap), and Swap (shmem_swap). The performance results indicate that MV2X-SHMEM provides much lower latency for all of the different atomic routines. In MV2X-SHMEM, the atomic routines are implemented directly over Remote Direct Memory Access (RDMA). The latencies reported for a shmem_fadd operation are 4.52, 3.04, 17.11, and 25.74 μs for UH-SHMEM, MV2X-SHMEM, Scalable-SHMEM, and OMPI-SHMEM, respectively. The verbs level numbers for fetch-add and compare-swap operations reported are 2.54, and 2.71 μs, which are close to the latencies observed at OpenSHMEM level.

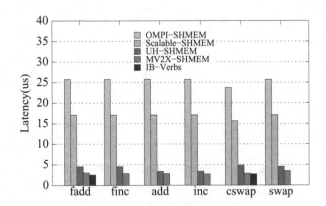

Fig. 4. Atomic Operation Performance (Inter-node)

4.4 Collectives Performance

In this section, we compare the performance of various collective operations in OpenSHMEM specification - shmem_broadcast, shmem_reduce, shmem_collect, and **shmem_barrier** - across various implementations and design choices, with a varying number of processes. We use OSU OpenSHMEM collective benchmarks for these evaluations. The benchmarks measure the average latency of the collective operation across N processes, for various message lengths, over multiple iterations. In these experiments, we vary the number of processes from 128 to 2,048. The results are presented in Figures 5, 6, 7, and 8. The Y-axis represents latency reported in μs and X-axis represents message size.

We compare the performance of each collective operation, among the OpenSHMEM libraries. In UH-SHMEM library, two versions of collective operations are available — linear and tree algorithm based implementations. We include these also in our evaluations, which are denoted as 'UH-SHMEM (Linear)' and 'UH-SHMEM (Tree)', respectively.

In Figure 5, we compare the performance of **shmem_reduce** operation. As we can see from the results, MV2X-SHMEM offers lower latency for all of the different system scales. The performance of Scalable-SHMEM and OMPI-SHMEM are similar, but the latencies are little higher. However, UH-SHMEM linear and tree versions show very high latency. Thus, we show UH-SHMEM results for smaller system sizes (128 and 256 processes) and exclude these results for higher system sizes. For 2,048 processes, the latencies measured for a 4 byte **shmem_reduce** operation for MV2-X SHMEM, OMPI-SHMEM, and Scalable-SHMEM are 27, 240, and 316 μs, respectively.

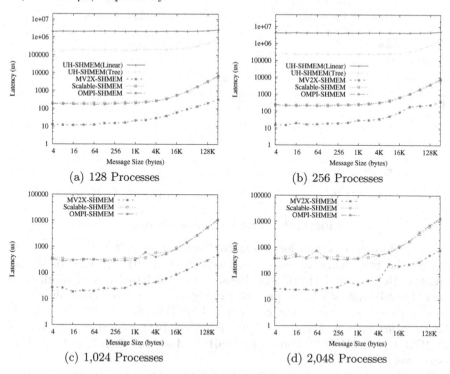

(a) 128 Processes   (b) 256 Processes

(c) 1,024 Processes   (d) 2,048 Processes

Fig. 5. Reduce Performance Results

shmem_broadcast latency results are presented in Figure 6. These results also exhibit same pattern as the shmem_reduce results. MV2X-SHMEM offers lower latencies for all the message sizes for varying system sizes. MV2X-SHMEM utilizes a combination of hardware based multicast scheme and tuned algorithms realized in software for implementing the broadcast operation. Since the collective operations are implemented over point-to-point operations, the impact of point-to-point performance is reflected in collective operation performance. At 2,048 system scale, the latencies measured for a 4 byte shmem_broadcast operation for MV2-X SHMEM, OMPI-SHMEM, and Scalable-SHMEM are 7, 149, and 110 μs, respectively.

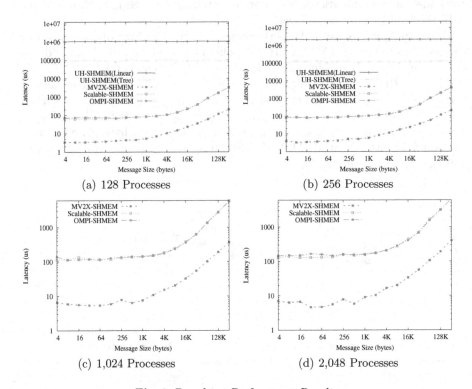

Fig. 6. Broadcast Performance Results

The performance results for shmem_collect also exhibit a similar pattern. There is no tree-algorithm-based implementation in UH-SHMEM for shmem_collect. Results for UH-SHMEM linear algorithm based design results and other OpenSHMEM stacks are presented in Figure 7. There is no tree-algorithm-based implementation of shmem_collect in UH-SHMEM. At 2,048 system size, the latencies measured for a 4 byte shmem_collect operation for MV2-X SHMEM, OMPI-SHMEM, and Scalable-SHMEM are 237, 28261, and 22599 μs, respectively.

shmem_barrier and shmem_barrier_all performance results are presented in Figure 8. The only difference between these barrier operations is that in

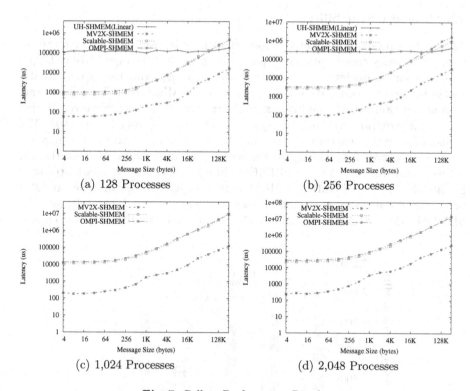

Fig. 7. Collect Performance Results

shmem_barrier, the participating processes can be dynamically specified, but in shmem_barrier_all, all the PEs participate in barrier operation (just like MPI_Barrier(MPI_COMM_WORLD)). The time for shmem_barrier operation with 2,048 processes are 83, 141, and 357 μs, for MV2X-SHMEM, Scalable-SHMEM, and OMPI-SHMEM, respectively. There is no tree-algorithm-based implementation of shmem_barrier_all. At 2,048 processes, the latency reported for shmem_barrier_all operation are 83, 250, 361μs, for MV2X-SHMEM, Scalable-SHMEM, and OMPI-SHMEM, respectively.

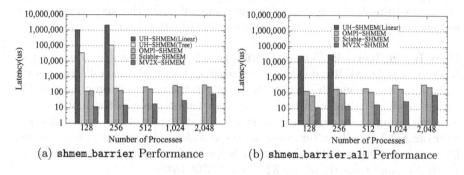

Fig. 8. Barrier Performance Results

4.5 Memory Scalability

This section presents the memory footprint analysis results. Memory footprint refers to memory consumption of a particular process. It is imperative to keep a lower memory footprint for scalability, especially considering the modern multi/many-core architectures. We used a simple OpenSHMEM 'Hello World' program with `shmem_barrier_all` and `shmem_collect32` calls for this evaluation. We executed this program over different system scales ranging from 128 to 2,048. The memory footprint is measured by reading the `VmHWM` entry in `/proc/self/status`. As it can observed from the figure, the memory requirement of MV2X-SHMEM is lower compared to other OpenSHMEM libraries. Also, the memory footprint of Scalable-SHMEM and OMPI-SHMEM increases with increase in scale. At 2,048 processes, the memory footprints are 1,646, 1,111, 967, and 344 MB, for UH-SHMEM, OMPI-SHMEM, Scalable-SHMEM, and MV2X-SHMEM, respectively.

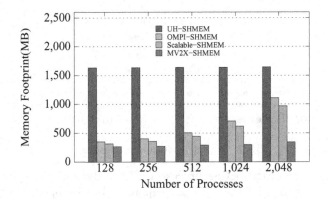

Fig. 9. Memory Scalability Evaluation

4.6 Application Performance

In this section, we present the application kernel evaluation results. We consider two application kernels — Heat Image and DAXPY. These are part of OpenSH-MEM test suite [9]. We first explain the communication characteristics of these kernels and then we present the performance evaluation results.

Heat Image Kernel: This application kernel solves the heat conduction task based on row-based distribution of the matrix. The application distributes the matrix in rows among PEs and then exchanges the result of computation. The major communication operation is the data transfer across the matrix rows/columns (using `shmem_put`) and the synchronization operations (using `shmem_barrier_all`.) Finally, after doing all the transfers, the output is written to a file in an image format. The matrix size is specified as input. In our experiments, we used an input matrix of size 32,768 × 32,768 bytes.

The performance results of the Heat Image kernel is presented in Figure 10(a). In these experiments, we kept the input size constant ($32\,K \times 32\,K$) and varied the system scale from 256 processes to 4,096 processes. We plot the execution time (in seconds) in the Y-axis and the system scale is plotted on X-axis. We present the results for all the OpenSHMEM stacks. For UH-SHMEM, we evaluate using both 'Linear' and 'Tree' based algorithms, and denote these as 'UH-SHMEM (Linear)' and 'UH-SHMEM (Tree)', respectively. As it can be observed from the results, the execution time reduces for MV2X-SHMEM, OMPI-SHMEM, and Scalable-SHMEM, as the system size increases. However, the execution time remains constant for linear and tree based UH-SHMEM versions. For all the system sizes, MV2X-SHMEM performs better compared to other OpenSHMEM libraries. At 4,096 processes, the Heat Image kernel execution time reported are 538, 537, 19, 257, and 361 seconds, for UH-SHMEM (Linear), UH-SHMEM (Tree), MV2X-SHMEM, Scalable-SHMEM, and OMPI-SHMEM, respectively.

Figure 10(b) presents the profiling results (obtained using HPC Toolkit [4]) of the kernel at 1,024 cores, and provides the time taken for each of the OpenSHMEM routines. The results indicate that the time for shmem_barrier, and startpes, are the major factors contributing to overall execution time. The barrier time for UH-SHMEM linear and tree are similar, as explained in Section 4.4. The initialization time for OMPI-SHMEM and Scalable-SHMEM are observed to be higher than other libraries. As it can be observed from the figure, MV2X-SHMEM offers lower execution time for startpes and shmem_barrier.

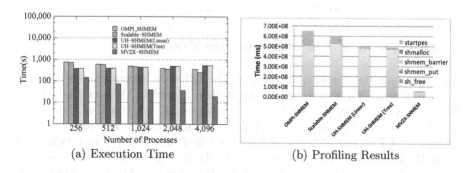

(a) Execution Time   (b) Profiling Results

Fig. 10. Heat Image Performance Results

DAXPY Kernel: This kernel is a simple DAXPY like kernel with computation and communication. It simulates a typical application that uses one dimensional array for local computation and does a reduction collective operation of the result. Here the data transfer is done using shmem_put operation, synchronization using shmem_barrier_all, and reduction using shmem_reduce operations. The execution time reported by the benchmark involves the OpenSHMEM initialization time also. The performance results are presented in Figure 11(a). The execution time (in seconds) is plotted in the Y-axis and the system size is presented in the X-axis.

In the benchmark, the problem size increases with increase in the system size. However, there is a significant difference in performance between different OpenSHMEM libraries. OMPI-SHMEM and Scalable-SHMEM execution times are much higher compared to UH-SHMEM and MV2X-SHMEM. Profiling results (for a system size of 1,024 cores) presented in Figure 11(b) indicate that the initialization time (indicated as 'startpes') is the major contributor to the overall execution time for these stacks. Also, time for reduce operation is higher for UH-SHMEM (Linear) and UH-SHMEM (Tree). At 4,096 processes, the execution times reported are 151, 83, 29, 1594, 1776 seconds, for UH-SHMEM (Linear), UH-SHMEM (Tree), MV2X-SHMEM, Scalable-SHMEM, and OMPI-SHMEM, respectively. For both the application kernels, MV2X-SHMEM performs better as compared to other OpenSHMEM libraries.

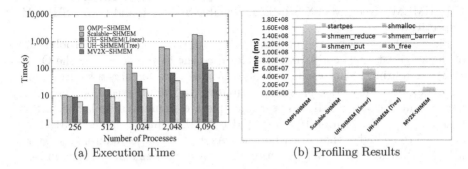

(a) Execution Time   (b) Profiling Results

Fig. 11. DAXPY Performance Results

5   Discussion of Performance Results

We summarize the comparison between the different libraries using the five-pronged diagram presented earlier, depicted in Figure 12. We see that all the libraries perform very similar to one another, when we consider the performance of Put and Get operations. This is because of the direct simple implementation of Put and Get operations over underlying RDMA operations. For OpenSHMEM atomics, we see that MV2X-SHMEM and UH-SHMEM perform considerably better than the other two implementations. MV2X-SHMEM outperforms UH-SHMEM due to its IB atomics-based implementation. We see a distinct difference in the performance of OpenSHMEM collectives between the different implementations owing to the different algorithms used. We see that MV2X-SHMEM outperforms all other implementations for all the collectives. When memory scalability is considered, we see that MV2X-SHMEM, Scalable-SHMEM, and OMPI-SHMEM have much smaller memory footprints compared to the reference implementation. For application level performance, we see that MV2X-SHMEM outperforms other libraries, owing to the better atomics and collective implementation.

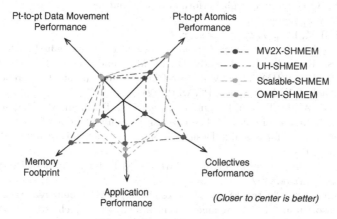

Fig. 12. Evaluation Results

6   Conclusion

In this paper we provided a comprehensive performance evaluation of different OpenSHMEM implementations over InfiniBand. We compare University of Houston OpenSHMEM, Mellanox Scalable-SHMEM, OpenMPI OpenSHMEM, and MVAPICH2-X OpenSHMEM. We presented a detailed comparison of the performance of different OpenSHMEM implementations using point-to-point and collective micro-benchmarks. We also provided a detailed analysis of the performance trends observed in different OpenSHMEM implementations. We analyzed the performance of two application kernels - Heat Image and DAXPY. The study indicates that MVAPICH2-X OpenSHMEM stack delivers best performance and scalability. The study also demonstrates how application developers can draw a correlation between the micro-benchmark results and application performance using various OpenSHMEM stacks on InfiniBand clusters.

References

1. Co-Array Fortran, http://www.co-array.org
2. Brightwell, R., Pedretti, K.: An Intra-Node Implementation of OpenSHMEM Using Virtual Address Space Mapping. In: The 5th Conference on Partitioned Global Address Space (PGAS) (2011)
3. Bonachea, D.: GASNet Specification v1.1. Tech. Rep. UCB/CSD-02-1207, U. C. Berkeley (2008)
4. HPCToolkit, http://hpctoolkit.org/
5. Jose, J., Kandalla, K., Luo, M., Panda, D.: Supporting Hybrid MPI and OpenSHMEM over InfiniBand: Design and Performance Evaluation. In: 41st International Conference on Parallel Processing, ICPP (2012)
6. Mellanox Scalable SHMEM, http://www.mellanox.com/page/products_dyn?product_family=133&mtag=scalableshmem
7. MVAPICH2-X: Unified MPI+PGAS Communication Runtime over OpenFabrics/Gen2 for Exascale Systems, http://mvapich.cse.ohio-state.edu/

8. OpenMPI: Open Source High Performance Computing,
   http://www.open-mpi.org/
9. OpenSHMEM, http://openshmem.org/
10. OSU Micro-benchmarks, http://mvapich.cse.ohio-state.edu/benchmarks/
11. Potluri, S., Kandalla, K., Bureddy, D., Li, M., Panda, D.K.: Efficient Intranode
    Desgins for OpenSHMEM on Multicore Clusters. In: The 6th Conference on Partitioned Global Address Space, PGAS (2012)
12. Shainer, G., Wilde, T., Lui, P., Liu, T., Kagan, M., Dubman, M., Shahar, Y., Graham, R., Shamis, P., Poole, S.: The Co-design Architecture for Exascale Systems, a Novel Approach for Scalable Designs. Computer Science-Research and Development, 1–7 (2013)
13. Silicon Graphics International: SHMEM API for Parallel Programming, http://www.shmem.org/
14. TACC Stampede Cluster, http://www.xsede.org/resources/overview
15. UPC Consortium: UPC Language Specifications, v1.2. Tech. Rep. LBNL-59208, Lawrence Berkeley National Lab (2005)

Benchmarking Parallel Performance
on Many-Core Processors

Bryant C. Lam, Ajay Barboza, Ravi Agrawal,
Alan D. George, and Herman Lam

NSF Center for High-Performance Reconfigurable Computing (CHREC)
Department of Electrical and Computer Engineering
University of Florida
Gainesville, FL 32611-6200
{blam,barboza,ragrawal,george,hlam}@chrec.org

Abstract. With the emergence of many-core processor architectures
onto the HPC scene, concerns arise regarding the performance and productivity of numerous existing parallel-programming tools, models, and
languages. As these devices begin augmenting conventional distributed
cluster systems in an evolving age of heterogeneous supercomputing,
proper evaluation and profiling of many-core processors must occur in
order to understand their performance and architectural strengths with
existing parallel-programming environments and HPC applications. This
paper presents and evaluates the comparative performance between two
many-core processors, the Tilera TILE-Gx8036 and the Intel Xeon Phi
5110P, in the context of their applications performance with the SHMEM
and OpenMP parallel-programming environments. Several applications
written or provided in SHMEM and OpenMP are evaluated in order to
analyze the scalability of existing tools and libraries on these many-core
platforms. Our results show that SHMEM and OpenMP parallel applications scale well on the TILE-Gx and Xeon Phi, but heavily depend on
optimized libraries and instrumentation.

Keywords: PGAS, SHMEM, OpenMP, many-core, parallel programming, performance analysis, high-performance computing, parallel architectures.

1 Introduction

With the emergence of many-core processors into the high-performance computing (HPC) scene, there is strong interest in evaluating and evolving existing
parallel-programming models, tools, and libraries. This evolution is necessary to
best exploit the increasing single-device parallelism from multi- and many-core
processors, especially in a field focused on massively distributed supercomputers. Although many-core devices offer exciting new opportunities for application
acceleration, these devices need to be properly evaluated between each other and
the conventional servers they potentially supplement or replace.

S. Poole, O. Hernandez, and P. Shamis (Eds.): OpenSHMEM 2014, LNCS 8356, pp. 29–43, 2014.
© Springer International Publishing Switzerland 2014

A very popular parallelization method for HPC applications is a hybrid mix of shared-memory threads with OpenMP [3] for intra-node communication between processor cores and single-program, multiple-data (SPMD) processes with MPI [5] for inter-node communication. Partitioned global address space (PGAS) languages and libraries, however, are experiencing rising interest with their potential to provide high-performance around a straightforward memory and communication model. Notable members of the PGAS family include Unified Parallel C (UPC), X10, Chapel, Co-Array Fortran (CAF), Titanium, and SHMEM [9].

In this paper, we present and evaluate the performance of SHMEM and OpenMP applications on two current-generation many-core devices, the Tilera TILE-Gx and the Intel Xeon Phi. The SHMEM applications are evaluated with two library implementations: the OpenSHMEM reference implementation [11] on both platforms, and TSHMEM [7]—an OpenSHMEM library optimized specifically for Tilera many-core processors—on the TILE-Gx. OpenMP implementations are provided by the native compiler for each platforms. Results from these applications emphasize comparative performance of our many-core devices and the effectiveness of each parallel-programming environment.

The remainder of the paper is organized as follows. Section 2 provides background on the SHMEM library and OpenSHMEM efforts, our previous research with TSHMEM (SHMEM for Tilera processors), OpenMP, and brief architectural descriptions of the Tilera TILE-Gx and Intel Xeon Phi. Section 3 presents and evaluates several SHMEM and OpenMP applications on the two many-core platforms. Finally, Section 4 provides conclusions and directions for future work.

2   Background

This section provides brief background of the parallel-programming environments under analysis (SHMEM, OpenSHMEM, TSHMEM, and OpenMP) and the Tilera and Intel many-core platforms that will execute these applications.

2.1   SHMEM and OpenSHMEM

The SHMEM communication library adheres to a strict PGAS model whereby each cooperating parallel process (also known as a processing element, or PE) consists of a shared symmetric partition within the global address space. Each symmetric partition consists of symmetric objects (variables or arrays) of the same size, type, and relative address on all PEs. Originally developed to provide shared-memory semantics on the distributed-memory Cray T3D supercomputer, SHMEM closely models SPMD via its symmetric, partitioned, global address space.

There are two types of symmetric objects that can reside in the symmetric partitions: static and dynamic. Static variables reside in the heap segment of the program executable and are allocated during link time. These static variables, when parallelized as multiple processes, appear at the same virtual address to all processes running the same executable, thus ensuring its symmetry across all partitions. Dynamic symmetric variables, in contrast, are allocated at runtime on all PEs via SHMEM's dynamic memory allocation function *shmalloc()*. These dynamic variables, however, may or may not be allocated at the same virtual address on all PEs, but are typically at the same offset relative to the start of each symmetric partition.

SHMEM provides several routines for explicit communication between PEs, including one-sided data transfers (puts and gets), blocking barrier synchronization, and collective operations. In addition to being a high-performance, lightweight library, SHMEM has historically provided for atomic memory operations not available in popular library alternatives until recently (e.g., MPI 3.0).

Due to the lightweight nature of SHMEM, commercial variants have emerged from vendors such as Cray, SGI, and Quadrics. Application portability between variants, however, proved difficult due to different functional semantics, incompatible APIs, or system-specific implementations. This situation had regrettably fragmented developer adoption in the HPC community. Fortunately, SHMEM has seen renewed interest in the form of OpenSHMEM, a community-led effort to create a standard specification for SHMEM functions and semantics. Version 1.0 of the OpenSHMEM specification has already seen commercial adoption by vendors such as Mellanox [8].

2.2   GASNet and the OpenSHMEM Reference Implementation

The OpenSHMEM community provides a reference implementation of their library with primary source-code contributions from the University of Houston and Oak Ridge National Laboratory [11]. This reference implementation is compliant with version 1.0 of the OpenSHMEM specification and is implemented atop GASNet [2], a low-level networking layer and communication system for supporting SPMD parallel-programming models such as PGAS. GASNet defines a core and an extended networking API that are implemented via conduits. These conduits enable support for numerous networking technologies and systems. By leveraging GASNet's conduit abstraction, the OpenSHMEM reference implementation is portable to numerous cluster-based systems.

2.3   TSHMEM for Tilera Many-Core Processors

Our prior work with OpenSHMEM involved the design and evaluation of a library called TSHMEM (TileSHMEM) for Tilera many-core processors [7]. Along with improving developer productivity via the lightweight SHMEM API, TSHMEM delivers a high-performance many-core programming library and enables SHMEM application portability for the Tilera TILE-Gx and TILE*Pro* architectures. With the purpose of leveraging many-core capabilities and optimizations, TSHMEM is built atop Tilera-provided libraries and evaluated via microbenchmarking in order to demonstrate realizable performance and minimal overhead between the underlying libraries and TSHMEM functionality. Notable optimizations in TSHMEM include leveraging the Tilera on-chip mesh network for very-low-latency barriers. Optimization and evolution of TSHMEM continues as we research and experiment with functionality for current and future OpenSHMEM standards.

2.4 OpenMP

The OpenMP specification defines a collection of library routines, compiler directives, and environment variables that enable application parallelization via multiple threads of execution [3]. Standardized in 1997, OpenMP has been widely adopted and is portable across multiple platforms.

OpenMP commonly exploits SMP architectures by enabling both data-level and thread-level parallelism. Parallelization is typically achieved via a fork-and-join approach controlled by compiler directives whereby a master thread will fork several child threads when encountering an OpenMP parallelization section. The child threads may be assigned to different processing cores and operate independently, thereby sharing the computational load with the master. Threads are also capable of accessing shared-memory variables and data structures to assist computation. At the end of each parallel section, child threads are joined with the master thread and the parallel section closes. The master thread continues on with sequential code execution until another parallel section is encountered.

While other multi-threading APIs exist (e.g., POSIX threads), OpenMP is comparatively easier to use for developers that desire an incremental path to application parallelization for their existing sequential code. With the emergence of many-core processors such as the TILE-Gx and Xeon Phi, OpenMP is evolving to become a viable choice for single-device supercomputing tasks.

2.5 Tilera TILE-Gx

Tilera Corporation, based in San Jose, California, develops commercial many-core processors with emphases on high performance and low power in the cloud computing, general server, and embedded devices markets. Each Tilera many-core processor is designed as a scalable 2D mesh of tiles, with each tile consisting of a processing core and cache system. These tiles are attached to several on-chip networks via non-blocking cut-through switches. Referred to as the Tilera iMesh (intelligent Mesh), this scalable 2D mesh consists of dynamic networks that provide data routing between memory controllers, caches, and external I/O and enables developers to explicitly transfer data between tiles via a low-level user-accessible dynamic network.

Our research focuses on the current-generation Tilera TILE-Gx8036. The TILE-Gx is Tilera's new generation of 64-bit many-core processors. Differentiated by a substantially redesigned architecture from its 32-bit predecessor—the TILE*Pro*—the TILE-Gx exhibits upgraded processing cores, improved iMesh interconnects, and novel on-chip accelerators. Each 64-bit processing core is attached to five dynamic networks on the iMesh. The TILE-Gx8036 (a specific model of the TILE-Gx36) has 36 tiles, each consisting of a 64-bit VLIW processor with 32k L1i, 32k L1d, and 256k L2 cache. Furthermore, the L2 cache of each core is aggregated to form a large unified L3 cache. The TILE-Gx8036 offers up to 500 Gbps of memory bandwidth and over 60 Tbps of on-chip mesh interconnect bandwidth. An operating frequency from 1.0 to 1.2 GHz allows this processor to perform up to 750 billion operations per second at 10 to 55W (22W typical) TDP. Other members of the TILE-Gx family include the TILE-Gx9, TILE-Gx16, and TILE-Gx72. In addition, the TILE-Gx includes hardware accelerators not found on previous Tilera processors: mPIPE (multicore Programmable Intelligent Packet Engine) for wire-speed packet classification, distribution, and load balancing; and MiCA (Multicore iMesh Coprocessing Accelerator) for cryptographic and compression acceleration.

2.6 Intel Xeon Phi

The Xeon Phi is Intel's line of many-core coprocessors. With processing cores based on the original Intel Pentium architecture, the Xeon Phi architecture is comprised of up to 61 x86-like cores with an in-order memory model on a ring-bus topology. Its performance strength is derived from the 512-bit SIMD vector units on each core, providing maximum performance to highly vectorized applications. With four hardware-thread units per core (up to 244), the Xeon Phi can theoretically achieve more than 1 TFLOPS of double-precision performance.

Each core of the Xeon Phi consists of an x86-like processor with hardware support for four threads and 32k L1i, 32k L1d, and 512k L2 caches. The unification of the L2 caches are globally available to the cores as an L3 cache and are kept coherent via a globally distributed tag directory. Several wide high-bandwidth bidirectional ring interconnects connect the cores to each other and to the on-board GDDR5 memory modules. Data movement is facilitated by this bidirectional hardware ring bus. The main BL ring carries 64-byte wide data in each direction while the narrower AD and AK carry address and coherence information respectively.

With the Xeon Phi, Intel aims to offer a general-purpose application coprocessor and accelerator for large-scale heterogeneous systems. Housed in a GPU form factor, the Xeon Phi attaches to the PCIe bus of a standard host server and provides application acceleration via three modes of operation: offload for highly parallel work while the host processor executes typically serial work, symmetric for parallel work sharing between the host and coprocessor, and native for only-coprocessor application executions. Multiple Xeon Phi coprocessors can be attached to a single server for very high computational throughput per unit area. By supporting tools and libraries (e.g., OpenMP, Intel Clik, Intel MKL) available for code acceleration on Xeon processors, code portability to the Xeon Phi is relatively straightforward. Further performance optimizations for the Xeon Phi generally enable higher parallelism for the application on other platforms.

Our research focuses on the Intel Xeon Phi 5110P coprocessor. This coprocessor model is comprised of 60 cores with 240 hardware threads, 30 MB of on-chip cache, and 8 GB GDDR5 memory with peak bandwidth of 320 GB/s. Operating at 1.053 GHz, this passively-cooled coprocessor operates at 225W TDP.

3   SHMEM and OpenMP Performance Studies

SHMEM and OpenMP are highly amenable programming environments for SMP architectures due to their shared-memory semantics. With many-core processors emerging onto the HPC scene, developers are exceedingly interested in the performance and scalability of their applications for these devices. This section attempts to fairly analyze several applications, written in both SHMEM and OpenMP, on the TILE-Gx and Xeon Phi many-core processors. We then analyze several SHMEM-only applications to showcase performance differences between SHMEM-library implementations and conclude the section with observational experiences with both SHMEM and OpenMP, emphasizing their respective strengths and weaknesses.

3.1   Experimental Setup

The many-core platforms targeted by our research are the Tilera TILEmpower-Gx stand-alone server with a single TILE-Gx8036 [10] operating at 1.0 GHz, and the Intel Xeon Phi 5110P [6] passively-cooled PCIe card operating at 1.053 GHz attached to a standard host server. While the Xeon Phi is also designed as a coprocessor capable of offloaded workloads when paired with a Xeon host processor, we conduct our application executions with the Xeon Phi in native-execution mode only. All workloads execute only on the Xeon Phi with no significant influence from the host processor.

The SHMEM implementations under analysis include the OpenSHMEM reference implementation version 1.0d (referred to afterward as simply OpenSHMEM) and our TSHMEM library. The underlying API in OpenSHMEM is provided by GASNet version 1.20.2. GASNet was straightforwardly cross-compiled for the TILE-Gx, but cross-compiling for the Xeon Phi required minor source-code modifications to resolve missing x86 assembly instructions from the instruction-set architecture (ISA). Because the Xeon Phi has an in-order memory model, several x86 instructions related to memory fencing (i.e., sfence, lfence, mfence) are not necessary and are not included in the Xeon Phi ISA. These memory-fence instructions in GASNet were replaced with compiler barriers that effectively resolve into no-ops. In contrast, the OpenSHMEM library cleanly cross-compiles for both the TILE-Gx and Xeon Phi due to its use of the GASNet API. We leverage the GASNet SMP conduit for our experiments with OpenSHMEM. The second SHMEM implementation is our TSHMEM library which natively builds for the TILE-Gx. Due to significant use of Tilera libraries, TSHMEM portability to other platforms is under investigation for future work.

OpenMP is supported on both platforms via their native compiler. The TILE-Gx uses GCC version 4.4.6. OpenMP programs are compiled for the Xeon Phi with ICC version 13.0.1. Unless otherwise mentioned, all SHMEM and OpenMP applications are compiled with O2 optimizations.

3.2   SHMEM and OpenMP Applications

Our performance analysis of parallel-programming environments consists of three applications written each in both SHMEM and OpenMP. These applications are presented as follows: matrix multiply, linear curve fitting, and exponential curve fitting. In conducting our performance evaluation, we attempt to be impartial by evaluating how well an application's algorithm will map to the programming environment. When possible, specific optimizations were made only when the computational algorithm remained unchanged for both versions of the application. Scalability results are presented with increasing number of PEs, where PEs are either processes in SHMEM or threads in OpenMP. Serial-baseline executions were written only in the C programming language and are used for both OpenMP and SHMEM scalability at 1 PE. Results are reported in execution times for each application with power-of-two PEs as well as the realistic maximum number of PEs per device: 36 for the TILE-Gx and 240 for the Xeon Phi (60 cores).

Matrix Multiply. Matrix multiplication is a fundamental kernel in HPC and the computational sciences. The matrix-multiplication algorithm chosen for instrumentation was a partial-row dissemination with loop-interchange optimization for three matrices: $C = A \times B$. Each PE is partitioned a block of sequential rows to compute the partial result. In the case of OpenMP, the A, B, and C matrices are shared among the threads via compiler directives. Because of SHMEM's symmetric heap, the A and C matrices can be easily partitioned among the PEs, but each PE receives a private copy of the B matrix due to the pattern of computation. There are other parallelization strategies that do not require private matrix copies, but the pattern of computation and communication would have differentiated from the OpenMP version. In addition to row dissemination, loop interchange can easily occur since each matrix element in C has no data dependency with its other elements. By interchanging the inner-most loop with one of its outer loops, locality of reference and cache-hit rates drastically increase.

Execution times for SHMEM and OpenMP matrix multiplication are presented in Figure 1a. While the TILE-Gx execution times are significantly longer than the Xeon Phi's, normalizing the results with device power consumption will show more competitive conclusions. This power normalization, however, is only mentioned casually and will be investigated in the future.

For both platforms, OpenMP, OpenSHMEM, and TSHMEM execution times scale with each other up to 8 PEs. At this point, OpenSHMEM begins to stop scaling as closely with OpenMP and TSHMEM and eventually increases in execution time with higher PE counts. The performance of TSHMEM, however, follows closely with OpenMP for the TILE-Gx. Due to the Xeon Phi's 4-way SMT processing cores, each core's L1 and L2 caches are shared amongst its hardware-thread engines. Our Xeon Phi is equipped with 60 cores, therefore scalability beyond 60 is highly impacted by cache-hit rates as threads begin competing for per-core resources. For this specific OpenMP matrix multiplication, the Xeon Phi stops scaling around 128 threads. For the TILE-Gx, TSHMEM outperforms OpenSHMEM for all PE counts.

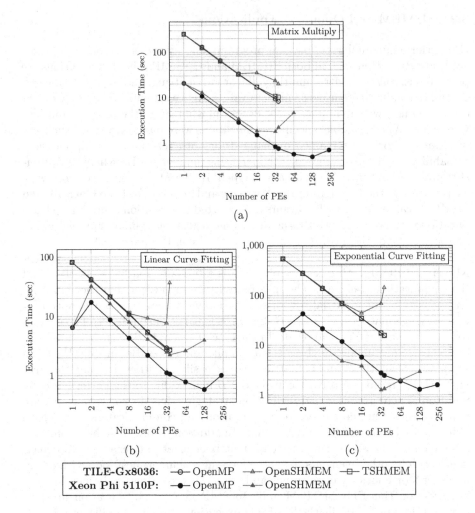

Fig. 1. Execution times for (a) matrix multiplication (2048×2048, double); (b) linear curve fitting (400M points, float); and (c) exponential curve fitting (400M points, float). For TILE-Gx, TSHMEM and OpenMP execution times commonly overlap.

Linear Curve Fitting. The second application is curve fitting via linear least-squares approximation. By using the least-mean-squares approximation, we can define a best-fit curve with minimal sum-of-squared deviation from an existing data set. If the data points are $(x_1, y_1), (x_2, y_2), \ldots, (x_n, y_n)$ where x and y are variables such that x is independent and y is dependent, then $f(x)$ can be defined as a curve with deviation d from each point in the data set. Least-squares approximation defines the best curve fit with the following deviation property:

$$\prod = d_1^2 + d_2^2 + \cdots + d_n^2 = \sum_{i=1}^{n} d_i^2 = \sum_{i=1}^{n} [y_i - f(x_i)]^2 = \text{minimum}$$

For a straight line given by the equation $f(a, b) = a + bx$, the slope and intercept can be calculated as follows: $b = \sum(dx\,dy)/\sum dx^2$; $a = \bar{y} - b\bar{x}$.

The implementation of linear curve fitting can be highly parallelized since the points distributed among the PEs can be used to compute the partial sum and the intermediate values of the deviations. These partial results can then be combined with summation reduction operations. This application provides a contrast between these two programming environments as the application is lightweight and primarily consists of memory-bound computation.

Figure 1b presents execution times for linear curve fitting for each programming environment and device. Similar to matrix multiplication on the TILE-Gx, the execution times of TSHMEM, OpenSHMEM, and OpenMP track each other until OpenSHMEM begins to stop scaling significantly after 8 PEs. Our TSHMEM library continues to outperform OpenSHMEM on TILE-Gx for all PE counts. The Xeon Phi performance shows similar scaling for OpenSHMEM and OpenMP, with a runtime disadvantage to OpenSHMEM. Interestingly, the serial baseline performs exceedingly well on the Xeon Phi without any parallelization due to aggressive cache prefetching, locality of reference across the unified L3 of the device, and strong memory performance for streaming data from arrays. The performance of this application begins increasing at 4 PEs for the OpenMP version and 8 PEs for the SHMEM version. OpenSHMEM on the Xeon Phi stops scaling after 36 PEs.

Exponential Curve Fitting. Our final application for SHMEM and OpenMP performance analysis on the TILE-Gx and Xeon Phi is curve fitting via exponential approximation. An exponential equation of the form $y = ae^{bx}$ can be represented in linear format via logarithm: $ln(y) = ln(a) + bx$. This form allows us to leverage the previous linear curve-fitting application and supplement it with logarithm functions for exponential approximation. Once this transformation is achieved, linear curve fitting is executed and the final result is transformed back by taking the inverse logarithm. Exponential curve fit is computationally intensive as compared to linear curve fit as it involves logarithmic transformation of points.

The execution times are presented in Figure 1c. For the TILE-Gx, the performance for OpenMP, OpenSHMEM, and TSHMEM follow the same pattern as the previous two applications. TSHMEM and OpenMP continue to track each other's execution times on the TILE-Gx, while OpenSHMEM does not scale as well with more than 16 PEs. The Xeon Phi, however, shows a surprisingly different trend. Unlike the two previous applications, OpenSHMEM outperforms the OpenMP version until it eventually stops scaling soon after 36 PEs. The performance difference was determined to be a log-deviation calculation whereby its reduction operation in OpenMP was seven times slower at 2 PEs than the same reduction with OpenSHMEM. Similar to linear curve fit, the serial baseline for exponential curve fit performs well when compared to OpenMP. OpenMP has parity performance with the serial baseline around 4 PEs. In comparison, OpenSHMEM is at parity performance with the serial baseline at 2 PEs. Both OpenMP and OpenSHMEM continue to increase speedup as PEs increase until 32 for OpenSHMEM and 128 for OpenMP.

3.3   SHMEM-only Applications

In conducting our analyses with SHMEM and OpenMP, writing applications to be algorithmically similar creates a disadvantage on optimization techniques available from each parallel-programming environment. While we pursued that approach in order to facilitate fair many-core platform comparisons for the computation and communication patterns of those algorithms, this subsection offers an alternative look. In this subsection, we present several parallel applications that were independently developed with the SHMEM programming library: matrix multiply and heat image from the OpenSHMEM test suite [11], a huge radix sort implementation, and process-based parallelization of the FFTW library with SHMEM. These applications are meant to showcase high performance with SHMEM as well as its specific tradeoffs.

OSH Matrix Multiply. The OpenSHMEM (OSH) website provides a test suite with benchmarks and applications [11]. One of the applications provided from the 1.0d test suite is a matrix multiplication kernel. The performance of this kernel is shown in Figure 2a for OpenSHMEM and TSHMEM for our many-core platforms. The serial baseline used is identical to the one from Figure 1a.

The execution times from Figures 1a and 2a show that OSH matrix multiplication is around 1.5 to 2 times slower than our own matrix multiplication presented in Section 3.2 when executed on the TILE-Gx. The Xeon Phi also performed worse for this application, reaching parity performance with the serial baseline at 16 PEs and stopped scaling soon after 36 PEs. The fundamental reason is due to the algorithm used in this implementation. As mentioned before, our matrix multiplication has to obtain a private copy of the second matrix, forcing the memory requirements to scale with the number of PEs and the size of the matrix. For large matrix sizes, these private copies become a problem as more and more PEs increasingly coexist on a single device. The communication time of obtaining this private copy also increases with more PEs in the system, explaining the slight increase in execution time at 32 and 36 PEs for TSHMEM compared to OpenMP in Figure 1a. The OSH matrix multiplication, however, uses a distributed data structure that divides up all matrices among the PEs. This data distribution results in more communication time to obtain non-local elements of the second matrix to perform matrix multiplication on its managed elements, but the advantage is substantially lower memory use for increasing PE sizes. While this approach is slower for these devices, it is more amenable for very large matrices, higher PE counts, or distributed systems with long latencies.

While the communication pattern plays a role in this application, TSHMEM on the TILE-Gx achieves the same runtime as OpenSHMEM on the Xeon Phi

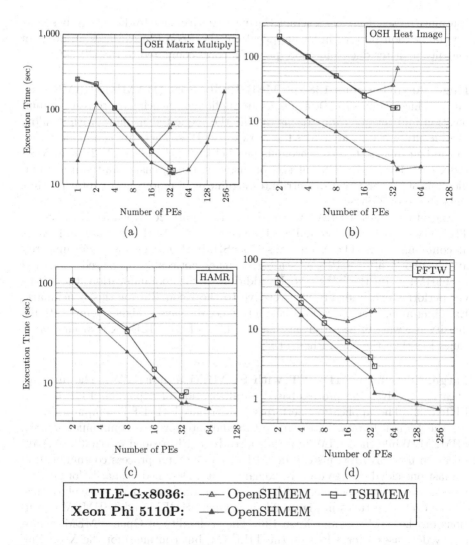

Fig. 2. Execution times for (a) OSH matrix multiply (2048×2048, double); (b) OSH heat image (1024×1024); (c) HAMR (3.8 GB); and (d) FFTW with SHMEM (8192 FFT operations on 8192-length float arrays)

at or around 36 PEs. This result is worthy of mention due to the difference in power consumption of the two devices.

OSH Heat Image. The second application is also from the OpenSHMEM test suite: heat-conduction modeling. This application takes width and height parameters as inputs and solves a heat-conduction task. Each PE generates its own initial data, performs computation, reduction, and finally generates an output image.

Execution times are shown in Figure 2b. Trends in execution time show that OpenSHMEM stops scaling around 16 PEs on the TILE-Gx whereas TSHMEM continues on to effectively leverage the entire device. Due to the relatively sparse communication pattern in this application, the Xeon Phi executes an order of magnitude faster due to its more powerful cores compared to the TILE-Gx.

Huge, Asynchronous 128-bit MSB Radix Sort (HAMR). HAMR is an in-place huge radix sort. Designed as an application benchmark to test communication and integer comparisons, it fills the requested memory with random 128-bit integers and subdivides the work to the PEs. There are two main phases to the benchmark: (1) asynchronous parallel key exchange, and (2) local MSB radix sort. For any significant size of memory, the intensive all-to-all communication of the first phase contributes significantly more toward total runtime than the second phase.

Execution times for HAMR are shown in Figure 2c. OpenSHMEM on the TILE-Gx stops scaling around 8 PEs whereas TSHMEM continues and excels at communication. The Xeon Phi's OpenSHMEM also begins performing relatively poorly after 8 PEs as scaling becomes noticeably decreased compared to TSHMEM on the TILE-Gx. In addition to the communication, the TILE-Gx performs exceptionally well relative to the Xeon Phi for this benchmark. Excelling at integer operations, the TILE-Gx displays a higher computational density per watt of power given that the TDP of the TILE-Gx is around eight times less than the Xeon Phi's TDP.

Large, Distributed 1D-FFT with SHMEM and FFTW. The final application involves the process-based parallelization of a popular FFT library, FFTW [4]. The application performs a distributed 1D-DFT computation using the FFTW library, with data setup and inter-process communication via SHMEM. While the FFTW library is already multithreaded internally, this application uses SHMEM instead of MPI to handle inter-process communication via fast one-sided puts to quickly exchange data. Designed primarily for cluster-based systems, we experiment with this application on our many-core platforms.

The execution times in Figure 2d show OpenSHMEM and TSHMEM executions on the TILE-Gx and Xeon Phi. The scalability of OpenSHMEM significantly decreases after 8 PEs on the TILE-Gx, but continues for the Xeon Phi. While previous applications showed slightly better performance with TSHMEM compared to OpenSHMEM at 8 PEs or less, execution times with FFTW show significantly superior performance for TSHMEM on the TILE-Gx. TSHMEM executions were approximately 20% faster than OpenSHMEM TILE-Gx executions. The weaker performance for OpenSHMEM with FFTW may have also manifested on the Xeon Phi, possibly explaining the close performance of TSHMEM on TILE-Gx to that of OpenSHMEM on the Xeon Phi.

3.4   Observational Experiences with SHMEM and OpenMP

To conclude our application analyses with OpenMP and SHMEM, we recap recurring themes and provide observational experiences with both of these programming environments.

In our experience with developing OpenMP and SHMEM applications, several advantages and disadvantages arose for both. OpenMP's main advantage is incremental parallelization of existing sequential applications. Through profiling, sequential code can be iterated on and gradually parallelized until the desired performance criteria are met. However, due to the use of compiler directives and developer-hidden parallelization, difficult-to-debug issues such as unnecessary synchronization, code serialization, or race conditions may occur. Additionally, OpenMP is typically unavailable for development on distributed systems and requires the use of other parallel-programming environments such as MPI for inter-node communication. The advantages of OpenMP's shared-memory model, however, allow it to remain a strong and viable choice for SMP-centric parallelization.

As alluded to previously, the OpenMP matrix multiplication application from Section 3.2 efficiently shares the three matrices with its child threads. When designing the same algorithm in SHMEM, sharing large data structures stored locally necessitates converting them into distributed data structures. For many-core devices, these distributed structures are not necessarily an advantage as the structures would still reside in the globally shared memory of SHMEM's symmetric PGAS, but incur more work for the developer to realize the same performance outcome for a single device. However, as shown from the results, SHMEM excels at large symmetric workloads whereby each PE receives computationally equivalent data and tasks. Asymmetric communication is also a strong suit for both SHMEM and OpenMP, but SHMEM performs them via standard library function calls. OpenMP, however, requires compiler support to implement these communication calls. As a result, SHMEM is highly suited for both local and distributed parallel programming (as was the original SHMEM on the Cray T3D distributed supercomputer) and is capable of taking the role of both MPI and OpenMP in a large, distributed, modern SMP-based cluster.

In all applications tested on the TILE-Gx, TSHMEM was able to successfully outperform the OpenSHMEM reference implementation. OpenSHMEM has scaling issues beyond 8 or 16 PEs, less than one-fourth or one-half of the device, and is partially attributed to less optimization for the TILE-Gx. Despite the underlying GASNet libraries cross-compiling successfully, the TILE-Gx is only generically supported. In contrast, OpenSHMEM on the Xeon Phi shows increased promise for scalability due to additional x86-based optimizations in the GASNet libraries, but several applications still display a surprisingly lower level of performance, especially relative to TSHMEM on the TILE-Gx (e.g., OpenSHMEM's matrix multiply, Figure 2a, 32 PEs). TSHMEM and OpenMP consistently scale together for these applications, demonstrating TSHMEM's potential for a hardware-aware bare-metal approach to designing a SHMEM library for many-core devices.

4   Conclusions

We have presented and evaluated three applications written in both OpenMP and SHMEM on the TILE-Gx and Xeon Phi. SHMEM implementations used include the OpenSHMEM reference implementation and our prior work with TSHMEM for Tilera many-core processors. In addition, four independently developed SHMEM applications were evaluated on our many-core platforms in order to emphasize comparative performance of the devices and the SHMEM-library implementations.

Several major contributions are illustrated with this work. The performance of SHMEM and OpenMP applications for our many-core platforms show scalability concerns for GASNet and the OpenSHMEM reference implementation on both platforms. When applicable, TSHMEM and OpenMP performance are comparable and scale similarly on the TILE-Gx. Furthermore, TSHMEM outperforms OpenSHMEM in execution times and scalability for all SHMEM applications evaluated. This conclusion provides validation to a bare-metal library design for TSHMEM on many-core devices.

Future work for this research includes power normalization of results to quantify each platform's computational density per watt, and additional results for the TILE-Gx and Xeon Phi with NAS Parallel Benchmarks [1] to evaluate their architectural strengths at different categories of computation and communication common among HPC applications.

Acknowledgements. This work was supported in part by the I/UCRC Program of the National Science Foundation under Grant Nos. EEC-0642422 and IIP-1161022.

References

1. Bailey, D., Barszcz, E., Barton, J., Browning, D., Carter, R., Dagum, L., Fatoohi, R., Fineberg, S., Frederickson, P., Lasinski, T., Schreiber, R., Simon, H., Venkatakrishnan, V., Weeratunga, S.: The NAS Parallel Benchmarks. Tech. Rep. RNR-94-007, NASA Advanced Supercomputing Division (1994)
2. Bonachea, D.: GASNet specification, v1.1. Tech. rep., University of California at Berkeley, Berkeley, CA, USA (2002)
3. Dagum, L., Menon, R.: OpenMP: an industry standard API for shared-memory programming. IEEE Computational Science Engineering 5(1), 46–55 (1998)
4. Frigo, M., Johnson, S.G.: The design and implementation of FFTW3. Proceedings of the IEEE 93(2), 216–231 (2005)
5. Gropp, W., Lusk, E., Doss, N., Skjellum, A.: A high-performance, portable implementation of the MPI message passing interface standard. Parallel Computing 22(6), 789–828 (1996)
6. Intel Corporation: Intel Xeon Phi coprocessor 5110P (2013),
   http://ark.intel.com/products/71992/
7. Lam, B.C., George, A.D., Lam, H.: TSHMEM: shared-memory parallel computing on Tilera many-core processors. In: Proc. of 18th International Workshop on High-Level Parallel Programming Models and Supportive Environments, HIPS 2013. IEEE (2013)

8. Mellanox Technologies: Mellanox ScalableSHMEM (2013), http://www.mellanox.com/related-docs/prod_software/PB_ScalableSHMEM.pdf
9. Silicon Graphics International Corp.: SHMEM API for parallel programming (2013), http://www.shmem.org/
10. Tilera Corporation: TILE-Gx8036 processor family (2013), http://www.tilera.com/products/processors/TILE-Gx_Family
11. University of Houston: OpenSHMEM source releases (2013), http://openshmem.org/site/Downloads/Source

Implementing OpenSHMEM Using MPI-3 One-Sided Communication*

Jeff R. Hammond[1], Sayan Ghosh[2], and Barbara M. Chapman[2]

[1] Argonne National Laboratory
Argonne IL, 60439
jhammond@alcf.anl.gov
[2] Dept. of Computer Science
University of Houston
Houston, Texas
{sgo,chapman}@cs.uh.edu

Abstract. This paper reports the design and implementation of Open-SHMEM over MPI using new one-sided communication features in MPI-3, which include not only new functions (e.g. remote atomics) but also a new memory model that is consistent with that of SHMEM. We use a new, non-collective MPI communicator creation routine to allow SHMEM collectives to use their MPI counterparts. Finally, we leverage MPI shared-memory windows within a node, which allows direct (load-store) access. Performance evaluations are conducted for shared-memory and InfiniBand conduits using microbenchmarks.

Keywords: SHMEM, MPI-3, RMA, one-sided communication.

1 Introduction

SHMEM [1,10] is a one-sided communication interface originally developed for Cray systems but subsequently adopted by numerous vendors (SGI, Quadrics, IBM, Mellanox, etc.) for use in high-performance computing. OpenSHMEM [7] represents a community effort to standardize SHMEM in order to enable portable applications and grow the user base. There are essentially two kinds of SHMEM implementations: (1) platform-specific, proprietary i.e. closed-source, highly optimized implementations and (2) portable (at least to some extent), open-source reference implementations. Examples of the former include SGI-SHMEM and CraySHMEM, while the latter includes the OpenSHMEM reference implementation from University of Houston, based upon widely portable GASNet [5] and

---

* This manuscript has been created by UChicago Argonne, LLC, Operator of Argonne National Laboratory ("Argonne"). Argonne, a U.S. Department of Energy Office of Science laboratory, is operated under Contract No. DEAC02-06CH11357. The U.S. Government retains for itself, and others acting on its behalf, a paid-up, nonexclusive, irrevocable worldwide license in said article to reproduce, prepare derivative works, distribute copies to the public, and perform publicly and display publicly, by or on behalf of the Government.

S. Poole, O. Hernandez, and P. Shamis (Eds.): OpenSHMEM 2014, LNCS 8356, pp. 44–58, 2014.
© Springer International Publishing Switzerland 2014

SHMEM based upon Portals4 [4], which is portable to the most common commodity networks. MVAPICH2-X [14] is not proprietary in the sense that it is freely available and not distributed by any platform vendor, but it is currently closed-source and only supports InfiniBand, for which it is highly optimized.

Among the current reference implementations – that is, the ones based upon GASNet and Portals4, respectively – are limited in portability only by their underlying conduits. GASNet has broad support of both commodity and HPC networks; we are not aware of any widely used platform that is not supported. Despite the wide portability of GASNet, it is not supported directly by vendors nor is it shipped in binary form for commodity systems (in part due to the different ways PGAS compilers use it, which require different configurations) and it lacks explicit support for atomic operations, which prevents the use of native hardware implementations when available. On the other hand, the Portals4 implementation is itself a reference implementation of the Portals4 specification [3], which aims to have optimized implementations where at least some of the features have customized hardware support. The Portals4 reference implementation currently supports shared memory, TCP/IP and InfiniBand. In contrast to the aforementioned conduits, MPI is supported on the widest variety of platforms, is supported by all major HPC vendors and can be trivially installed via the appropriate package management system on the most common platforms. Broad portability and vendor support are not the only advantages of an MPI-based implementation. The MPI ecosystem includes powerful performance and debugging tools as well as parallel math and I/O libraries (as just two examples), all of which are now available for use in SHMEM applications. Finally, because GASNet nor Portals4 provide collective operations, any implementation of these must be implemented on top of point-to-point operations inside of the SHMEM library. On the other hand, an MPI-based implementation immediately leverages many years of algorithm and software development of MPI collectives. The relatively recent release of the MPI-3 standard has made possible – for the first time – a direct implementation of SHMEM and PGAS programming models using the one-sided functionality therein. Prior to MPI-3, lack of important atomic operations (e.g. fetch-and-add and compare-and-swap), inconvenient memory model (designed to support non-cache coherent systems), and awkward synchronization functions made MPI one-sided communication an inadequate conduit for models like SHMEM. Additional criticism and analysis of the MPI-2 one-sided communication in the context of PGAS can be found in Bonachea and Duell [6] and Dinan, et al. [8]. With the features provided in MPI-3, it is possible to implement SHMEM relatively efficiently since essentially all SHMEM calls map directly to one or two MPI calls and the synchronization modes in MPI-3 are not excessive relative to SHMEM semantics. Given this, the limiting factor in SHMEM performance when implemented using MPI-3 is the quality of the MPI implementation. The purpose of this paper is to demonstrate the first implementation of OpenSHMEM using MPI-3 as the conduit. We leave performance analysis/profiling and discussion on RMA implementation quality for future work. We refer to our implementation of OpenSHMEM over MPI-3 as OSHMPI. We compare our implementation to existing implementations for shared memory and InfiniBand, which include those based upon GASNet and Portals4 as well as the optimized MVAPICH2-X implementation. We also compare OSHMPI with a vendor implementation of OpenSHMEM from Mellanox, called Mellanox-ScalableSHMEM which works with the OpenFabrics RDMA for Linux stack (OFED).

2 Background

In order to motivate our design choices, we summarize the important semantics of the SHMEM and MPI-3 models to understand how they must be reconciled in the implementation and the performance effects associated therewith.

2.1 SHMEM

One-Sided Communication. SHMEM one-sided communication operations are locally blocking, meaning they return once the local buffer is available for reuse. Single-element, contiguous and strided variants of Put (remote write) and Get (remote read) are provided. For each of these, the type is encoded in the function name, which enables compiler type-checking (for example, this is not available in MPI C code except via collaboration of compiler extensions and metadata in the MPI header file [11]). SHMEM also supports the common atomic operations of swap, compare-and-swap, add, fetch-and-add, increment and fetch-and-increment, all of which block on local completion, which entails a round trip in four of the six cases.

The synchronization primitives for one-sided operations are Fence and Quiet, with the former corresponding to point-wise ordering and the latter to ordering with respect to all remote targets. Some implementations specify that these ordering points correspond to remote completion, which is sufficient but not always necessary to ensure ordering. In any case, we choose the conservative interpretation - these functions enforce remote completion of one-sided operations.

Collective Communication. SHMEM provides Barrier, Broadcast, Reduction and Gather operations with type support encoded into the function names, just as for one-sided operations. Subsets of processes (referred as PEs or Processing Elements in SHMEM) are described using (PE_start, logPE_stride, PE_size) tuples, which is not fully general, but are still useful for some applications. With the exception of shmem_barrier_all, collectives take an argument pSync, which presumably allows for the implementation to avoid additional internal state for collectives.

2.2 MPI-3

Barrett, et al. discussed MPI-3 RMA semantics in detail in Ref. [2]; we summarize only the salient points related to SHMEM here.

One-Sided Communication. The MPI 3.0 standard [17] represents a significant change from previous iterations of MPI, particularly with respect to one-sided communication (RMA). New semantics for memory consistency, ordering and passive-target synchronization were introduced, all three of which have a significant (positive) impact on an MPI-based implementation of SHMEM.

The unified memory model of MPI-3 RMA stipulates that direct local access and RMA-based access to the memory associated with a window[1] see the same data (but not necessarily *immediately*) without explicit synchronization. This model is not required, rather the user must query for it, but it should be possible for implementations to support this on cache-coherent architectures.

Prior to MPI-3, RMA operations were specified as unordered and the only means for ordering operations was to remote-complete them. This entails a rather high overhead and so MPI-3 now specifies that accumulate operations are ordered by default; these operations have always been specified as element-wise atomic, unlike Put and Get. The user can inform the implementation that ordering is not required but then the user is required to enforce ordering via remote completion in the application.

In MPI-2, passive target synchronization was specified in the form of an epoch delineated with calls to `MPI_Win_lock` and `MPI_Win_unlock`. Only upon returning from the latter call was any synchronization implied and it implied global visibility, i.e. remote completion. MPI-3 provides the user the ability to specify local and remote completion separately and to do so without terminating an epoch. These semantics are more consistent with SHMEM and ARMCI [18] as well as many modern networks.

Collective Communication. MPI collective communication occurs on a communicator, which is an opaque object associated with a group processes. Communication on one communicator is independent of communication on another, which enables strict separation of different sets of messages in the case of point-to-point and allows for a well-defined semantic for collective operations on overlapping groups of processes. In MPI-2, communicators could only be created collectively on the parent communicator, meaning that a subcommunicator to be derived from the default (world) communicator (containing all processes) could not be created without the participation of all processes. This precluded their use in SHMEM collectives unless all possible subcommunicators were created at initialization, which is obviously unreasonable.

MPI-3 introduced a new function for creating subcommunicators that is collective only on the group of processes that are included in the new communicator [9]. This enables subcommunicators associated with (`PE_start`, `logPE_stride`, `PE_size`) tuples to be created on the fly as necessary. Of course, creating subcommunicators on the fly is potentially expensive relative to a particular collective operation, so a high-quality implementation of SHMEM over MPI-3 would maintain a cache of these since it is reasonable to assume that they will be reused. The MVAPICH2-X implementation of OpenSHMEM does this internally despite

---

[1] A window is the opaque memory registration object of MPI RMA upon which all one-sided operations act.

not explicitly using the MPI-3 interface for collectives [16]. Another potential bottleneck in this process is the translation of the root PE (necessary only for broadcast operations) to a process in the subcommunicator, which is $O(N)$ in space and time [23]. However, we can avoid this translation routine if necessary due to the restricted usage necessary in SHMEM collectives.

3   Implementation Design

In this section, we outline the design of the mapping from SHMEM to MPI-3. The mapping of SHMEM functions to MPI-3 ones is mostly straightforward due to the flexibility MPI-3 RMA, but there are a few key issues that must be addressed.

Symmetric Heap: The use of symmetric variables is a unique concept in one-sided communication that deserves special mention [20]. SHMEM communication operations act on virtual addresses associated with symmetric variables, which include data in the symmetric heap (dynamically allocated) and statically allocated data, such as global variables and variables declared with the static attribute. Communication with stack variables is not supported within OpenSHMEM. On the other hand, the MPI window object is opaque and communication operations act on data in the window specified via offsets relative to the window base, which can be different on every PE. Whereas SHMEM requires all allocations from the symmetric heap be symmetric (i.e. uniform across all PEs), MPI supports the general case where PEs can pass different sizes (including zero) to the window constructor routine. Prior to MPI-3, the only window constructor routine was MPI_Win_create, which was a registration routine that took local memory buffers as input. This precluded the use of symmetric allocations for scalable metadata; it had to be assumed that the base address was different at every PE, thus requiring $O(N)$ metadata in the window object. MPI-3 provides a new routine for constructing windows that includes memory allocation (MPI_Win_allocate), hence permits the implementation to allocate symmetrically. It also permits the use of shared memory segments for intranode optimization. This is available explicitly to the user via MPI_Win_allocate_shared and implicitly in the case of MPI_Win_allocate. By explicit, we mean that the user can query the virtual address associated with a window segment in another PE on the same node and access it via load-store; the implicit case is where the implementation uses shared memory to bypass the network interface when the user makes MPI communication calls.

Put and Get: SHMEM performs communication against symmetric data, which can be either global, static or symmetric heap (*sheap*) data. The latter is quite easy to deal with; we allocate an MPI window of sufficient size (controlled by an environment variable) and allocate memory out of it. To access this data remotely, one merely translates the local address into a remote offset within the sheap window, which is not expensive. Global data is registered with MPI using MPI_Win_create at initialization using the appropriate operating system mechanism to get the base address and size of this region. We use one window for *bss* and *data* segments (global data can reside in both places) but two may be required in some cases. The lookup function (`__shmem_window_offset`) differentiates between the two windows. We use a much simpler special case as that of [8] because valid symmetric variables always fall within one of two windows. Because the symmetric heap window is allocated rather than just registered, it supports directly local access within a node, so for this case, we use direct access when all PEs reside in a single node. This can be generalized to multiple nodes using overlapping windows – one each for internode and intranode communication[2] – but this has not yet been implemented.

```
void __shmem_put(MPI_Datatype type, int type_size, void *target,
                 const void *source, size_t len, int pe)
{
    enum shmem_window_id_e win_id;
    shmem_offset_t offset;
    __shmem_window_offset(target, pe, &win_id, &offset));
    if (world_is_smp && win_id==SHEAP_WINDOW) {
        void * ptr = smp_sheap_ptrs[pe] + (target - sheap_base_ptr);
        memcpy(ptr, source, len*type_size);
    } else {
        MPI_Win win = (win_id==SHEAP_WINDOW) ? sheap_win : text_win;
        int n = (int)len; assert(len<(size_t)INT32_MAX);
        MPI_Accumulate(source, n, type, pe, offset, n, type, MPI_REPLACE, win);
        MPI_Win_flush_local(pe, win);
    }
}

void shmem_int_put(int *target, const int *source, size_t len, int pe)
{    __shmem_put(MPI_INT, 4, target, source, len, pe);    }
```

Fig. 1. The implementation of SHMEM put using MPI for one type-variant. The code is modified from the original for presentation purposes.

Synchronization: The synchronization primitives `shmem_fence` and `shmem_quiet` are both mapped to `MPI_Win_flush_all` in order to ensure pairwise and global ordering of one-sided operations. Because `shmem_fence` does not take a specific PE as an argument, the implementation would like have to maintain $O(N)$ state to implement the minimum synchronization required. We assume that the MPI implementation already tracks the remote processes and only flushes those that are the the target of communication and thus it is redundant for our implementation to do this. The assumption that `MPI_Win_flush_all` is an efficient way to implement `shmem_fence` may not always be true, but it is perhaps worth noting that the Portals4 implementation does something similar to avoid $O(N)$ state.

Atomics. Atomic operations map from SHMEM to MPI similarly as with Put and Get. Table 1 specifies how each SHMEM function translates to an MPI function. Because `shmem_inc` and `shmem_finc` are just special cases of `shmem_add` and `shmem_fadd`, respectively, we do not list them.

---

[2] The need for two windows may be obviated in a future version of the MPI standard.

Table 1. Correspondance between SHMEM and MPI atomic operations

SHMEM function	MPI function	Accumulate operation
shmem_cswap	MPI_Compare_and_swap	-
shmem_swap	MPI_Fetch_and_op	MPI_REPLACE
shmem_fadd	MPI_Fetch_and_op	MPI_SUM
shmem_add	MPI_Accumulate	MPI_SUM

Collective Operations. We follow the same approach as [16] with respect to non-collective communicator creation [9]. Figure 2 shows the code that is used to translate a SHMEM PE group triplet to an MPI subcommunicator. Only Broadcast requires the rank translation of the root; when an invalid rank (e.g. -1) is passed to this function, translation is skipped. The use of a cache for communicators is an obvious optimization but one that is not yet implemented in OSHMPI.

Table 2 shows the mapping from SHMEM to MPI with respect to collective operations. Because the shmem_collect routine provides only the count at each PE, the MPI implementation requires an MPI_Allgather to form the vector of counts. The translation from SHMEM reduction operators to their MPI counterparts is trivial and is left as an exercise for the reader.

```
void __shmem_acquire_comm(int pe_start, int pe_logs, int pe_size,
                          MPI_Comm * comm, int pe_root, int * broot)
{
    if (pe_start==0 && pe_logs==0 && pe_size==shmem_world_size) {
        *comm = SHMEM_COMM_WORLD; *broot = pe_root;
    } else {
        MPI_Group strgrp;
        int * pe_list = malloc(pe_size*sizeof(int)); assert(pe_list!=NULL);
        int pe_stride = 1<<pe_logs;
        for (int i=0; i<pe_size; i++) pe_list[i] = pe_start + i*pe_stride;
        MPI_Group_incl(SHMEM_GROUP_WORLD, pe_size, pe_list, &strgrp);
        MPI_Comm_create_group(SHMEM_COMM_WORLD, strgrp, pe_start, comm);
        if (pe_root>=0) *broot = __shmem_translate_root(strgrp, pe_root);
        MPI_Group_free(&strgrp);
        free(pe_list);
    }
}
```

Fig. 2. Code to create an MPI sub communicator associated with a PE subgroup

Table 2. Mapping of SHMEM collectives to MPI collective functions

SHMEM	MPI
shmem_barrier	MPI_Barrier
shmem_broadcast	MPI_Bcast
shmem_collect	MPI_Allgatherv
shmem_fcollect	MPI_Allgather
shmem_<op>_to_all	MPI_Allreduce(op)

4 Results

In this section, we evaluate the performance of OSHMPI versus other implementations of OpenSHMEM (GASNet, Portals4, MVAPICH2-X and Mellanox).
While these are not the only OpenSHMEM implementations available, they are
a representative set and sufficient to make a reasonable evaluation of the quality
of our implementation and of MPI-3 as a conduit. In particular, the comparison
of OSHMPI using the MPI-3 implementation found in MVAPICH2 to the Open-
SHMEM implementation in MVAPICH2-X is particularly useful, since this uses
at least some of the same implementation features and thus exposes more of the
semantic differences. However, as will be shown below, there appear to be implementation issues that prevent MPI-3 from achieving its full potential, i.e. not all
the differences are due to semantics. Most of the test cases are taken from publicly available benchmarks or example codes packaged with the OpenSHMEM
reference API.

The evaluation platform used is a dual-socket AMD 6128 (8 cores/socket) cluster with QDR InfiniBand from Mellanox and 64 GB of memory per node. We
use the latest release of each of the implementations considered. OSHMPI uses
MPICH 3.1b2 for SMP, and MVAPICH2 2.0a for distributed cases. The Open-
SHMEM reference implementation uses GASNet 1.20 configured for GASNet
"smp" and "ibv" conduits only; this implementation is referred to as GASNet.
For SHMEM-Portals and Portals4 (henceforth, Portals4), the repository trunk
is used, configured with --with-implementation=ib --enable-ib-shmem.

MVAPICH2-X 2.0a provides the OpenSHMEM implementation, which is denoted as MVAPICH2-X. Mellanox-ScalableSHMEM version 2.0 is also included
in our evaluation (configured with only --with-oshmem), denoted as MLNX.

4.1 OpenSHMEM versus MPI-3 – Implementation Effects

Figure 3 compares the message rate for messages from 8 byte to 8 MB using tests written for the MPI-3 and OpenSHMEM interfaces and implemented
with MVAPICH2 and MVAPICH2-X, respectively. The purpose of this test is
to elucidate differences in the implementation of the two protocols within a presumably similar implementation. The differences need not necessarily be so large
but MVAPICH2 inherits an implementation design for one-sided that is not targeting one-sided networks, whereas the OpenSHMEM implementation clearly
exploits the one-sided nature of InfiniBand in a direct way.

4.2 Latency and Message-Rate Evaluation

In this section, we evaluate the performance of the OSHMPI, Portals4, GASNet,
Mellanox-ScalableSHMEM and MVAPICH2-X implementations using the OSU
microbenchmarks [15]. These tests measures the message rate, average latencies
for varying message sizes and types of one-sided operations. Figures 4a, 4b, 4c
and 4d show the average latencies on a shared memory system or across the
network on distributed nodes with increasing data sizes from 1 to 2^{20} bytes.

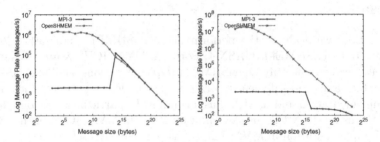

Fig. 3. Internode and intranode (both with 2 PEs) message rate (**long** *puts*) of MPI-3 and OpenSHMEM interfaces as implemented with MVAPICH2 and MVAPICH2-X, respectively

Figure 5 shows aggregate unidirectional put injection rate with message size varying from 1 to 2^{22} bytes on shared-memory and distributed nodes.

The shared-memory performance of OSHMPI is generally superior as compared to others, which is due to the use of MPI-3 shared memory windows that allows direct load-store access on the target memory without any additional overhead. Portals4 cannot do this due to the lack of XPMEM support and GASNet appears to require additional overhead, either due to locking or copying through shared segments. Mellanox-ScalableSHMEM has performance close to GASNet for distributed nodes, the sharp drop/rise in the performance plot (Figure 5) suggests message-transfer protocol crossover at certain sizes. On the other hand, OSHMPI suffers from poor message rate/latency on distributed nodes. This is mostly due to the implementation quality but a small portion of the overhead can be attributed to the requirement of two MPI function calls to implement a blocking Put operation – since MPI_Put is nonblocking, it must be followed by MPI_Win_flush_local – which may entail more software overhead than implementations that use only a single call to the conduit API.

The operation rate test for OpenSHMEM atomic routines are similar to the Put message-rate test. The benchmark measures the performance of atomic fetch-operate routines supported in OpenSHMEM by issuing back-to-back atomic operations of a type from the origin to the target PE. Figure 6 shows the average latency and aggregate message rate per atomic operation for all the atomic operations between two PEs on two nodes.

4.3   SHMEM Barrier Performance

Barriers are used extensively in parallel programs, perhaps unnecessarily in some cases, but they are nonetheless an essential collective operation that needs to be efficient. Figure 7 shows barrier latencies for the shared memory and distributed cases (on 2, 4, 8, and 16 PEs). OSHMPI and MVAPICH2-X have nearly identical performance, indicating the same underlying implementation (using the MPI collective infrastructure in MVAPICH2). The OSHMPI routine shmem_barrier also performs local and remote synchronization, meaning a memory barrier and a

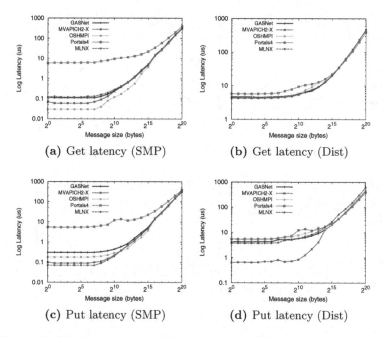

Fig. 4. Get/Put latencies on 2 PEs of one node (SMP) and two nodes (Dist)

remote flush of all outstanding communication operations, which is not explicitly required by the OpenSHMEM specification but is implied by examples programs therein. Barrier illustrates a significant benefit of using MPI as a conduit for SHMEM; collective operations are heavily optimized in MPI implementations and often use the best available algorithms. Building collectives on top of point-to-point operations in a SHMEM-oriented conduit may make it difficult or even impossible to achieve the same performance as MPI. For example, MPI leverages hardware implementations of collectives on systems such as IBM Blue Gene. Alternatively, a SHMEM-oriented conduit may not provide the most appropriate point-to-point operations for implementing synchronous collectives, thereby requiring the SHMEM collective implementation to poll on memory locations or use other inefficient protocols.

4.4 Solving 2D Heat Equation

The 2D heat benchmark predicts the heat distribution, resulting from conduction in a 2D domain and could be solved iteratively using - Jacobi, Gauss-Seidel and Successive Over-relaxation methods. The benchmark code (`shmem_2dheat.c`) is available with the OpenSHMEM reference API package. In the 2D heat benchmark, data is distributed evenly across PEs (plus one or more rows to facilitate "ghost" transfers from neighbors). Rows of data are communicated between adjacent PEs, with the communication overhead of $(2*npes - 1)$ per iteration. The results of the 2D heat benchmark on 128, 256, 512, and 1024 PEs for OSHMPI,

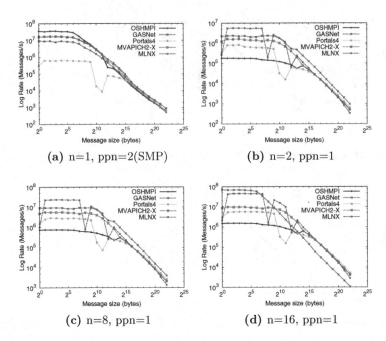

(a) n=1, ppn=2(SMP)   **(b)** n=2, ppn=1

(c) n=8, ppn=1   **(d)** n=16, ppn=1

Fig. 5. Unidirectional Put message-rate on 2, 8, and 16 PEs within a node (top-left) and across nodes

MVAPICH2-X, GASNet, Mellanox-ScalableSHMEM and Portals4 on a (32K × 32K) matrix are shown in Figure 8. For this particular benchmark, some of the GASNet runs terminated with a segmentation fault, hence we are unable to show GASNet results beyond 256 PEs.

5   Observations

For shared memory systems, the performance of OSHMPI and MVAPICH2-X is comparable, which is not surprising given that the implementations are documented to use the same optimizations. The Portals4 intranode performance is not surprisingly slow given that XPMEM could not be used due to the inability to install this kernel module because it requires elevated privileges. [3] Additional performance artifacts are seen in Portals4 for messages between 1 and 64 KiB in internode tests, which may be the result of protocol crossover effects.

In distributed case however, both in terms of latency and message rate, OSHMPI is noticeably worse than other implementations. One can only assume that the MPI-3 implementation in MVAPICH2 is not as optimized as the SHMEM implementation in MVAPICH2-X (see Figure 3). For larger messages, however, both the direct and indirect (that is, via MPI-3) performance is similar,

---

[3] XPMEM is a Linux kernel module (originally developed by SGI) that enables a process to attach memory segments from another process to it's address space.

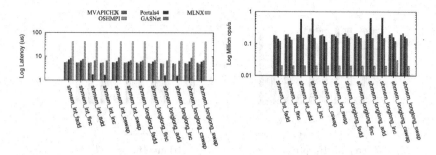

Fig. 6. Atomic latency and operations rate between 2 PEs across 2 nodes

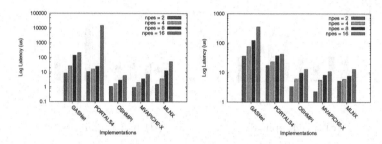

Fig. 7. Barrier latencies on 2, 4, 8, and 16 PEs within a node (left) and across nodes (right). n=1,ppn=*npes* for SMP and n=*npes*,ppn=1 for Dist.

so the MPI-3 implementation appears to be related to the short-message implementation, which one hopes will be optimized in future releases of MVAPICH2. GASNet performs the best for short-to-medium messages but is not as robust as the others when a larger number of PEs are used; we were unable to run the 2D heat test for 256 PEs or larger with this implementation.

The atomic latency and message rate performance of MVAPICH2-X and OSHMPI for distributed nodes are found to be very similar, as evident from Figure 6, suggesting that the MVAPICH2 SHMEM and MPI-3 implementations are of similar quality.

We notice significant latency variations across SHMEM implementations of barrier routines (shown in Figure 7). Particularly, GASNet and Portals4 latencies are a minimum ~10x to that of OSHMPI and MVAPICH2-X on two nodes. GASNet performance significantly degrades for 16 distributed PEs.

We had also performed other collective tests – broadcast, reduce and collect – and observed that GASNet performance was substantially worse for collect/reduce (for both SMP and distributed nodes). On the other hand, OSHMPI and MVAPICH2-X have identical performance for both shared and distributed cases, which is not surprising given their use of the same infrastructure internally.

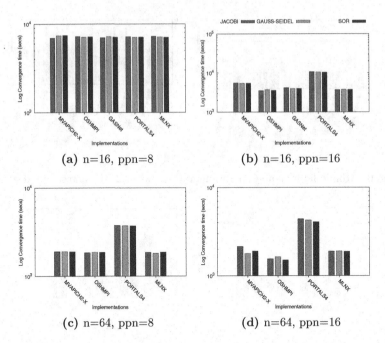

(a) n=16, ppn=8   **(b)** n=16, ppn=16

(c) n=64, ppn=8   **(d)** n=64, ppn=16

Fig. 8. 2D-Heat benchmark performance of SHMEM implementations on 128/256/512/1024 PEs for 32K × 32K matrix

6 Related Work

Since the introduction of SHMEM for Cray T3D, there have been several other implementations, including QSHMEM [21], HP-SHMEM [12], SGI-SHMEM [24], GPSHMEM [19], and IBM TurboSHMEM [13], each with distinct API specifications. In addition to MVAPICH2-X and Portals-SHMEM, Gator-SHMEM [25] and Mellanox ScalableSHMEM [22] are additional implementations of the Open-SHMEM API.

7 Conclusions and Future Work

This paper describes the initial design and implementation of an OpenSHMEM implementation using MPI-3 as a communication conduit. With the recent improvements in the MPI-3 specification, particularly related to RMA, MPI is now a suitable conduit for PGAS programming models like SHMEM. The simplicity of our implementation indicates a good semantic match between the two models. Additionally, the performance is similar to existing PGAS runtimes such as GAS-Net, Portals4, Mellanox-ScalableSHMEM and MVAPICH2-X for many cases, although clearly there is room for improvement for distributed memory. On the other hand, the intranode, i.e. shared-memory, performance was excellent and in many cases better than the others, suggesting that MPI shared-memory windows are an effective way to optimize one-sided communication within a node.

The performance of collective operations was excellent with the MPI implementation, as one might expect given the substantial investment in these over the last 20 years. While SHMEM is primarily about one-sided communication, SHMEM applications may rely upon collective operations, particularly in certain mathematical procedures (e.g. Krylov solvers), where dot products are essential.

In the future, we will generalize our intranode optimizations to work in the general case where PEs are spread across multiple nodes, i.e. shared-memory access will be used within a node while MPI operations will be used between nodes. This usage is permitted using the unified memory model of MPI-3 that can be supported on cache-coherent systems. OSHMPI currently lacks intranode optimizations for atomics and strided operations but it is straightforward to add these, the former using compiler intrinsics instead of inline assembly to maintain a high degree of portability. MPI datatypes will be used to support SHMEM operations on more than 2^{31} elements, which may be required on 64-bit systems with abundant memory.

Acknowledgment. This research used resources of the Argonne Leadership Computing Facility at Argonne National Laboratory, which is supported by the Office of Science of the U.S. Department of Energy under contract DE-AC02-06CH11357. We are thankful to all the anonymous reviewers who helped us improve the paper.

References

1. Bariuso, R., Knies, A.: Shmem user's guide (1994)
2. Barrett, B., Hoefler, T., Dinan, J., Thakur, R., Balaji, P., Gropp, B., Underwood, K.D.: Remote memory access programming in MPI-3. Preprint, Argonne National Laboratory (April 2013)
3. Barrett, B.W., Brightwell, R., Hemmert, S., Pedretti, K., Wheeler, K., Underwood, K., Riesen, R., Maccabe, A.B., Hudson, T.: The Portals 4.0 message passing interface (SAND2013-3181) (April 2013)
4. Barrett, B.W., Brigthwell, R., Scott Hemmert, K., Pedretti, K., Wheeler, K., Underwood, K.D.: Enhanced support for OpenSHMEM communication in Portals. In: Symposium on High-Performance Interconnects, pp. 61–69 (2011)
5. Bonachea, D.: GASNet specification, v1.1. Technical Report UCB/CSD-02-1207, U.C. Berkeley (2002)
6. Bonachea, D., Duell, J.: Problems with using MPI 1.1 and 2.0 as compilation targets for parallel language implementations. Int. J. High Perform. Comput. Netw. 1, 91–99 (2004)
7. Chapman, B., Curtis, T., Pophale, S., Poole, S., Kuehn, J., Koelbel, C., Smith, L.: Introducing OpenSHMEM: SHMEM for the PGAS community. In: Proceedings of the Fourth Conference on Partitioned Global Address Space Programming Model, p. 2. ACM (2010)

8. Dinan, J., Balaji, P., Hammond, J.R., Krishnamoorthy, S., Tipparaju, V.: Supporting the Global Arrays PGAS model using MPI one-sided communication. In: Proceedings of the International Parallel and Distributed Processing Symposium (IPDPS) (May 2012)
9. Dinan, J., Krishnamoorthy, S., Balaji, P., Hammond, J.R., Krishnan, M., Tipparaju, V., Vishnu, A.: Noncollective communicator creation in MPI. In: Cotronis, Y., Danalis, A., Nikolopoulos, D.S., Dongarra, J. (eds.) EuroMPI 2011. LNCS, vol. 6960, pp. 282–291. Springer, Heidelberg (2011)
10. Feind, K.: Shared memory access (shmem) routines. In: Cray User Group, CUG 2005 (1995)
11. Gribenko, D., Zinenko, A.: Enabling Clang to statically check MPI type safety. In: International Conferences on High Performance Computing (HPC-UA) (October 2012)
12. HP. HP Alphaserver SC 40, http://h18002.www1.hp.com/alphaserver/archive/sc/sys_sc40_features.html
13. IBM. HPC Toolkit, https://computing.llnl.gov/mpi/klepacki.pdf (2004)
14. Jose, J., Kandalla, K., Luo, M., Panda, D.K.: Supporting hybrid MPI and OpenSHMEM over InfiniBand: Design and performance evaluation. In: 2012 41st International Conference on Parallel Processing (ICPP), pp. 219–228 (2012)
15. Jose, J., Kandalla, K., Luo, M., Panda, D.K.: Supporting hybrid MPI and OpenSHMEM over InfiniBand: Design and performance evaluation. In: 2012 41st International Conference on Parallel Processing (ICPP), pp. 219–228. IEEE (2012)
16. Jose, J., Kandalla, K., Zhang, J., Potluri, S., Panda, D.K.: Optimizing collective communication in OpenSHMEM (October 2013)
17. MPI Forum. MPI: A message-passing interface standard. Version 3.0 (November 2012)
18. Nieplocha, J., Carpenter, B.: ARMCI: A portable remote memory copy library for distributed array libraries and compiler run-time systems. In: Rolim, J., et al. (eds.) IPPS-WS 1999 and SPDP-WS 1999. LNCS, vol. 1586, pp. 533–546. Springer, Heidelberg (1999)
19. Parzyszek, K., Nieplocha, J., Kendall, R.A.: A generalized portable SHMEM library for high performance computing. Technical report, Ames Lab., Ames, IA, US (2000)
20. Poole, S.W., Hernandez, O., Kuehn, J.A., Shipman, G.M., Curtis, A., Feind, K.: OpenSHMEM - toward a unified RMA model. In: Encyclopedia of Parallel Computing, pp. 1379–1391. Springer (2011)
21. Quadrics. Quadrics/SHMEM programming manual (2001)
22. Shainer, G., Wilde, T., Lui, P., Liu, T., Kagan, M., Dubman, M., Shahar, Y., Graham, R., Shamis, P., Poole, S.: The co-design architecture for exascale systems, a novel approach for scalable designs. In: Computer Science-Research and Development, pp. 1–7 (2013)
23. Träff, J.L.: Compact and efficient implementation of the MPI group operations, pp. 170–178 (2010)
24. Woodacre, M., Robb, D., Roe, D., Feind, K.: The SGI AltixTM 3000 global shared-memory architecture (2005)
25. Yoon, C., Aggarwal, V., Hajare, V., George, A.D., Billingsley III, M.: GSHMEM: A portable library for lightweight, shared-memory, parallel programming. In: Proceedings of Partitioned Global Address Space, Galveston, Texas (2011)

Analyzing the Energy and Power Consumption of Remote Memory Accesses in the OpenSHMEM Model

Siddhartha Jana[1], Oscar Hernandez[2], Stephen Poole[2],
Chung-Hsing Hsu[2], and Barbara M. Chapman[1]

[1] HPCTools, Computer Science Department,
University of Houston,
Houston, Texas
{sidjana,chapman}@cs.uh.edu
[2] Computer Science and Mathematics Division
Oak Ridge National Laboratory,
Oak Ridge, Tennessee
{oscar,spoole,hsuc}@ornl.gov

Abstract. PGAS models like OpenSHMEM provide interfaces to explicitly initiate one-sided remote memory accesses among processes. In addition, the model also provides synchronizing barriers to ensure a consistent view of the distributed memory at different phases of an application. The incorrect use of such interfaces affects the scalability achievable while using a parallel programming model. This study aims at understanding the effects of these constructs on the energy and power consumption behavior of OpenSHMEM applications. Our experiments show that cost incurred in terms of the total energy and power consumed depends on multiple factors across the software and hardware stack. We conclude that there is a significant impact on the power consumed by the CPU and DRAM due to multiple factors including the design of the data transfer patterns within an application, the design of the communication protocols within a middleware, the architectural constraints laid by the interconnect solutions, and also the levels of memory hierarchy within a compute node. This work motivates treating energy and power consumption as important factors while designing compute solutions for current and future distributed systems.

1 Introduction

Recent studies on the challenges facing the Exascale era express a need for understanding the energy profile of applications that depend on inter-process communication on large-scale systems. The amount of energy consumed due to data movement poses a serious threat to the usability of distributed memory models on future systems. One-sided communication in PGAS models are analogous to memory accesses in shared-memory models. However, its impact on the performance and power consumption is different.

Shared memory models are characterized by implicit data transfers that are bounded by the distance between the CPU and the different levels of the memory

S. Poole, O. Hernandez, and P. Shamis (Eds.): OpenSHMEM 2014, LNCS 8356, pp. 59–73, 2014.

hierarchy. Such data transfers include intra-node cache and memory accesses that consume very low energy, typically of the order of 800-1000 pico Joules [7]. In contrast, inter-process communication patterns in PGAS models are initiated by the programmer and bounded by a number of factors internal and external to a single compute node. In this paper, we present our study of the factors affecting the energy and power consumption behavior of parallel programming models. These can be categorized as either internal or external based on the associated layers of the hardware and the software stack. Benedict [6] and Hoefler [12] list some of the factors that have the potential to affect the energy consumption of interconnect solutions. They include the router/switch organization, flow control, congestion control, routing and deadlock handling, network topology, load balancing, reliability, and QoS support.

The scope of this paper is to discuss the energy consumption by the CPU and the memory hierarchy while servicing remote data transfers and synchronization constructs provided by the OpenSHMEM model.

PGAS implementations like OpenSHMEM stand out with respect to their memory consistency model. To maintain a consistent view of the progress of execution and the globally-shared memory among multiple processes (or *processing elements*), OpenSHMEM provides synchronizing constructs like *shmem_barrier_all()*, *shmem_fence()*, and *shmem_quiet()*. The impact of such barriers on the performance and scalability of distributed applications is well known [17]. In Section 3, we discuss our findings on the factors affecting the power consumption of applications that use such barriers.

The OpenSHMEM memory model permits RDMA operations. Our studies indicate that during the progress of such operations, there is a significant impact on the power consumed by the CPU and DRAM due to multiple factors including the design of the data transfer patterns within an application, the design of the communication protocols within a middleware, the architectural constraints laid by the interconnect solutions, and also the levels of memory hierarchy within a compute node. We present a study of the parameters that affect the power consumption behavior of such interfaces in Section 4.

Our empirical study was carried out at the granularity of various OpenSHMEM constructs. Because of the fine level of granularity, it was essential to reduce the impact on the power readings by external noise like the host Operating system and background processes. In Section 2, we describe our experimental setup for collecting the energy and power readings under such conditions.

2   Notes on Experimental Setup

The details of the test environment used to obtain the empirical results in this paper are listed in Table 1.

2.1   Setup for Monitoring Energy and Power Consumption

In order to monitor energy consumption by different components of a compute node (cores, socket, memory), we used Intel's Running Average Power Limiting

Table 1. Test machine and environment details

Processor	Intel Xeon CPU E5-2670
Microarchitecture	Intel's Sandy Bridge
Maximum Thermal Design Power (TDP)	115 Watts
Hyperthreading support	Disabled
Sockets	2
Cores/socket	8
L1 cache size (per core)	32KB
L2 cache size (per core)	256KB
L3 cache size (shared - 1/socket)	20MB
Infiniband card	Mellanox MT26428 [ConnectX VPI PCIe 2.0 5GT/s]
Infiniband switch	InfiniScale IV 36-Port QSFP 40 Gb/s, MTS 3600
Compiler	gcc version 4.4.6
Compiler flags used	-O3
OpenSHMEM version	Mellanox OpenSHMEM ver. 2.2-23513

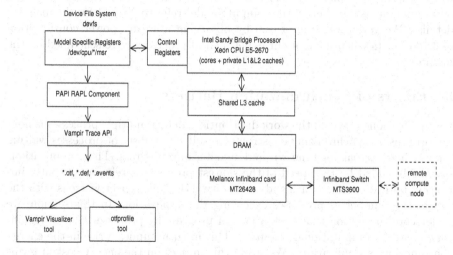

Fig. 1. Experimental Setup incorporating Intel's RAPL interface for fine-grained power monitoring

(RAPL) interface [1]. Fig. 1 illustrates our experimental setup which incorporates this interface by monitoring the thermal and power management values of the model-specific registers (MSRs) exposed by the Intel Sandy Bridge processor, E5-2670. In order to read the RAPL counters in MSRs from the device file system (/dev/cpu/*/msr on *devfs*), we used the RAPL component provided by PAPI v5.1 [18]. In addition, we used Vampir Trace [14] for fine-grained instrumentation of our synthetic microbenchmarks.

Verifications by David et al. [8], Hackenberg et al. [11], and Dongarra et al. [9] provide empirical evidence of a high correlation between the energy consumption readings provided by the RAPL interface and direct power measurements. However, readings provided by this interface have certain shortcomings due to its model-based approach for estimating the metrics [11]. The fact that energy values of DRAM as reported by RAPL only take into account the memory accesses initiated by the CPU and not other I/O devices (e.g. the network card), was a major obstacle in this study. Nevertheless, these DRAM-specific values are a good estimation of the impact of the energy consumption due to data transfers between the CPU and the memory. Any direct memory accesses by the interconnect (without the participation of the CPU) would only lead to further increase in the impact of the power/energy consumption. Due to space constraints, we do not present these in this paper.

2.2 Reducing Noise in Readings Due to the OS and Background Processes

To reduce OS noise and avoid other processes from being scheduled on the monitored socket, we used Linux *CPU shielding* [13]. This ensured that all unrelated processes/threads (including most OS service threads) were scheduled on the extra unmonitored socket on the compute node (refer to Table 1 for the machine details). We verified this approach by observing a steady power consumption of 3.786 Watts when none of our experimental processes were scheduled on the monitored socket.

3   Effects of Synchronization Barriers

For applications in which the work distribution among multiple processes is non-uniform, using synchronizing constructs[1] result in a subset of processes waiting for varying intervals of time without making any progress. Thus, applications become bounded by the speed of the slowest process, thereby significantly impacting both its performance and scalability [17]. This impact worsens with the rise in the number of processes executing the application. In this section, we underscore the notion that such a lack of progress by processes lead to significant waste of computational resources. This in turn implies a rise in the energy consumption of applications. We study this impact on the energy cost in terms of two factors - the cost incurred by processes waiting for different time periods within a barrier, and the cost incurred by the entire system with a rise in the number of processes participating in a barrier.

PGAS implementations like OpenSHMEM decouple communication and synchronization operations [10]. A process may progress in its execution of code segments while being oblivious to communication operations initiated by other processes. In other words, processes are permitted to have an inconsistent view of the globally shared memory during a phase of an application. To ensure sequential consistency and an ordering of remote data transfer operations, OpenSHMEM applications may use synchronizing constructs like *shmem_barrier_all()*, *shmem_fence()*, and *shmem_quiet()*. We discuss the impact of using the global barrier - *shmem_barrier_all()* below:

---

[1] In the rest of the text, we use the words 'synchronizing construct' and 'barriers' interchangeably.

Table 2. Microbenchmark and line charts for studying the impact of barrier on energy and power cost
(i) varying wait periods within a barrier (ii) varying number of processes participating in a barrier

Line charts	Code snippets
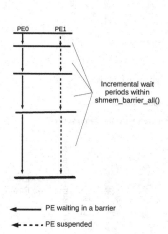 —— PE waiting in a barrier ◄ - - - - PE suspended	```for (sleep_cnt =0;
         sleep_cnt >=MAX_SLEEP
         ; sleep_cnt +=5)
{

   shmem_barrier_all ( ) ;
    if (me == 0)
         sleep (sleep_cnt) ;
   else
         sleep (MAX_SLEEP) ;
   // START monitoring
   shmem_barrier_all ( ) ;
   // STOP monitoring

}``` |
| 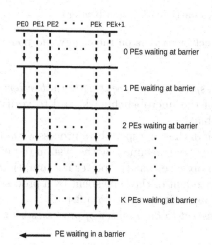

—— PE waiting in a barrier
◄ - - - - PE suspended | ```for (cnt=num_pes ( ) −1;
        cnt >=0; cnt −−)
{

   shmem_barrier_all ( ) ;
    if (me <= cnt)
         sleep (CONST_SLEEP) ;
   // START   monitoring
   shmem_barrier_all ( ) ;
   // STOP   monitoring

}``` |

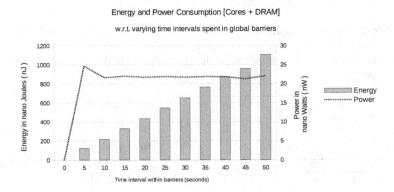

(a) Impact of wait period within a barrier

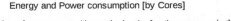
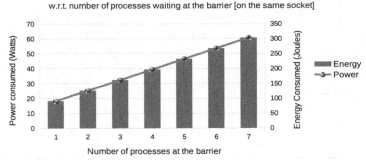

(b) Impact of number of processes participating in a barrier

Fig. 2. Empirical results illustrating the impact of barriers on the energy and power cost of the system

- *Energy and power consumption with respect to time spent within a barrier*:
  The line chart and the code snippet of the microbenchmark used to verify this is presented in the first row of Table 2.

  Fig.2a illustrates that a linear growth in the time spent by a process within a barrier leads to a linear rise in total energy consumed by the system (cores and the DRAM)[2]. In addition, we also observe that the power consumption or the rate of change in energy, is independent of the time spent by a process waiting at a barriers. We discuss this observation in Section 3.1

- *Energy and power consumption with respect to the number of processes waiting at a barrier*:
  The line chart and the code snippet of the microbenchmark used to verify this is presented in the second row of Table 2

---

[2] For our experiments, the linear relationship between the energy (E) consumed and the time (T) spent within a barrier was: $E = (33.1446*T)-1.88467$. As expected, the model was characterized with a high Coefficient of determination ($r^2=0.999027$).

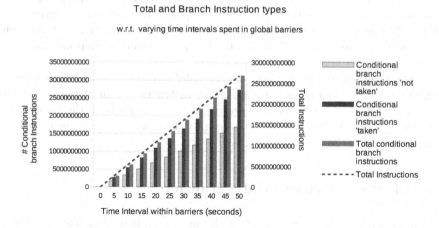

Fig. 3. Comparing the types of instructions executed by the CPU while waiting at a barrier. The count includes (i) Total number of instructions (ii) Number of conditional branch instructions (iii) Number of conditional branch instructions that are 'taken' (iv) The number of conditional branch instructions that are 'not taken'.

The results depicted in Fig. 2b verify the claim that an increase in the number of processes waiting at a barrier leads to a linear rise in the energy consumed over the entire system which, in turn implies a linear rise in the average power consumption.

3.1 A Note on Implementation of Barriers

Common implementations of a barrier incorporate the use of shared semaphores which are subjected to repeated atomic polling by each process. The purpose of this polling is to keep track of the state of the semaphore objects. These are typically *globally shared* so that they remain accessible by other processes[3]. The polling is always *atomic* in nature to ensure that only one process can test or set it at any point in time. Furthermore, this polling is typically performed directly over the copy of the semaphore object within the remotely accessible memory, thus avoiding accesses to stale cached versions. This in turn increases the pressure on the memory. Additionally, the polling is *continuous*, to ensure that there is no significant delay between the time each process signals entering the barrier and the time this event is detected.

Such *software-based* implementations of barriers result in the CPU repeatedly executing the same set of instructions without making any progress in the application. It is only when a semaphore signals the end of the barrier, that the CPU executes a code fragment that prepares the process to exit the barrier region. In

---

[3] If RDMA is supported by the interconnect, the overhead of the management of semaphores reduces when they are remotely accessible.

accordance with this design, Fig. 3 depicts the change in the energy and power consumption pattern with respect to the types of instructions executed by the CPU. The waste in CPU cycles can be observed by the linear rise in the difference between the number of conditional-branch instructions that are 'taken' and 'not taken'.

Also, the high correlation between the *total* number of instructions executed and the total number of *conditional-branch* instructions hint at the execution of the same set of instructions, irrespective of the time spent in the barrier. This *homogeneity* in the instruction types result in a constant power consumption by the system (Fig. 2a)

4   Effects of Remote Data Transfers

This section discusses the impact of the use of explicit data transfer routines on the energy cost of OpenSHMEM applications. While using these routines, a programmer may decide to transfer the program data in multiple fragments based on the design of an application. While this practice makes it easier to align the semantics of an algorithm to an implementing program, our studies indicate that such practices come at a significant cost.

Thus, we identify two application characteristics to analyze the communication patterns in OpenSHMEM programs:

- *Total size of the data to be transferred*
  This factor is governed by the problem size of the application and granularity of parallelism chosen[4].
- *Number of explicit calls (or fragments) used to transfer the data*
  This factor is dependent on the nature of the design of the application by the programmer.

However, it must be noted that the actual progress of the data movement depends on a number of factors related to the design and the capabilities of the underlying software and hardware stack. Fig. 4 categorizes these factors depending on whether they impact the energy and power profiles of internal system-components like the CPU and DRAM i.e. the *intra-node* factors, or external components like the interconnect solutions i.e. *inter-node* factors.

The study of the effects of inter-node factors on the energy profile of remote data transfers is outside the scope of this paper. Nevertheless, in order to account for their impact, we abstract their effects in terms of the net achievable bandwidth. Fig. 5 illustrates this constraint with respect to the two communication-based parameters discussed above. We observe that for any given data transfer size, maximum bandwidth is achievable with minimum amount of fragmentation.

The impact of the intra-node factors on the energy and power cost incurred in Sections 4.1 and 4.2, respectively.

---

[4] The granularity of parallelism is typically determined by the number of processes participating in the data/task distribution.

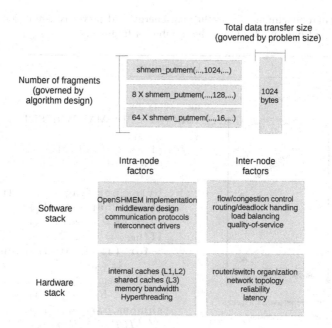

Fig. 4. Top: Parameters that define communication patterns from an OpenSHMEM programmer's point of view. Bottom: Underlying factors within the software and hardware stack that impact the power and energy cost of interfaces for remote data transfer.

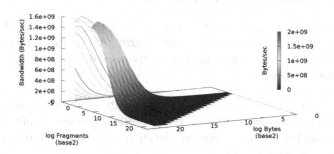

Fig. 5. The impact of the interconnect solution can be summarized by the achievable bandwidth with respect to:
(i) size of the total data to be transferred
(ii) number of fragments into which the transfer is divided into.

Table 3. Microbenchmark for evaluating energy and power consumption by varying
the total size of data payload and the number of fragments

Line chart	Code snippet
| 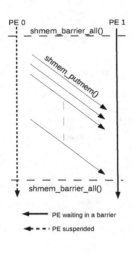 | ```
me = my_pe();
for(j=1 ; j<=MAX_WRK_SIZE ; j*=2)
{
    for(frag_cnt=MIN_MSG_NUM;
        frag_cnt<=j; frag_cnt*=2)
    {
        bytes_per_frag = j / frag_cnt;
        shmem_barrier_all();
        // START monitoring
        if(me == 0)
            for (it=0; it<frag_cnt;
                 it++)
                shmem_putmem( ..... ,
                    bytes_per_frag , 1);
        shmem_barrier_all();
        // STOP monitoring
    }
}
``` |

4.1   Energy Consumption Observations

Fig. 6 illustrates the energy consumption by the CPU and the DRAM with
respect to the different message sizes of data transferred (in bytes along X-axis)
and the number of fragments used to transfer the total data (along Y-axis). The
noteworthy observations are:

- Energy consumed holds a correlation to the number of instructions executed.
  Since an increase in the number of data transfers initiated implies a rise in
  the number of instructions executed, the energy consumption increases with
  rise in fragmentation.
- For large bulk transfers with a fixed message size, the energy consumed
  remains independent of the *initial* rise in fragmentation.
- Using a constant number of fragments, the energy consumed in servicing the
  transfer of small to medium sized messages (2 to 65536 bytes) is independent
  of the total size of the data transferred. This behavior can also be observed
  in terms of the spectrum of the achievable bandwidth shown in Fig.5. This
  behavior can be explained by the fact that for such small-sized messages,
  the cost in managing the data buffers for remote transfers overshadows the
```

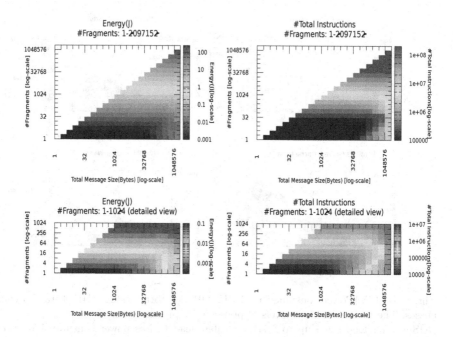

Fig. 6. Relationship between energy consumption by cores(left) and the total number of instructions executed(right). Top: Results for cases where: $Fragments \in [1, 2097152]$. Bottom: Results for cases where: $Fragments \in [1, 1024]$.

actual movement of the data. This cost is independent of the message size and hence leads to a steady bandwidth and energy consumption.

– For large bulk transfers (>65536 bytes), the energy consumed increases with the size of the data to be transferred. This can be attributed to cost incurred in handling data buffers. For large messages, this becomes dependent on the actual size of data that is being transferred.

4.2   Power Consumption Observations

Fig.s 7 depicts the power consumption by the CPU cores and the DRAM for different message sizes and number of fragments.

– For small data transfer sizes, the power consumed by the CPU (16 Watts) and the DRAM (7 Watts) is low.
– The power consumed by the CPU during transfer of large bulk data payloads (16.2 Watts) is marginally more (1.25%) than that consumed during small data transfers.
– The power consumed by the DRAM during transfer of large bulk data payloads (9 Watts) is significantly more (22%) than that consumed during small data transfers.

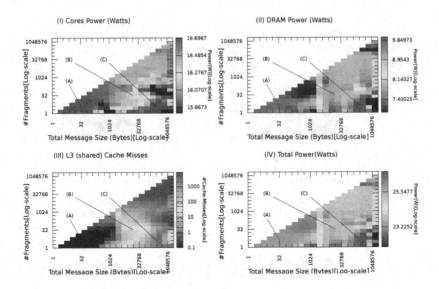

Fig. 7. (I,II,IV)Power consumed by CPU, DRAM, total system (III) Total L3 cache misses. The various distinct levels of power are represented as:
(A)Small payload sized(up to 2KB) transfers lead to less power consumption by the cores and DRAM;
(B)Medium to large message sizes(4K and beyond) imply accesses of large memory regions and this impacts power consumption;
(C)Large payload sizes with minimum fragmentation leads to higher power consumption by the cores. The underlying NIC is generally responsible for chunking such large transfers, the effect on which is not accounted for by the cores.

- With very low fragmentation, the CPU consumes more power than with fragmented data payload.
- As the message size is increased (along x-axis), the transition of the change in the power consumption behavior by the CPU appears to hold a correlation to the sizes of the intermediate levels of the cache hierarchy. The transition levels correspond to the sizes of the L1 and L2 caches - 32KB and 256KB respectively. Since the caches were flushed after every set of readings, one can speculate that every cache miss in L1 and L2 adds on to the memory pressure on the shared L3 cache thereby resulting in a proportional rise in cache misses. This effect can be observed in Fig. 7(III), which illustrates the number of L3 cache misses.
- From Fig. 7, the average power consumption by the system (CPU+DRAM) while servicing large bulk message sizes (28 Watts) is 21.73% higher than that consumed by small message sizes (23 Watts).

5   Related Work

There has been a great deal of research directed towards measuring and managing the energy and power consumption of applications. Proposals like Thrifty [2] have been put forth to direct large-scale research towards redesigning the complete computing stack. The goal of such efforts is directed towards building power-aware Exascale platforms.

Some of the model-based techniques provided by chip manufacturers to dynamically monitor and manage the power or energy consumption include: Intel's RAPL [1], AMD's APM module [3], NVIDIA's NVML [4].

Hoefler [12] mentions discussions by the IEEE standard on energy efficient Ethernet specifications including - dynamic link-speed reduction, receiver modification, network routing, and deep sleep states. However, initial research indicates latencies and network jitter with these techniques.

Past efforts towards understanding and managing the power consumption trends of applications have been significant. One of the static based approaches for managing power consumption by processes is for the compiler to evaluate a program and determine sections within the code where the energy consumption profile changes. This knowledge in the form of *power management hints* can then be conveyed to the runtime to adjust the voltage/frequency scaling of applications [5]. Korthikanti and Agha [15] study the power consumption behavior of shared memory architectures while handling applications with different problem sizes. Li et al. [16] use DCT and DVFS techniques to study the opportunities of reducing power consumption of hybrid MPI-OpenMP applications. The focus of our work has been to perform a fine-grained study of OpenSHMEM communication interfaces which are responsible for remote memory accesses.

6   Conclusion

In this paper we presented our study of the energy and power consumption behavior of a system while participating in synchronizing global barriers and remote data transfers.

We observed that the energy and power cost is dependent on the time spent within barriers and the number of processes participating in the barriers.

Additionally, our study indicates that the energy and power cost incurred by a system while servicing remote data transfers are dependent on a number of factors characterizing the underlying the hardware and software stack. These include the sizes of the memory hierarchy, design of the communication protocols, and the capabilities of the interconnect solutions.

The impact of these factors depend on the size of the total data to be transferred within a communication phase of an application. In addition, the number of data transfers initiated to transfer this load also impact the energy and power consumption behavior of OpenSHMEM-like PGAS applications.

The results put forth in this paper motivate the need for taking energy and power costs into account while designing efficient PGAS libraries for large-scale systems.

Acknowledgments. This work is supported by the U.S. Department of Defense and used resources of the Extreme Scale Systems Center located at the Oak Ridge National Laboratory. Experiments included resources of the Oak Ridge Leadership Computing Facility, which is supported by the Office of Science of the U.S. Department of Energy under Contract No. DE-AC05-00OR22725. Vampir trace is developed at the Center for Information Services and HPC of Technische Universität Dresden in Germany. PAPI is an open-source research project of the Innovative Research Laboratory of the University of Tennessee, Knoxville in the U.S.

Thanks are due to Joseph Schuchart and the Vampir-support team at Technische Universität Dresden, for offering support with Vampir. Special thanks are also due to Pavel Shamis from ORNL for his input on the usage of Infiniband verbs.

References

1. Intel 64 and ia-32 architectures software developers manual volume 3b: System programming guide, part 2
2. Thrifty: An exascale architecture for energy-proportional computing, http://science.energy.gov/~/media/ascr/pdf/research/cs/aa/A_oph_uiuc_thrifty_110215.pdf
3. Linux tuning guide, amd opteron 6200 series processors (April 2012)
4. Nvml api reference manual, ver.5.319.43 (August 2013)
5. Aboughazaleh, N., Childers, B., Melhem, R., Craven, M.: Collaborative compiler-os power management for time-sensitive applications. Tech. rep., Department of Computer Science, University of Pittsburgh (2002)
6. Benedict, S.: Review: Energy-aware performance analysis methodologies for hpc architectures-an exploratory study. J. Netw. Comput. Appl. 35(6), 1709–1719 (2012), http://dx.doi.org/10.1016/j.jnca.2012.08.003
7. Choi, J.W., Bedard, D., Fowler, R., Vuduc, R.: A theoretical framework for algorithm-architecture co-design. In: Proc. IEEE Int'l. Parallel and Distributed Processing Symp. (IPDPS), Boston, MA, USA (May 2013)
8. David, H., Gorbatov, E., Hanebutte, U.R., Khanna, R., Le, C.: Rapl: Memory power estimation and capping. In: 2010 ACM/IEEE International Symposium on Low-Power Electronics and Design (ISLPED), pp. 189–194 (2010)
9. Dongarra, J., Ltaief, H., Luszczek, P., Weaver, V.M.: Energy Footprint of Advanced Dense Numerical Linear Algebra Using Tile Algorithms on Multicore Architectures. In: 2012 Second International Conference on Cloud and Green Computing, pp. 274–281 (2012), http://ieeexplore.ieee.org/lpdocs/epic03/wrapper.htm?arnumber=6382829
10. High Performance Computing Tools group and at UH, Extreme Scale Systems Center at ORNL: Openshmem application programming interface, version 1.0. Tech. rep., University of Houston (UH), Oak Ridge National Laboratory, ORNL (2012), http://www.openshmem.org
11. Hackenberg, D., Ilsche, T., Schone, R., Molka, D., Schmidt, M., Nagel, W.: Power measurement techniques on standard compute nodes: A quantitative comparison. In: 2013 IEEE International Symposium on Performance Analysis of Systems and Software (ISPASS), pp. 194–204 (2013)

12. Hoefler, T.: Software and hardware techniques for power-efficient hpc networking. Computing in Science Engineering 12(6), 30–37 (2010)
13. Kerrisk, M.: Linux programmer's manual (2012), http://man7.org/linux/man-pages/man7/cpuset.7.html
14. Knüpfer, A., Brunst, H., Doleschal, J., Jurenz, M., Lieber, M., Mickler, H., Müller, M., Nagel, W.: The vampir performance analysis tool-set. In: Resch, M., Keller, R., Himmler, V., Krammer, B., Schulz, A. (eds.) Tools for High Performance Computing, pp. 139–155. Springer, Heidelberg (2008), http://dx.doi.org/10.1007/978-3-540-68564-7_9
15. Korthikanti, V.A., Agha, G.: Towards optimizing energy costs of algorithms for shared memory architectures. In: Proceedings of the 22nd ACM Symposium on Parallelism in Algorithms and Architectures, SPAA 2010, p. 157 (2010), http://portal.acm.org/citation.cfm?doid=1810479.1810510
16. Li, D., de Supinski, B.R., Schulz, M., Cameron, K., Nikolopoulos, D.S.: Hybrid MPI/OpenMP power-aware computing. In: 2010 IEEE International Symposium on Parallel & Distributed Processing (IPDPS), pp. 1–12 (2010), http://ieeexplore.ieee.org/lpdocs/epic03/wrapper.htm?arnumber=5470463
17. Markatos, E., Crovella, M., Das, P., Dubnicki, C., LeBlanc, T.: The effects of multiprogramming on barrier synchronization. In: Proceedings of the Third IEEE Symposium on Parallel and Distributed Processing, pp. 662–669 (1991)
18. Mucci, P.J., Browne, S., Deane, C., Ho, G.: Papi: A portable interface to hardware performance counters. In: Proceedings of the Department of Defense HPCMP Users Group Conference, pp. 7–10 (1999)

Hybrid Programming Using OpenSHMEM and OpenACC

Matthew Baker[1], Swaroop Pophale[3], Jean-Charles Vasnier[4], Haoqiang Jin[2], and Oscar Hernandez[1]

[1] Oak Ridge National Laboratory, Oak Ridge, Tennessee, 37840, USA
`bakermb@ornl.gov,oscar@ornl.gov`
[2] NASA Ames, Moffet Field, California USA
`haoqiang.jin@nasa.gov`
[3] University of Houston, Houston, Texas 77004, USA
`spophale@cs.uh.edu`
[4] CAPS Entreprise, France
`jvasnier@caps-entreprise.com`

Abstract. With high performance systems exploiting multicore and accelerator-based architectures on a distributed shared memory system, heterogenous hybrid programming models are the natural choice to exploit all the hardware made available on these systems. Previous efforts looking into hybrid models have primarily focused on using OpenMP directives (for shared memory programming) with MPI (for inter-node programming on a cluster), using OpenMP to spawn threads on a node and communication libraries like MPI to communicate across nodes. As accelerators get added into the mix, and there is better hardware support for PGAS languages/APIs, this means that new and unexplored heterogenous hybrid models will be needed to effectively leverage the new hardware. In this paper we explore the use of OpenACC directives to program GPUs and the use of OpenSHMEM, a PGAS library for one-sided communication between nodes. We use the NAS-BT Multi-zone benchmark that was converted to use the OpenSHMEM library API for network communication between nodes and OpenACC to exploit accelerators that are present within a node. We evaluate the performance of the benchmark and discuss our experiences during the development of the OpenSHMEM+OpenACC hybrid program.

1 Introduction

New HPC systems are increasingly turning to accelerators to increase compute power while mitigating the rising cost of power [1]. For example, four of the top ten super computers use GPUs as their main devices to perform the majority of the computations. Oak Ridge National Laboratories Titan [2], a DOE leadership class machine, makes extensive use of GPUs, using one Nvidia Kepler GPU per node. Without a major breakthrough in technology, the future of the fastest super computers will consist of clusters with multiple cores and attached to specialized devices for accelerators, interconnects and I/O. Modern cluster nodes

S. Poole, O. Hernandez, and P. Shamis (Eds.): OpenSHMEM 2014, LNCS 8356, pp. 74–89, 2014.

have many different types of hardware that need to be exploited efficiently to make the maximum use of the provided resources. Current nodes have multiple sockets with attached memory, each socket has a CPU with multiple cores. On top of this the node usually has an attached accelerator, currently the most common one is the GPU. In addition the nodes are all connected with network hardware that provides better support for PGAS languages/libraries to allow them to communicate. This means that each node has three different major components that need to be programmed for. Each of these components has its own programming model with its own challenges. When these models are used together for hybrid programming models, new challenges arise, specially when one of the models deals with heterogeneous programming. In this paper we explore a new hybrid programming model OpenSHMEM+OpenACC.

OpenSHMEM is the result of standardizing several shmem libraries [3]. It is a one-sided communication library where individual processes do one-sided puts and gets, as compared to MPI that does synchronized send/receive between pairs of processes. This allows for data to be sent without having to wait on remote nodes to do communication. OpenACC is the result of standardizing compiler directives for accelerator programming sanctioned by the OpenACC organization. It allows for an OpenMP-like programming with support for incremental parallelism. This includes the ability to incrementally add directives to a code to program for GPUs, rather than having to do a considerable amount of code restructure to just start using an accelerator (like with the OpenCL standard). We use the NASA Advanced Supercomputing (NAS) Block Tri-diagonal (BT) Multizone benchmark [4] to evaluate our results. This benchmark is structured so that there are multiple zones that can be solved independently with the boundary values of each zone exchanged on each iteration, making it well suited to experimentation with heterogeneous hybrid programming model.

This paper is organized into 5 sections. In Section 2 we discuss the other research done on hybrid programming models and provide background information on the BT-MZ benchmark used, the OpenACC directives, and the OpenSHMEM library in Section 3 . In Section 4 we discuss the implementation details of how OpenSHMEM and OpenACC are used together. The results are presented in Section 5. We discuss the platforms used and the timings from running BT-MZ on those platforms. In Section 6 we interpret the results we obtain and discuss the future paths for exploration in this hybrid programming.

2   Related Work

Hybrid models that explore shared-memory and distributed-memory programming have been researched over the last few decades. The idea is to exploit the strengths of the different models, including the in-node efficiency, memory savings, accelerator programming, and the scalability characteristics within a distributed memory system. The shared and distributed programming models models have been evolving separately and an attempt to unify them resulted in the creation of new languages and models such as the HPCS and PGAS languages (X10, Chapel, Fortress, UPC, etc). In terms of heterogenous programming, there have been attempts to explore the use of message passing libraries and accelerator languages and APIs (i.e. CUDA, OpenCL). Recently, a high-level approach to program accelerators has been released, called OpenACC that improves portability across accelerators. Some applications have successfully used the model of MPI/OpenACC, MPI/OpenCL, MPI/CUDA. Very little work has been done to explore OpenSHMEM with accelerator programming models.

3   Background

In this section we introduce the different models that we used to experiment with heterogenous hybrid programming.

3.1   OpenSHMEM

The OpenSHMEM library is a PGAS library that provides a library API for programmers using the Single Program Multiple Data (SPMD) programming paradigm for programs written in C, C++ and Fortran. The OpenSHMEM Specification [5] provides the definition, functionality and expected behavior of these powerful library calls that are meant for communicating and processing data. The SGI SHMEM library specification and implementation motivated Open-SHMEM Specification 1.0 which was finalized by the OpenSHMEM community in early 2012. OpenSHMEM is an evolving open standard for all SHMEM library implementations and we expect many useful changes to the API and library in the near future to be able to cater to the growing and ever changing high performance computing environment. The current library specification provides API for *one-sided* reads and writes, remote atomic memory operations, broadcasts, reductions, collects, distributed locking, and collective and point-to-point synchronization and ordering primitives. OpenSHMEM *put/get* calls provide excellent opportunities for hiding communication latency by overlapping communication with computation when the underlying hardware supports true one-sided remote direct memory access (RDMA). Along with performance, application programmers require both portability and productivity and the OpenSHMEM library facilitates this by providing a standard and simple API.

3.2   OpenACC

Directives comprise a mechanism that allows a program to "direct" (or "hint") the compiler as to what it should do about a region of code that is often in proximity to the directive's occurrence in the program. In the C/C++ and Fortran languages directives appear as lines prefixed with #pragma *id* or !$*id*, respectively, where *id* signifies the directives API that these directives belong to. In the case of Fortran, for instance, OpenMP and HPF use omp and hpf respectively. It is the directive's API specification that designates what is legal – when put this way, directive APIs can be thought of as separate languages meant to annotate C & Fortran sources.

Using directives to program accelerators is not new. Data and executable code placement on National Semiconductors' NAPA1000 reprogrammable chips is steered from pragma-annotated C [6], while intelligent memory operations can be offloaded onto a FlexRAM array by using the the CFlex pragmas for the C language [7]. IBM's Cell BE is programmable with the Cell Superscalar (CellSs) [8]. The accessibility to GPUs saw the emergence of OpenHMPP [9] and hiCUDA [10], while for the more recent Intel Many Integrated Cores (MIC), it was shown how work offloading can be achieved by OpenMP offloading (`#pragma offload target(mic)` combined with OpenMP directives) [11].

The OpenACC specification comprises a programming model supported by a directives-based API that was put together by a consortium of four, namely CAPS enterprise, Cray Inc, the Portland Group Inc (PGI) and NVIDIA. The specification was put together to provide a prototype implementation to speedup the OpenMP accelerator directive process, which constantly gets merged in the OpenMP accelerator model [12]. The OpenACC defines a host and accelerator programming model where accelerated regions are used to define which parts of the program can be (1) offloaded to an accelerator and/or (2) data regions describe the data motion between the accelerator and the CPU, where some host variables become available on the device. (`acc_data`).

The data regions address concerns with the (mostly) disjoint CPU and accelerator memory spaces and the lifetime of data objects. Similar to OpenMP where the programmer tags objects as `private`, `shared`, `lastprivate`, OpenACC offers a number of clauses. Some of the supported clauses are the following: (1) the `copyin` clause for objects that are to copied over to the accelerator at the begining of the region, (2) the `copyout` and then copied back to the CPU at the end of the region, (3) the `present` clause for checking if an object is already available on the accelerator (in order to avoid redundant or outdated copies) and (4) `copy` that combines `copyin` and `copyout`.

In recognition of existing accelerators' processing element (PE) topology, OpenACC orchestrates the work to be assigned to the accelerator's PE in a hierarchical fashion: there are *gangs* of *workers* where each worker performs a *vector* operation. The actual mapping is both target and compiler specific. In the case of NVIDIA GPUs, for instance, the number of gangs corresponds to the number of CUDA threadblocks, the number of workers determines the size of the warps or the Y dimension of the threadblock while the vector suggests the SIMD length [13]. To designate work for offloading onto the accelerator, OpenACC makes available the `parallel` directive, which will, essentially, launch work on the device according to a compiler-selected or user-selected configuration of gangs, workers and vectors.

In addition to the `parallel` directive, OpenACC offers the `kernel` and `loop` directives. Given a region of sequential statements, where statements may be loops or less complex statements, the `kernel` directive instructs the compiler to organize the statements into *kernels* and execute them sequentially on the accelerator. An implementation is free to modify the organization of gangs, workers and vectors between launches. The reader may assume that a mapping to CUDA would suggest that the kernels have been queued up for serial launching over a

CUDA stream. The `loop` directive is meant to map loop nests onto the gang, worker and vector hierarchy.

3.3 Hybrid Programming with OpenSHMEM and OpenACC

Using the OpenSHMEM and OpenACC programming models together is a new type of hybrid model. The low latency characteristic of OpenSHMEM combined with accelerator programming of OpenACC makes it an attractive model to explore. However, there are limitations from both APIs that makes it hard for them to interoperate. For example, the accelerator memory is not part of the *symmetric memory* required and used by the OpenSHMEM library. Also, the current OpenSHMEM 1.0 specification is not thread safe which limits the use of OpenSHMEM library API to outside of OpenACC regions.

3.4 BT Multizone Benchmark

The Block Tri-diagonal (BT) benchmark is part of the NPB benchmark suite. The benchmark simulates a CFD application that solves 3-dimensional compressible Navier-Stokes equations using Alternating Direction Implicit (ADI) to find the finite difference solution to the problem by solving three sets of uncoupled systems of equations in x, y and z directions. These equations are block tridiagonal with a 5x5 block size. The multi-zone version of the benchmark a logically rectangular discretization mesh is divided into a two-dimensional horizontal tiling of three-dimensional zones [4] and the aspect ratios are changed from the original NPB to avoid pathologically shaped zones. In the reference BT-MZ implementation (MPI+OpenMP) a MPI process executes the initialization step and after initial setup and synchronization of all processes the benchmark loops over the computation kernels. Communication between processes occurs after the computations are completed and the *root* process verifies the results obtained for the problem size class chosen. The number of zones grows with the problem size and the ratio of the largest zone over the smallest zone is about 20. The zones span a signifiant range and can be modulated by using different classes of input data.

4   Implementation

The OpenSHMEM+OpenACC version of the BT-MZ benchmark is structured into five distinct steps (similar to the reference BT-MZ implementation). The first setup is to set up the zones, then all the zones are initialized. These two steps are done independently on each node and without accelerators. The next step is the boundary exchange and OpenSHMEM is used to communicate between nodes as they exchange boundary values. The next step is the BT solver, where using OpenACC directives computation is offloaded to the accelerator. These two steps that consist of the boundary exchange and the solver, are looped over for a fixed number of iterations. After this a verification step is performed to ensure that the solver produced the correct result. Conversion of the benchmark from using MPI+OpenMP to OpenSHMEM+OpenACC is a two step process where we first replace all MPI calls be equivalent OpenSHMEM calls to get an intermediate OpenSHMEM+OpenMP BT-MZ version. This is used as the starting point for OpenACC related modifications.

4.1 Inter Process Communication Using OpenSHMEM

We use the OpenSHMEM communication library to communicate between processes. It effectively accomplishes the same role as Message Passing Interface (MPI) did in the reference implementation of the NPB-MZ hybrid parallel benchmark. The difference emanates from the fact that all communication in OpenSHMEM is *one-sided*, thus not requiring the participation of the target process. In the Open-SHMEM+OpenACC hybrid benchmark OpenSHMEM communicates data related to overlap regions of *zones*, and OpenACC parallelizes loops within each zone.

The BT-MZ benchmark has distinct communication and computation phases. There is no communication during the solving stage (*x-solve, y-solve and z-solve*). While porting the BT-MZ benchmark to use OpenSHMEM certain design choices have to be made which include decisions regarding the program variables that need to be *symmetric*, the choice of communication primitives (*put* vs *get*) and synchronization points. Since OpenSHMEM does not have matching sends and receives (refer Listing 1.1) this exchange has to be ordered with an extra communication to indicate the correct offset location (Listing 1.2, line 1) and point to point synchronization (Listing 1.2, lines 4, 6, 7) that guarantees that the correct data has been communicated. Listing 1.2 shows how the exchange is effected using OpenSHMEM communication and synchronization calls. Moreover there is a significant benefit in using *put* as (unlike *get*) it returns as soon as the buffer is available for reuse [5]. The final verification stage performs a reduction of solutions over all processes and computes residues from over all zones.

```
1  if (iodd == 0) {
2  MPI_Isend(&qbc_ou[qoffset],m_size,
3            dp_type,ip,tag+myid,
4            comm_setup,&requests[nr]);
5  MPI_Irecv(&qbc_in[qoffset],m_size,
6            dp_type,ip,tag+ip,
7            comm_setup,
8            &requests[nr+1]);
9  }
10 else {
11 MPI_Irecv(&qbc_in[qoffset],m_size,
12           dp_type, ip, tag+ip,
13           comm_setup,
14           &requests[nr]);
15 MPI_Isend(&qbc_ou[qoffset],m_size,
16           dp_type, ip,tag+myid,
17           comm_setup,
18           &requests[nr+1]);
19 }
```

Listing 1.1. MPI buffer exchange in reference BT-MZ *exch qbc* routine

```
1  shmem_putmem(&dest_qoffset,
2               &qoffset,
3               sizeof(idx_t),ip);
4  shmem_fence();
5  shmem_long_put(&done, &x,1,ip);
6  shmem_quiet();
7  shmem_wait(&done, 0);
8  shmem_double_put(
9               &qbc_in[dest_qoffset],
10              &qbc_ou[qoffset],
11              m_size, ip);
12 shmem_quiet();
```

Listing 1.2. OpenSHMEM buffer exchange in *exch qbc* routine

4.2 Targeting Hybrid Architectures with OpenACC Directives

4.2.1 Introducing the OpenACC Directives

We started with the OpenSHMEM and OpenMP version of BT-MZ. We first find the OpenMP pragmas, which indicates code kernels that are already parallel and replaced them with OpenACC pragmas. We started by replacing OpenMP pragma (refer Listing 1.3) with OpenACC *#pragma acc kernels* around the main computational loops of *x-solve, y-solve, z-solve compute_rhs*, and *add* (refer Listing 1.4). This pragma indicates to the compiler that it should generate accelerated kernels for each loop nest. Only with this approach we do not expect to see performance gain since for every kernel the runtime will transfer the data back and forth to the accelerator and at this stage the kernels are not optimized at all. Unlike OpenMP where a subroutine called in a OpenMP parallel context is the same machine code as the host core, OpenACC regions are compiled to CUDA code and then compile by the Nvidia CUDA compiler for the GPU. This means that the compiler must either know that a function will be called in OpenACC or the function must be inlined. Because of this the subroutines lhs_init, matvec_sub, matmul_sub, binvcrhs and bincrhs have to be manually copied to the same source file so they be inlined by the OpenACC compiler. The new OpenACC 2.0 solves this problem using the routine directive. [1]

```
1  #pragma omp parallel for
2  for (k = 1; k <= nz-2; k++) {
3    for (j = 1; j <= ny-2; j++) {
4      for (i = 1; i <= nx-2; i++) {
5        for (m = 0; m < 5; m++) {
6          u(m,i,j,k) = u(m,i,j,k)
                   + rhs(m,i,j,k);
7        }
8      }
9    }
10 }
```

```
1  #pragma acc kernels
2  for (k = 1; k <= nz-2; k++) {
3    for (j = 1; j <= ny-2; j++) {
4      for (i = 1; i <= nx-2; i++) {
5        for (m = 0; m < 5; m++) {
6          u(m,i,j,k) = u(m,i,j,k)
                   + rhs(m,i,j,k);
7        }
8      }
9    }
10 }
```

Listing 1.3. Original OpenMP pragmas in *add* routine

Listing 1.4. New OpenACC pragma *add* routine

4.2.2 Split Loop Nests

After inlining these subroutines the loops in the OpenACC regions were very large with high memory utilization. By experience, we know that splitting a huge loop nest into smaller ones will allow both OpenACC compiler, capsmc, and NVCC, to generate more optimized code for the GPU. This has advantages as it allows the compiler to find more parallelism to exploit, reduce register pressure and the device shared memory footprint. It does not negatively affect performance since maximum data is kept on the GPU between the different calls to the OpenACC kernels, prefetch to local caches and memories, which improves performance.

After splitting the solver loop nests into smaller ones, these loop nests are not anymore parallel. In order to enable the parallelization on the two outer

---

[1] This directive will be available in the CAPS OpenACC compiler later this year.

loops, two additional dimensions were added to the fjac, njac, and lhs arrays
(refer Listing 1.5 and Listing 1.6). We had to redeclare those arrays because the
dimensions depend on the external loop levels. In the x-solve file (similarly for
y-solve and z-solve), the external loop levels are based on the nz and ny sizes
(respectively on, nz and nx, ny and nx). This enables the compiler to parallelize
this loop nest by removing the dependencies between the different iterations of
the outer loop accessing these arrays. While this puts additional pressure on the
GPU memory, it allows us to reestablish the parallelism lost by splitting the
loop nest.

```
1  for (k = 1; k <= nz-2; k++) {
2    for (j = 1; j <= ny-2; j++) {
3      for (i = 1; i <= nx-2; i++) {
4  ...
5
6        fjac[i][0][1] = -(u(1,i,j,k) * tmp2 *
7          u(1,i,j,k))
8          + c2 * qs(i,j,k);
9        fjac[i][1][1] = ( 2.e0 - c2 )
10         * ( u(1,i,j,k) / u(0,i,j,k) );
11        fjac[i][2][1] = - c2 * ( u(2,i,j,k) * tmp1 );
12        fjac[i][3][1] = - c2 * ( u(3,i,j,k) * tmp1 );
13        fjac[i][4][1] = c2;
14  ...
15      }
16    }
17  }
```

Listing 1.5. Original arrays in *x_solve* routine

```
1  double fjacX[5][5][PROBLEM_SIZE+1][ny][nz];
2  #pragma acc kernels loop independent present(up[0:size5],rhsp[0:size5])
3  for (k = 1; k <= nz-2; k++) {
4    for (j = 1; j <= ny-2; j++) {
5      for (i = 1; i <= nx-2; i++) {
6  ...
7        fjacX[i][1][0][j][k] = -(u(1,i,j,k) * temp2 * u(1,i,j,k))
8          + c2 * qs(i,j,k);
9        fjacX[i][1][1][j][k] = ( 2.0 - c2 ) * ( u(1,i,j,k) / u(0,i,j,k) );
10        fjacX[i][1][2][j][k] = - c2 * ( u(2,i,j,k) * temp1 );
11        fjacX[i][1][3][j][k] = - c2 * ( u(3,i,j,k) * temp1 );
12        fjacX[i][1][4][j][k] = c2;
13  ...
14      }
15    }
16  }
```

Listing 1.6. Expanded arrays and OpenACC pragma *x_sovle* routine

4.2.3   Reducing Data Transfers

To reduce the data transfer between the different OpenACC kernels we make
the data reside on the GPU. We allocate the data on the GPU with the pragma
#pragma acc enter data create for all the data at the beginning of the BT-MZ
benchmark. The *#pragma acc data present* pragma is used to indicate to the
kernels that the data already resides on the accelerator when the kernels block
arrives. The *#pragma acc update host* and *#pragma acc update device* pragmas
are used to manually update the data on the host or device after the data on
the other side is modified.

To allocate the memory for the different matrices, we used the OpenACC enter data directive from OpenACC 2.0 was already available in the CAPS OpenACC compiler. As shown in Listing 1.7, we allocate all the zones for each matrices. We cannot do only one allocation per matrix because the OpenACC's present table maps the addresses between the hosts and device pointers using the address of the first element. In our case, the matrix is a double linked vector and these addresses will in not available in the solver functions.

```
1        u = (double *)shmalloc(sizeof(double)*PROC_MAX_SIZE5);
2        for (iz = 0; iz < proc_num_zones; iz++) {
3           zone = proc_zone_id[iz];
4           size=nxmax[zone]*ny[zone]*nz[zone]*5;
5           up=&u[start5[iz]];

7   #pragma acc enter data create(up[0:size], ...)

9           initialize(&u[start5[iz]], ...);
10  ...
11        }
```

Listing 1.7. Allocates in *main* routine to create data on GPU

In the solver functions, to indicate the data is already available on the device, we used the *#pragma acc data* directive with the present clause. This allows the runtime to know this data is already on the device and ready to be used. On this data directive we also specify to the runtime to allocate the locals lhs, fjac and njac buffer, if not already done, using the pcreate clause. The Listing 1.8 illustrates this.

```
1   #pragma acc data present(up[0:size5],...) pcreate(lhsX,fjacX,njacX)
2   {
3     #pragma acc kernels loop independent
4       for (i = 0; i <= isize; i++)
5   ...
6   } //end data
```

Listing 1.8. Data clauses in *x_solve* routine

Two operations compose the timestep loop, the exchange boundaries function call and the solver function calls. At every timestep, we need to update U matrix on the host with the values from the device before updating the boundary values. Then perform the OpenSHMEM communications to update the other PEs and afterwards, we update the U matrix from the host to the device. We use the *#pragma acc update device—host* directive around the OpenSHMEM calls (Refer to Listing 1.9).

```
1   #pragma acc update host(u[0:size])
2   ...
3   //OpenSHMEM communications
4   ...
5   #pragma acc update device(u[0:size])
```

Listing 1.9. Update clauses in *exch_qbc* routine

4.2.4   Improve Kernels Performance

After improving the cumulative time taken for transfers by reducing their occurrences we focus on optimizing the kernels. There are many ways to improve the performance of these kernels. The optimization we applied are the following: increased the threads to execute the different kernels, take care of the coalescing, unrolled some of the loops and pre-accessing some data.

To improve the global performance of the kernels, a first step consist in indicating the compiler that it can parallelize on more loop levels. To do so, the use of the *#pragma acc loop independent* indicates that the user knows for sure this particular loop level is parallel and can be executed by multiple OpenACC threads. As a result, the kernel in itself is executed by more number of threads and each thread does less work.

A well-known performance issue on the Nvidia GPU is the non-contiguous global memory accesses, also known as un-coalesced accesses (refer to Listing 1.10). The goal of this optimization is to allow contiguous accelerator threads in the thread grid to work on contiguous data in the memory. This way the memory controller can reduce the number of memory loads and stores to the data. When a thread is accessing data in the GPU memory, the memory controller will load the memory segment that contains this particular data. So if contiguous threads are accessing contiguous data at the same time, the memory controller will load the needed memory segment for all this threads only once. To do so, we will ensure that the inner parallelized loop level corresponds to the most contiguous dimension of the main arrays of each loop nest (refer to Listing 1.11).

```
#pragma acc kernels loop independent present(up[0:size5],rhsp[0:size5])
for (k = 1; k <= nz-2; k++) {
  #pragma acc loop independent
  for (j = 1; j <= ny-2; j++) {
  #pragma acc loop independent
    for (i = 1; i <= nx-2; i++) {
...
      fjacX[1][0][i][j][k] = -(u(1,i,j,k) * temp2 * u(1,i,j,k))
           + c2 * qs(i,j,k);
      fjacX[1][1][i][j][k] = ( 2.0 - c2 ) * ( u(1,i,j,k) / u(0,i,j,k) );
      fjacX[1][2][i][j][k] = - c2 * ( u(2,i,j,k) * temp1 );
      fjacX[1][3][i][j][k] = - c2 * ( u(3,i,j,k) * temp1 );
      fjacX[1][4][i][j][k] = c2;
...
    }
  }
}
```

Listing 1.10. Un-coalesced array accesses in *x_solve* routine

```
1   #pragma acc kernels loop independent present(up[0:size5],rhsp[0:size5])
2   for (i = 1; i <= nx-2; i++) {
3     #pragma acc loop independent
4     for (j = 1; j <= ny-2; j++) {
5       #pragma acc loop independent
6       for (k = 1; k <= nz-2; k++) {
7   ...
8         fjacX[1][0][i][j][k] = -(u(1,i,j,k) * temp2 * u(1,i,j,k))
9               + c2 * qs(i,j,k);
10        fjacX[1][1][i][j][k] = ( 2.0 - c2 ) * ( u(1,i,j,k) / u(0,i,j,k) );
11        fjacX[1][2][i][j][k] = - c2 * ( u(2,i,j,k) * temp1 );
12        fjacX[1][3][i][j][k] = - c2 * ( u(3,i,j,k) * temp1 );
13        fjacX[1][4][i][j][k] = c2;
14  ...
15      }
16    }
17  }
```

Listing 1.11. Coalesced array access in *x_sovle* routine

Unrolling is a well-known technique to increase the global performance of kernels. It allows to increase the amount of work per thread and takes advantage of data reuse.

Finally, in order to help the CAPS OpenACC compiler get better performance, in some kernels, we pre-loaded some of the values in temporary variables (refer to Listing 1.12). At runtime, the data will be preloaded in a register which has a very low latency access latency (few memory cycles) compare to an access to gloabl memory (400-700 memory cycles). Otherwise, it accesses the same data in global memory multiple times resulting in higher latencies.

```
1   double tmprhs0, tmprhs1, tmprhs2, tmprhs3, tmprhs4;
2     tmprhs0 = rhs(0,i-1,j,k);
3     tmprhs1 = rhs(1,i-1,j,k);
4     tmprhs2 = rhs(2,i-1,j,k);
5     tmprhs3 = rhs(3,i-1,j,k);
6     tmprhs4 = rhs(4,i-1,j,k);
7
8   rhs(0,i,j,k) = rhs(0,i,j,k) - lhsX[0][0][AA][i][j][k]*tmprhs0
9                       - lhsX[0][1][AA][i][j][k]*tmprhs1
10                      - lhsX[0][2][AA][i][j][k]*tmprhs2
11                      - lhsX[0][3][AA][i][j][k]*tmprhs3
12                      - lhsX[0][4][AA][i][j][k]*tmprhs4;
```

Listing 1.12. Preloading temporary values *matvec_sub* routine

5   Results

5.1   Platform

These tests were run on the Titan supercomputer, a Cray XK7 supercomputer [14]. Titan has 18,688 compute nodes equipped with 1 GPU per node. The nodes are connected with Cray's Gemini interconnect. For OpenSHMEM Titan has installed Cray's shmem implementation version 5.6.3. For OpenACC Titan has capsmc version 3.3.4. For this paper we used a beta version of the CAPS compiler, version 3.3beta-r50937. Additionally the GNU compiler collection version 4.7.1, nvidia CUDA compiler version 5.5 and CUDA driver 5.0 were used.

5.2 Timing and Scalability

In the following figure you can see the different speedup. the Figure 1 shows the speed ups of the different configuration compared to the fully serial version 1 PE on 1 node of the class C. the Figure 2 shows the speed ups of the different configuration compared to the fully serial version 16 PEs on 16 nodes of the class D.

We focused on the execution of the OpenSHMEM version and the OpenSHMEM-OpenACC version of the BT-MZ benchmark. We choose to compare the class C and D. The class C is composed of 256 zones with zone sizes distributed from 13x8x28 to 57x38x28 elements and executes 200 iterations. The class D is composed of 1024 zones with zone sizes distributed from 22x16x34 to 98x73x34 elements and executes 250 iterations. We first run these tests against a serial version on a single node, then compare the speed up of using 8, 16, 32, 64, 128, and 256 nodes. We also compare the speed of using OpenACC as well, showing what benefits or deficits that are incurred for using GPU acceleration. We do this in a seperate graph for a class C run and a class D run.

In Figure 1 we can see that the OpenACC struggles to match the speedup from the pure OpenSHMEM version at first. Then after 64 nodes the performance of the pure OpenSHMEM version plateaus while the GPU version continues to see gains. The most likely explanation for this is that for class C after 64 nodes, OpenSHMEM is no longer able to extract additional parallelism. This may be a result of the simplistic nature of the port from MPI to OpenSHMEM. It may be possible to get additional performance gains by restructuring the communication patterns. OpenACC continues to see performance gains because distributing more zones across more PEs with more GPUs allows for fewer transfers of zones across the PCIe bus increasing the efficiency of the GPUs.

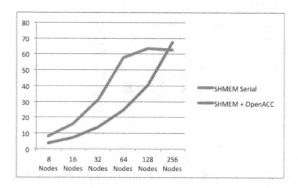

Fig. 1. Speed-up for the Class C of BT-MZ

In Figure 2 we can see that OpenACC and OpenSHMEM+OpenACC both continue to see the same amount of performance gain as we add more PEs. However, unlike in Class C where OpenSHMEM saw an early lead before dropping off in gains, both see the same amount of performance gain for the additional PEs.

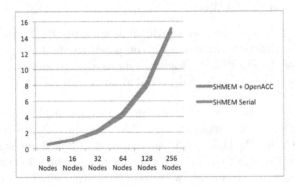

Fig. 2. Speed-up for the Class D pf BT-MZ

However, in this run we also see the version with OpenACC has a consistent performance advantage of 10%.

On the figure 3 we can see the percentage of the time spent in the exch_boundary function call for the OpenSHMEM-OpenACC version of the code. This function call is also where the updates to GPU memory occur, so in addition to the time spent in network communication it also encompasses the time spent transferring data between the GPU and the system memory. For the OpenSHMEM serial execution we observed up to 3% of time spent in exch_qbc for 256 PE. Concerning the OpenSHMEM-OpenACC version the time spent in exch_qbc goes up to 47%.

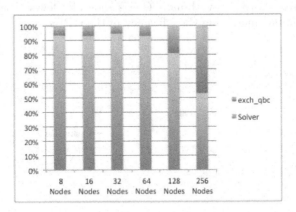

Fig. 3. Proportion of time spent in exch_qbc and the solver for the Class D Of BT-MZ

We also compared the performance of the Serial-C version [15] and the OpenACC version of the BT benchmark (non-MZ) for the class B and C. The B class computes on a matrix of 102x102x102 elements for 200 iterations. The C class computes on a matrix of 162x162x162 elements for 200 iterations. In the table 1, you can see the time of execution of the different class on 1 node of Titan.

Here we can see that increasing the size of the data to compute on the accelerator allows us to get some good speedup compare to the serial execution. It uses the same algorithm with the same code implementation for the BT solver. This isolates the performance of OpenACC versus the performance of OpenSHMEM for this algorithm. We do this to demonstrate the performance gains of using a GPU implementation without OpenSHMEM communication.

Table 1. Execution time of the NAS BT benchmark for Class B & C

Class	B	C
serial	427.53	1575.67
ACC	99.71	460.74
speed-up	4.29	3.42

6 Conclusions and Future Work

While the non multi-zone version of the BT benchmark showed great performance benefit, the Multizone version struggled to match serial performance. This was largely because, as seen in the time spent exchanging data, because as the zones got smaller the benefits extracted from the GPU became smaller, since the transfer times overwhelmed the computational benefits. Using larger problem sizes should also result in larger gains in speed, since we can see increases in the ratio of transfer versus computation as the number of nodes was increased for the same problem size.

In our OpenSHMEM and OpenACC hybrid most of the performance problems came from the need to communicate memory stored on the GPU across the network. Network performance was good but since the GPUs had to send their data to main memory to communicate over the network the performance gains of having accelerators was hard to realize in a distributed environment.

Using an accelerator that uses host memory should eliminate these problems. The AMD APUs would not suffer from the performance degradation associated with transferring memory from the accelerator to the host system and thus should not have problems associated with transferring small zones to and from the independent accelerator memory. This would solve a large part of the growth seen in figure 3 since the boundary exchange includes memory transfer from the accelerator.

We can see in Table 1 that OpenACC saw a solid performance gain when run in serial with one zone, so it is safe to say that we are not seeing performance degradation because of the execution on the accelerator. In figure 3 we can see that the memory exchange, including updating system memory and transfers across the network, quickly grew in the dominance of the total run time. In figure 1 we can see that the BT-MZ benchmark without OpenACC is initially faster, and with the evidence in table 1 and figure 3 it is reasonable to guess that most of this slowdown is the accelerator transfer. Because of this we believe it is reasonable to project that an integrated solution like an AMD APU will see performance closer to what we saw in figure 2.

Further work can include increasing the problem size, allowing the GPU to do more compute work for the zones between transfers. The ability to target the benchmark to fill the memory size of the GPU would expose the maximum benefits of the GPUs. It would also be interesting to see the results of exceeding the maximum size of the GPU memory to see how OpenACC would cope or suggest to future OpenACC specifications to support the swapping of memory from the GPU to the host.

One interesting avenue to explore for this purpose would be using the accelerator as the primary source of memory, as opposed to the system memory. In the current implementation, the benchmark still has to transfer memory to the system memory in order to communicate barrier conditions with OpenSHMEM. If something similar to the GPU direct with CUDA and MPI could be implemented for OpenSHMEM there would be no need to transfer this memory to the system memory. In fact, the host system could be made unnecessary in an extreme case. Further exploration of how OpenSHMEM and OpenACC can be utilized together represents a large challenge that also holds promise for excellent performance. The main hurdle to this remains an awareness of the GPU and how it works with memory transfers and it's impact on communication.

Acknowledgments. This work is supported by the United States Department of Defense and used resources of the Extreme Scale Systems Center located at the Oak Ridge National Laboratory.

References

1. Top500: Top 500 supercomputer sites (2013), http://www.top500.org/
2. Bland, B.: Titan - early experience with the titan system at oak ridge national laboratory. In: Proceedings of the 2012 SC Companion: High Performance Computing, Networking Storage and Analysis, SCC 2012, pp. 2189–2211. IEEE Computer Society (2012)
3. Poole, S., Hernandez, O., Kuehn, J., Shipman, G., Curtis, A., Feind, K.: Openshmem - toward a unified rma model. In: Padua, D. (ed.) Encyclopedia of Parallel Computing, pp. 1379–1391. Springer US (2011)
4. Jin, H., der Wijngaart, R.F.V.: Performance characteristics of the multi-zone nas parallel benchmarks. In: IPDPS. IEEE Computer Society (2004)
5. OpenSHMEM Org.: Openshmem specification (2011)
6. Gokhale, M., Stone, J.: Napa c: compiling for a hybrid risc/fpga architecture. In: Proceedings of the IEEE Symposium on FPGAs for Custom Computing Machines, pp. 126–135 (1998)
7. Fraguela, B.B., Renau, J., Feautrier, P., Padua, D., Torrellas, J.: Programming the flexram parallel intelligent memory system. SIGPLAN Not. 38, 49–60 (2003)
8. Bellens, P., Perez, J.M., Badia, R.M., Labarta, J.: Cellss: a programming model for the cell be architecture. In: Proceedings of the 2006 ACM/IEEE Conference on Supercomputing, SC 2006. ACM, New York (2006)
9. OpenHMPP: OpenHMPP: Concepts & Directives (2012)
10. Han, T.D., Abdelrahman, T.S.: hiCUDA: a high-level directive-based language for GPU programming. In: Proceedings of 2nd Workshop on General Purpose Processing on Graphics Processing Units, GPGPU-2, pp. 52–61. ACM, New York (2009)

11. Koesterke, L., Boisseau, J., Cazes, J., Milfeld, K., Stanzione, D.: Early Experiences with the Intel Many Integrated Cores Accelerated Computing Technology. In: Proceedings of the 2011 TeraGrid Conference: Extreme Digital Discovery, TG 2011, pp. 21:1–21:8. ACM, New York (2011)

12. OpenACC: How does the openacc api relate to openmp api? (2013)

13. NVIDIA: OpenACC Directives for Accelerators. In: NVIDIA Developer Zone (2012), http://developer.download.nvidia.com/CUDA/training/OpenACC_1_0_intro_jan2012.pdf

14. Oak Ridge Leadership Computing Facility: Introducing titan: Advancing the era of accelerated computing (2013), http://www.olcf.ornl.gov/titan/

15. Center for Manycore Programming, Seoul National University, Korea: Snu npb suite site (2013)

Towards Parallel Performance Analysis Tools for the OpenSHMEM Standard

Sebastian Oeste, Andreas Knüpfer, and Thomas Ilsche

Technische Universität Dresden, Center for Information Services and HPC (ZIH)

Abstract. This paper discusses theoretic and practical aspects when extending performance analysis tools to support the OpenSHMEM standard for parallel programming. The theoretical part covers the mapping of OpenSHMEM's communication primitives to a generic event record scheme that is compatible with a range of PGAS libraries. The visualization of the recorded events is included as well. The practical parts demonstrate an experimental extension for Cray-SHMEM in Vampir-Trace and Vampir and first results with a parallel example application. Since Cray-SHMEM is similar to OpenSHMEM in many respects, this serves as a realistic preview. Finally, an outlook on a native support for OpenSHMEM is given together with some recommendations for future revisions of the OpenSHMEM standard from the perspective of performance tools.

Keywords: OpenSHMEM, Performance Analysis, Tracing, Tools Infrastructure.

1 Introduction

In the field of High Performance Computing (HPC), MPI was and is the dominating parallelization standard. It provides a huge range of point-to-point and collective communication operations and is the de-facto standard in for highly parallel programming beyond multi-threading in High Performance Computing (HPC). Another model for parallel programming is gaining more and more attention lately, the Partitioned Global Address Space (PGAS) paradigm. It promotes the idea of shared memory parallelization even for large scale distributed memory parallel machines. For this purpose it employs Remote Direct Memory Access (RDMA) operations, also called one-sided communication. A number of efforts in the HPC community currently follow this paradigm. Among them may be promising candidates for a true rival for MPI. One of the main prospects of PGAS is the reduced complexity compared to hybrid MPI plus OpenMP parallelism. An indication that this may be true is the addition of one-sided operations to the MPI standard.

On the one hand, the set of PGAS approaches contains language extensions like Unified Parallel C (UPC) or Co-Array Fortran (CAF) which need their own compilers. On the other hand, it contains PGAS libraries that have the advantage that well-known languages like C/C++ and Fortran gain PGAS functionalities

S. Poole, O. Hernandez, and P. Shamis (Eds.): OpenSHMEM 2014, LNCS 8356, pp. 90–104, 2014.

and no extra compilers are needed. SHMEM is one flavor of such PGAS libraries. In the history of SHMEM there are several implementations like Cray-SHMEM, SGI-SHMEM or Quadrics SHMEM with quite different APIs. With OpenSH-MEM there is a new effort to create a open standard to make all vendor versions of SHMEM API-compatible.

This paper presents a concept for a generic infrastructure to record event traces from OpenSHMEM parallel application programs. Its goal is an integration in the Score-P monitoring system which produces event traces in the Open Trace Format 2 (OTF2) that are to be visualized and analyzed with the Vampir tool. In section 2 we describe the common techniques for the performance monitoring of parallel applications. Section 3 presents a concept for a generic tracing infrastructure for PGAS approaches in general and OpenSHMEM in particular. Section 4 gives an overview of an existing prototypical implementation for trace recording of SHMEM events using Cray-SHMEM and the VampirTrace package. The paper ends with an outlook on a native OpenSHMEM event tracing solution for the parallel performance analysis.

2 Parallel Performance Analysis Tools

Tools for parallel performance analysis are an important part of the HPC software ecosystem. Since the parallel execution performance and the scalability are most significant properties in HPC, developers need to pay attention to performance analysis and tuning. And they need support by appropriate tools.

Just like debugging is very difficult without dedicated debugging tools, the detailed investigation of the run-time behavior apart from the wall clock duration is almost impossible. And both kinds of task get notably more complicated in the parallel case.

2.1 Instrumentation

To monitor HPC applications it is necessary to be able to measure the run-time behavior inside target programs exactly. To reach this we need concrete run-time information from the application during execution. A way to to get run-time information of a program during execution is instrumentation. Instrumentation refers to a modification of the program code to measure certain events of interest. The measurement code is inserted before and after an event appears and triggers routines in the measurement environment to gather the information. Instrumentation can take place at different times of the program transformation process. There are several techniques to instrument a program.

- **Static instrumentation** The code will be inserted before execution.
- **Dynamic instrumentation** The code will be inserted during execution.
- **Manual instrumentation** The code is inserted manually this affords the most flexibility. The user can place measurement calls exactly on those parts of the program provides the most interest.

- **Automatic instrumentation** The code will be inserted automatically for example through certain linker options, or compiler functionalities. Which invokes corresponding functions with information like file name, line number, function name. Automatic instrumentation typically inserts enter and leave events.
- **Binary instrumentation** The instrumentation appears on the binary, executable file. Toolkits like the DyninstAPI are able to insert measurement code after the actual program is compiled [11].

The different ways to instrument an application makes instrumentation in general a flexible solution. We are currently developing an instrumentation tool for C and C++ sources which creates a wrapper library by parsing a header file and re-defining all symbols with performance annotations. This tools uses mechanisms for dynamic and static linking libraries and even supports profiling interfaces based on weak symbols.

2.2 Sampling

Another technique to record information is sampling. Sampling works without any modification of the programs source code or binary executable. During the execution of the program periodic interrupts occur to collect information about the state of the program. Popular information for sampling are values of performance counters or the state of the call stack. The granularity depends on the sampling frequency. An advantage of sampling compared with instrumentation is the ability to make forecasts about the overhead behavior. The overhead of program analysis using sampling grows linear with the sampling frequency.

2.3 Profiling

One way to present the acquired information from instrumentation or sampling is to create a so called profile. A profile in general is an summary of performance metrics e.g. the time difference between enter and leave events or the number of calls of a function. A profile can be created from information acquired by sampling or by instrumentation. Common kinds of profiles are the *flat profile* which is the simplest form of a profile. Because the aggregated information just depends on the regions or instrumented functions. Significantly for a flat profile is that it provides no caller context. Another form of a profile is a *call-path profile* which is a representation of the execution path. A call-path profile gives information about possible routes through a program - each route through the program is a own record.

2.4 Event Tracing

Parallel event tracing tools try to capture the run-time behavior of a target application by recording events of interest. Usually, event tracing relies on instrumentation to be notified about such events, but there are also sampling-based approaches. For every event a so called *event record* is stored. All records are stored separately in every processing element (PE) in temporal order. Every record contains at least the type (what), the time (when) and the location (where) of an event and might carry further type-specific data. Usually, the stream of event records is stored in a local memory buffer and is stored to the file system only at the end of the measurement. See [12] for more background.

The events of interest that are used for parallel event tracing of High Performance Computing (HPC) applications can be grouped into three groups: Sequential events, parallel events, and scalar values.

Sequential Execution Events. This includes all activities in all sequential phases of the parallel PEs. They have no direct effects on other PEs and are the same for all parallel programs no matter if they use MPI, Pthreads, or any other parallelization model. The monitoring system merely needs a way to find out the location (where) of the events. The granularity of such events may vary. Typical examples are the call to (enter event) or return from (leave event) for subroutine calls or the begin and end of loop bodies.

Events for Parallel Communication and Synchronization. Communication and synchronization event records cover the remaining parts of parallel programs. They represent all activities that directly affect two or more PEs. They are represented as local event records on some or all of the involved PEs. In particular, they allow to identify the communication peer(s) explicitly or implicitly.

This group of events is closely modeled according to the perspective of the programmer, i.e. the events represent the basic building blocks for communication and synchronization that the parallelization model provides. For parallelization libraries such as OpenSHMEM, this is close to their APIs.

There are a number of examples from established HPC parallelization models. First, there are point-to-point communication calls and collective communication calls from MPI [10], including both, the blocking and the non-blocking modes. Second, there are parallel regions and synchronization points from OpenMP which are not implemented as API calls but as code pragmas. Also there are data transfers calls between hosts and devices as well as synchronization points for GPGPU computing models such as CUDA and OpenCL. And there are PGAS-style communication and synchronization types which are applicable to OpenSHMEM and several other PGAS-libraries or PGAS language extensions, see also [8].

Usually, all communication and synchronization event records are surrounded by events for the API call to reference which exact API call was used and to capture the duration of the call (the time between the enter and the leave events).

Hardware Counters, System Metrics, and User-defined Metrics. In addition to the previous two groups, there are event records for *counters* or *metrics*. Usually, they provide summaries of events of interest which are too fine-grained to be recorded individually. The prime examples are CPU hardware performance counters counting floating point instructions, memory accesses, cache misses, TLB misses, and many more. Sampling such counters at the enter and leave points of subroutine calls provides interesting data about the floating point instructions, memory accesses, etc. that happened inside the call. Besides hardware performance counters, also system counters like memory consumption or temperature can be captured in this way, even though they are not strictly counting discrete events. Also external metrics like the power consumption or the throughput rates of storage subsystems can be captured like this. Last but not least, so called *user defined metrics* can be provided by the application code itself to indicate relevant properties of its inner workings. Examples could be the number of outstanding requests at a point in time, partition sizes of problem decompositions, or the residual value of an iterative solver.

2.5   Existing Tools and Related Work

There are a couple of performance analysis tools which support the techniques described above with a strong focus on High Performance Computing (HPC). The Tuning an Analysis Utilities (TAU) specialize in profiling with some tracing functionalities [17]. Scalasca focuses on automatic detection of well-known performance problems in parallel programs based on an event trace replay mechanism [5]. Vampir provides interactive visualization and exploration of parallel event traces [12]. All of the previously mentioned tools work together with the Score-P monitoring infrastructure for code instrumentation, profile collection and event trace recording [9]. There is also Vampir's previous default monitoring system called VampirTrace with a similar feature set. VampirTrace comes as a regular component of the Open MPI package and is therefore available on a large number of HPC machines worldwide [12]. HPCToolkit is one established example that relies on periodic sampling including call stack unwinding to capture the dynamic run-time behavior of parallel target applications [1].

With respect to performance tools for the rather young OpenSHMEM standard, there are very few pieces of related work. A prototypical extension to VampirTrace has been created by S. Jana and J. Schuchart at ORNL which capture traces of OpenSHMEM API calls but not data transfers. Using their extension, they facilitated an analysis of the energy consumption of certain OpenSHMEM library calls using the counter plug-in infrastructure of VampirTrace [7]. As far as we know this was not published yet. The extension of VampirTrace for the recording of API calls as well as data transfers for Cray-SHMEM, which was the basis for Section 4, was published in [16].

3   Concept of a Tracing Infrastructure for OpenSHMEM

The effort to provide recording of sequential events and counters or metrics for OpenSHMEM programs in existing monitoring systems is minimal. Yet, the PGAS-style communication scheme requires theoretical and practical changes in the recording and representation of events. Furthermore, the monitoring infrastructure needs to implement its internal communication with OpenSHMEM.

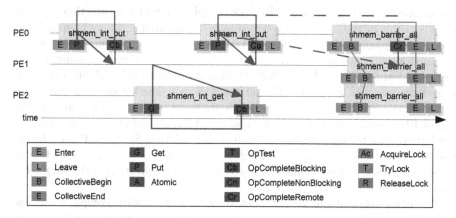

Fig. 1. Timeline visualization of put and get operations and their points of completion

3.1 Modeling and Recording PGAS Activities

While MPI is clearly clearly the dominating message passing model in the HPC landscape, there are several promising players in the PGAS realm. There are language extensions like Co-Array Fortran [15] and UPC [3] on the one hand and libraries like OpenSHMEM [4], GASPI [2], ARMCI [13], GlobalArrays [14] but also MPI 3.0 with the on-sided operations [10] on the other hand. All of them share the concept of the Partitioned Global Address Space with 'put' and 'get' operations (sometimes called 'write' and 'read', though) as the key communication operations. Therefore, there should be a single model and a single set of event records to represent all PGAS parallelization libraries. This allows analysis tools to be generic and usable for all PGAS libraries[1].

Still, there are semantic differences between all the flavors of 'put' and 'get' operations and there are various kinds of synchronization mechanisms. Furthermore, there are some more concepts present in some of the PGAS libraries but not in all of them. In [8] a combined model is presented covering all of them. In the remainder of this paper, only the OpenSHMEM operations are discussed.

Put and Get Operations. OpenSHMEM defines a variety of put and get operations. There are calls for individual numbers, for arrays or blocks, and strided ones for regular subarrays. All of them are blocking, i.e. the API calls only returns after the local completion of the operation. For get operations, local completion also ensures remote completion, that means the operation is not affected by following activities on the remote (passive) side. For put operations, only the local completion is given, i.e. following changes at the source address won't influence

---

[1] The model is also applicable to PGAS language extensions even though their 'put' and 'get' calls are hidden from the programmer. The compilers will generate them from the language constructs like loops. However, the remainder of this paper focuses on the PGAS libraries in general and OpenSHMEM in particular.

the locally completed operation. Remote completion, which means that the sent data is visible at the remote (passive) side, is not ensured and may happen later.

Put and get operations are recorded on the active PE only. Four event records are used for this, see also Fig.1. As first an last, an enter record (E) and a leave record (L) are written which denote the name of the called API function. The time between them is the duration of the API call. The actual data transfer is recorded as a RMA put event or an RMA get event, see Fig.2. They include the target PE, the transfer size in bytes, and a matching number. They also include a reference to a memory window, which is only relevant for other PGAS flavors which use multiple "memory windows" or "communicators". In OpenSHMEM there is always a single "symmetric heap" and the specification of the target PE always uses global IDs.

The completion of put or get operations is marked with completion event records on the same (active) PE. In all cases, the local completion has to be marked with an 'RmaOpCompleteBlocking' record with the same matching number. Since all OpenSHMEM 'put' or 'get' calls are blocking until the local completion, this completion event is put at the end of the associated API call, just before the leave event, see Fig.1 and Fig.2. For 'put' operations where there is a separate remote completion which may or may not be detectable. From the OpenSHMEM API level it is visible for example when there is a following call to 'shmem_barrier_all', see Fig.1(top right). In this case, an optional 'RmaOpCompleteRemote' record can be written. It is connected to the originating put event with the same matching number. However, an OpenSHMEM program may proceed without ever notifying the active PE (that issued the put operation) about the remote completion. In such cases, the remote completion record is left out, see Fig.1(top left).

Visualization of Put and Get Operations. The graphical visualization of put and get operations relies on the event records over time on the active PE. Besides depicting the API call, the data transfer will be shown with an arrow from the source PE to the destination PE. The start time of the arrow is the time of the respective put or get event and that is equal to the start time of

OTF2_Rma(Put|Get)		
OTF2_LocationRef	location	local PE
OTF2_TimeStamp	time	time stamp
OTF2_RmaWinRef	window	memory window
uint32_t	target	target PE in context of window
uint64_t	size	number of bytes transferred
uint64_t	matching	matching number

OTF2_RmaOp(Test|(Complete(Blocking|NonBlocking|Remote)))		
OTF2_LocationRef	location	process or thread of execution
OTF2_TimeStamp	time	time stamp
OTF2_RmaWinRef	window	memory window
uint64_t	matching	matching number

Fig. 2. OTF2 record definitions for put, get, and completion events

the API call. The end time for the arrows should be the time of completion. This is trivial for get operations where the local completion is the same as the remote completion. Thus, it is visualized as in Fig.1(bottom) giving a realistic impression of the duration and the speed of the data transfer.

It is not well defined for put operations, because local completion is not equal to remote completion and because remote completion might be invisible for the monitoring system. Even if the remote completion is visible, it is most probably visible only at a point in time later than the actual arrival of the data transfer. At least it is generally recommended by all PGAS programming models to issue individual remote memory accesses as early as possible and to uses barriers, fences, or other memory synchronization operations as late as possible. Since neither of the local or remote completion points give a good indication of the actual duration of a put data transfer, the local completion time is used because it is always available. It follows that the shown arrows for put operations need to be read differently. They are an indication when the put operation started and between which PEs it happens. Yet it does not indicate the transfer time.

Atomic RMA Operations. OpenSHMEM supports a number of atomic RMA operations that read and write remote variables in an atomicity manner, i.e. with the guarantee that no other local or remote memory access can interfere in between. A separate event record type is defined for atomic operations, see Fig.3. It is to be used like the put and get record types. In addition to those, it stores the type of atomic operations and it has separate fields to store the data volume sent and received. They should contain the number of bytes that two separate put and get operations would carry if they would try to mimic the effect of the atomic operation (without the atomicity).

OTF2_RmaAtomicType	
OTF2_RMA_ATOMIC_TYPE_SWAP	swap
OTF2_RMA_ATOMIC_TYPE_COMPARE_AND_SWAP	compare and swap
OTF2_RMA_ATOMIC_TYPE_FETCH_AND_ADD	fetch and add
OTF2_RMA_ATOMIC_TYPE_FETCH_AND_INCREMENT	fetch and increment
OTF2_RMA_ATOMIC_TYPE_ADD	remote add
OTF2_RMA_ATOMIC_TYPE_INCREMENT	remote increment
...	

OTF2_RmaAtomic		
OTF2_LocationRef	location	process or thread of execution
OTF2_TimeStamp	time	time stamp
OTF2_RmaWinRef	window	window
uint32_t	target	rank of target in context of window
OTF2_RmaAtomicType	type	type of atomic operation
uint64_t	size_sent	number of bytes transferred to target
uint64_t	size_received	number of bytes transferred from target
uint64_t	matching	matching number

Fig. 3. OTF2 record definitions for atomic events including the types of atomic operations that are relevant for OpenSHMEM

Like put and get records, atomic RMA records should be followed by a local complete record and an optional global complete record. For the visualization a single arrow like that of a put operation should be used. If the 'size_received' field is larger than 0 then a second arrow head pointing backward should be added.

Collective Operations. Collective operations in OpenSHMEM are operations performed simultaneously by a subset of PEs. They are represented by a pair of event records 'OTF2_RmaCollectiveBegin' and 'OTF2_RmaCollectiveEnd' as shown inf Fig.4. The former merely denotes the begin of the operation, the latter contains all information about it. This pair of records is to be written by every participating PE.

The field 'sync_level' is always set to 'OTF2_RMA_SYNC_LEVEL_ALL' for Open-SHMEM which means that memory and the execution is synchronized by Open-SHMEM collectives. Since OpenSHMEM collectives have no 'root' PE, the 'root' field is always set to a special value 'NONE'. The fields 'size_sent' and 'size_received' contain the number of bytes sent and received by the current PE if the collective operation would be mimicked by the minimal number of put and get operations. In the OpenSHMEM API these subsets of PE's in collective operations are known as *active set*. The participating PE's are managed in a group which refers to a memory window.

In the visualization all matching collective operations should be connected like shown in Fig.1(right) for the 'shmem_barrier_all' operation.

OTF2_RmaCollectiveBegin		
OTF2_LocationRef	location	process or thread of execution
OTF2_TimeStamp	time	time stamp

OTF2_RmaCollectiveEnd		
OTF2_LocationRef	location	process or thread of execution
OTF2_TimeStamp	time	time stamp
OTF2_RmaSyncLevel	sync_level	synchronization level
OTF2_RmaWinRef	window	memory window
uint32_t	root	root process/rank if there is one
uint64_t	size_sent	number of bytes sent
uint64_t	size_received	number of bytes received

Fig. 4. OTF2 record definitions for marking collective RMA operations

Locks. For the mutex lock concept, a separate set of events are introduced. Besides the API calls, they keep track of the lock type (exclusive lock or write lock vs. shared lock or read lock) and the lock instance. In the visualization, all operations working on the same lock on the same PE instance are connected until the lock is cleared. When several PEs compete for the same lock, then no connections are drawn between the PEs but when they are displayed side by side with aligned time axes, it becomes apparent, that only one can hold the lock at any time. See Fig.5 for an example.

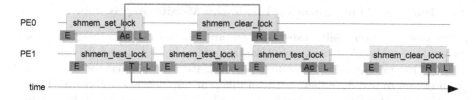

Fig. 5. Timeline visualization of two PEs performing competing lock operations

OTF2_LockType		
OTF2_LOCK_TYPE_EXCLUSIVE		only one lock allowed at the same time, e.g., write-lock, mutex, MPI exclusive lock
OTF2_LOCK_TYPE_SHARED		multiple shared locks allowed at the same time, e.g., read-lock, MPI shared lock
OTF2_(Request|Try)Lock		
OTF2_LocationRef	location	process or thread of execution
OTF2_TimeStamp	time	time stamp
OTF2_RmaWinRef	window	memory window
uint32_t	target	rank of target in context of window
OTF2_RmaLockType	lock_type	Type of lock (shared vs. exclusive)
uint64_t	lock_id	lock id in context of window
OTF2_ReleaseLock		
OTF2_LocationRef	location	process or thread of execution
OTF2_TimeStamp	time	time stamp
OTF2_RmaWinRef	window	
uint32_t	target	rank of target in context of window
uint64_t	lock_id	lock id in context of window

Fig. 6. OTF2 record definitions for lock operations

The record definitions are shown in Fig.6, see also [8]. The reference to a memory window and a reference to a target PE are not relevant for OpenSHMEM but only important for other PGAS flavors.

3.2   Communication on Lower Level Layers

All OpenSHMEM implementations will translate OpenSHMEM API functions to calls of lower transport layers. There are multiple such layers which may range from the second-level DMAPP library in Cray systems to the low-level Infiniband network layer, compare also the OSI model [6].

The presented event trace recording will only capture the OpenSHMEM layer but not the lower layers beneath. The primary reason for this is, that the performance analysis shall reflect the source code of the OpenSHMEM application. If a performance problem is detected in the way OpenSHMEM is used, then the (typical) optimization step will be to change the OpenSHMEM calls in the source code instead of changing details in the given OpenSHMEM library.

Should there be interest in the performance analysis of lower transport layers, then this should not be specific for OpenSHMEM but address this particular layer. For example, a monitoring extension for the low-level Infiniband layer might be used with OpenSHMEM, MPI, or GASPI. At the same time, it means that the connection between high-level API calls and low-level operations is lost.

3.3 Internal Communication Inside the Monitoring System

Apart from the user-visible aspects, there are internal tasks in the monitoring system for bookkeeping and synchronization which depend on parallel communication. They usually rely on the same parallelization method as used by the target program to avoid conflicts between different parallelization libraries. Those tasks include the collective initialization and finalization of the monitoring instances, the synchronization of the local timers used by every parallel instance, the unification of identifiers in the event records, and more.

While this constitutes a considerable part of the effort when porting an existing monitoring system to OpenSHMEM, this paper focuses on the user's perspective of performance analysis tools for parallel applications.

4   A Demonstration for Cray-SHMEM with VampirTrace

We already developed an experimental solution to monitor the communication of SHMEM applications based on Cray-SHMEM. Because Cray-SHMEM can co-exist with MPI and because it guarantees that all SHMEM PE numbers are equal to the MPI ranks (within `MPI_COMM_WORLD`), the steps from Section 3.3 could be re-used from the existing MPI monitoring infrastructure. This was accomplished with the VampirTrace library [12]. `MPI_Init` is called just before `start_pes` and `MPI_Finalize` after `shmem_finalize`. The communication semantics of the SHMEM operations were mapped to related MPI operations, for example a `shmem_int_put` was mapped to `MPI_Put`.

The instrumentation of SHMEM API functions was realized by using the weak symbols of the Cray-SHMEM library. The Cray SHMEM library provides weak symbols for all library functions that can be overwritten by so called wrapper functions. Inside the wrapper functions the real call to the Cray SHMEM library is executed, yet before and after the data to be recorded is collected and stored to memory buffers. Eventually, the memory buffers are flushed to traces files. At the very end, a post processing is performed before the parallel event traces are ready to be analyzed with the Vampir visualization tool (see also further down).

Demonstration Example

Our demonstration example is a 2D simulation of the heat equation which runs with 16 PEs on a $1500x1500$ matrix [16]. We ran the program several times on a the petascale Cray XE6 system Hermit at HLRS Stuttgart. The heat equation program use a regular block-wise data distribution. Each node computes its own area for every iteration whereupon a halo exchange with the four neighbors is performed using one-sided operations.

An Example of SHMEM Performance Analysis

For performance analysis the parts of communication are of particular interest. Fig.4 shows a zoomed view of one of the communication sections in Vampir.

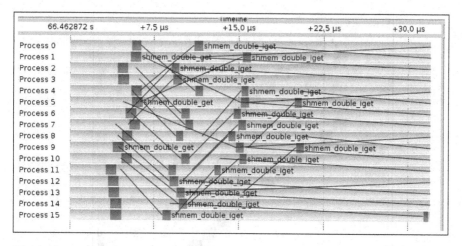

Fig. 7. Representation of a SHMEM communication section in Vampir. The run-time is shown horizontally from left to right while all PEs are arranged vertically.

The lines between the functions of the processes represent the direction of the communication. Vampir even provides further information such as the message size or the transfer rate in a more detailed view. The figure shows that the communication between the processes is done with the shmem_double_get and the shmem_double_iget functions. Besides individual communication operations, Vampir also provides a *communication matrix*, an overview of all communication operations between sender and receiver PEs.

Figure 8 shows the communication matrix for the average transfer time. The communication matrix indicates that the upper and lower borders (to/from the PE ±4) are transfered faster than the left and right borders (to/from the PE ±1). Yet, in all directions the same amount of data is transfered, as the same communication matrix view for the sum of message sizes would reveal.

The reason for the differing speeds are two different communication operations. For the horizontal halos shmem_double_get is used which can transfer the entire data block with a single low-level RMA operation. For the vertical halos the shmem_double_iget function has to be used, because the vertical halos of the two-dimensional array are not located in contiguous memory ranges. Thus, multiple small RMA operations have to be issued.

Overhead and Perturbation

The monitoring approach explained above including the instrumentation and run-time data collection will induce a certain overhead, of course. As long as this overhead is small enough and evenly distributed over the entire test run, the resulting perturbation of the recorded trace will be negligible, i.e. the recorded behavior is sufficiently close to the "real" behavior without the presence of the monitoring system. Then, it is sensible to reason about the parallel performance

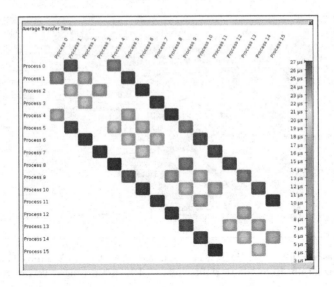

Fig. 8. View of Vampir communication matrix showing average transfer time

behavior of the "real" program run based on the event trace analysis. If used with some caution and with the help of some advanced features of VampirTrace such as selective instrumentation and filtering the overhead can be controlled.

In our example we compared the wall clock times of the un-instrumented and the instrumented cases for eight different configurations with 4 to 81 PEs. For averages of 10 runs in each configuration, the instrumented execution time was within 6 % of the original execution time.

5   Outlook to Native OpenSHMEM Support and Summary

The prototype solution described in the previous section shows an approach to the performance analysis of PGAS libraries. Implementing this for OpenSHMEM does pose some practical challenges. While the prototype assumes the direct relation to MPI, this is not generally the case for OpenSHMEM. Therefore the infrastructure of the monitoring library has to rely on OpenSHMEM for internal communication. OpenSHMEM does provide all the necessary communication primitives, including collectives, to implement measurement infrastructure such as the timer synchronization and the unification of distributed identifiers.

The instrumentation mechanism via weak symbols provides a reliable, portable and convenient way for the library wrapping step. While this functionality is optionally offered in the OpenSHMEM reference implementation, it is not currently defined by the standard. Performance analysis tools would greatly benefit if this was defined there. The MPI profiling interface (PMPI) has seeded a wide variety of tools - from lightweight profiling to flexible and complex measurement infrastructures. Alternatives using library pre-loading or linker wrapping are feasible but less straightforward, harder to make portable and generally divert the tool developers from core features.

Another open issue for implementing a parallel measurement infrastructure for OpenSHMEM is the lack of a finalization function. This would provide a reliable way to run measurement related code (e.g. combining results from multiple ranks) after the logical end of the application while it is still valid for the measurement infrastructure to use OpenSHMEM for communication. Also it would be guaranteed that the application does not call any other OpenSHMEM functions afterwards – so the recording is already complete at finalization time.

The possibilities for OpenSHMEM performance analysis described in this paper make no claim to be complete. It would be very interesting to hear from the OpenSHMEM user community what other information would be helpful to improve their applications. This extends to the developers of OpenSHMEM implementations that want to optimize their implementations. For instance, performance metrics that are internal to the OpenSHMEM implementation could be exposed to the monitoring infrastructure and recorded along with the application events. Examples might be the sizes of internal buffers or the current length of message queues.

Summary

In the first part of this paper we presented a concept for the event trace recording for OpenSHMEM applications, in particular the representation of one-sided communication primitives as event records and their suggested visualization. The second part shows a preliminary solution for the event trace recording of Cray-SHMEM applications. It includes results from an example case together with the Vampir visualization of the produced traces and a brief study of the introduced run-time overhead. Finally, an outlook for a native event tracing tool for OpenSHMEM is given.

Acknowledgments. This work is supported in a part by the German Research Foundation (DFG) in the Collaborative Research Center 912 "Highly Adaptive Energy-Efficient Computing". The authors would like to thank the HLRS for providing the compute time on *Hermit* used for the Cray-SHMEM demonstration.

References

1. Adhianto, L., Banerjee, S., Fagan, M., Krentel, M., Marin, G., Mellor-Crummey, J., Tallent, N.R.: Hpctoolkit: tools for performance analysis of optimized parallel programs. Concurrency and Computation: Practice and Experience 22(6), 685–701 (2010)
2. Alrutz, T., et al.: GASPI – A partitioned global address space programming interface. In: Keller, R., Kramer, D., Weiss, J.-P. (eds.) Facing the Multicore-Challenge III 2012. LNCS, vol. 7686, pp. 135–136. Springer, Heidelberg (2013)

3. Carlson, W.W., Draper, J.M., Culler, D.E.: S-246, 187 introduction to UPC and language specification
4. Chapman, B., Curtis, T., Pophale, S., Poole, S., Kuehn, J., Koelbel, C., Smith, L.: Introducing OpenSHMEM – SHMEM for the PGAS community (2010)
5. Geimer, M., Wolf, F., Wylie, B.J.N., Ábrahám, E., Becker, D., Mohr, B.: The Scalasca performance toolset architecture. Concurrency and Computation: Practice and Experience 22(6), 702–719 (2010)
6. Information technology – Open Systems Interconnection – Basic Reference Model (1994)
7. Jana, S., Schuchart, J.: Tracing and visualizing power consumption of OpenSH-MEM applications. Personal Communications (September 2013)
8. Knüpfer, A., Dietrich, R., Doleschal, J., Geimer, M., Hermanns, M.-A., Rössel, C., Tschüter, R., Wesarg, B., Wolf, F.: Generic support for remote memory access operations in Score-P and OTF2. In: Cheptsov, A., Brinkmann, S., Gracia, J., Resch, M.M., Nagel, W.E. (eds.) Tools for High Performance Computing 2012, pp. 57–74. Springer, Heidelberg (2013)
9. Knüpfer, A., Rössel, C., an Mey, D., Biersdorff, S., Diethelm, K., Eschweiler, D., Geimer, M., Gerndt, M., Lorenz, D., Malony, A., et al.: Score-p: A joint performance measurement run-time infrastructure for periscope, scalasca, tau, and vampir. In: Tools for High Performance Computing 2011, pp. 79–91. Springer, Heidelberg (2012)
10. Message Passing Interface Forum. MPI: A message-passing interface standard, version 2.2. Specification (September 2009)
11. Miller, B.P., Bernat, A.R.: Anywhere, any time binary instrumentation. In: ACM SIGPLAN-SIGSOFT Workshop on Program Analysis for Software Tools and Engineering (PASTE), Szeged, Hungary (September 2011)
12. Müller, M.S., Knüpfer, A., Jurenz, M., Lieber, M., Brunst, H., Mix, H., Nagel, W.E.: Developing scalable applications with vampir, vampirserver and vampirtrace. In: Parallel Computing: Architectures, Algorithms and Applications, vol. 15, pp. 637–644. IOS Press (2008)
13. Nieplocha, J., Carpenter, B.: ARMCI: A portable remote memory copy library for distributed array libraries and compiler run-time systems. In: Rolim, J., et al. (eds.) IPPS-WS 1999 and SPDP-WS 1999. LNCS, vol. 1586, pp. 533–546. Springer, Heidelberg (1999)
14. Nieplocha, J., Harrison, R.J., Littlefield, R.J.: Global arrays: A non-uniform-memory-access programming model for high-performance computers. The Journal of Supercomputing 10, 10–197 (1996)
15. Numrich, R.W., Reid, J.: Co-array fortran for parallel programming. ACM Fortran Forum 17(2), 1–31 (1998)
16. Oeste, S.: Aufzeichnung einseitiger Kommunikation zur Leistungsanalyse paralleler SHMEM-Anwendungen, Bachelor thesis in German (2012)
17. Shende, S.S., Malony, A.D.: The tau parallel performance system. Int. J. High Perform. Comput. Appl. 20(2), 287–311 (2006)

Profiling Non-numeric OpenSHMEM Applications with the TAU Performance System

John Linford[2], Tyler A. Simon[1,2], Sameer Shende[2,3], and Allen D. Malony[2,3]

[1] University of Maryland Baltimore County
[2] ParaTools Inc.
[3] University of Oregon

Abstract. The recent development of a unified SHMEM framework, OpenSHMEM, has enabled further study in the porting and scaling of applications that can benefit from the SHMEM programming model. This paper focuses on non-numerical graph algorithms, which typically have a low FLOPS/byte ratio. An overview of the space and time complexity of Kruskal's and Prim's algorithms for generating a minimum spanning tree (MST) is presented, along with an implementation of Kruskal's algorithm that uses OpenSHEM to generate the MST in parallel without intermediate communication. Additionally, a procedure for applying the TAU Performance System to OpenSHMEM applications to produce in-depth performance profiles showing time spent in code regions, memory access patterns, and network load is presented. Performance evaluations from the Cray XK7 "Titan" system at Oak Ridge National Laboratory and a 48 core shared memory system at University of Maryland, Baltimore County are provided.

1 Introduction

Non-numerical algorithms (NNA) are characterized by a low FLOPS/byte ratio and can be defined as those which spend most of their computational time doing either a search or sort. Memory locality, not computational load, is the primary performance factor. This class of algorithms is particularly challenging for HPC systems in the Top500 [11] as these systems are optimized for compute-intensive codes. NNAs often involve searching or traversing graphs, which are defined by a collection of *vertices* connected by *edges*. Graphs are used to model problems defined in terms of relationships or connections between objects. The mathematical properties of graphs facilitate the modeling of many useful computational problems, e.g. problems related to connectivity and routing optimization in networks.

Many graph algorithms begin by finding a *minimum spanning tree* (MST). Given a connected graph, a spanning tree is a subgraph that connects all the vertices and is a tree. For weighted graphs, the sum of the edge weights in a spanning tree is the weight of the spanning tree. A minimum spanning tree is a spanning tree with weight less than or equal to the weight of every other spanning tree. MSTs have many practical applications in communication networks,

S. Poole, O. Hernandez, and P. Shamis (Eds.): OpenSHMEM 2014, LNCS 8356, pp. 105–119, 2014.

network design and layout of highway systems. They provide a reasonable way to cluster points in space into natural groups and can be used to approximate solutions to hard problems, like the Traveling Salesman Problem [13].

Two common algorithms for finding an MST are Kruskal's [10] and Prim's [15]. The primary difference between these algorithms is the order of graph traversal (breadth first vs. depth first). We provide an overview of the space and time complexity of these algorithms and present an OpenSHMEM [3,7] implementation of Kruskal's algorithm. The implementation uses the symmetric hierarchical memory to generate the MST in parallel without intermediate communication, thereby minimizing network load. We use the TAU Performance System [16] to quantify the performance of our OpenSHMEM MST algorithm.

2   Background

2.1   The TAU Performance System

The challenge of developing parallel scientific and engineering applications for scalable, high-performance computer systems routinely involves the use of parallel performance tools to gain a deeper understanding of the code's execution characteristics and to guide optimizations. The evolving hardware technology of parallel computing platforms and the sophistication of software technologies to program them gives rise to complex performance interactions that requires careful measurement and analysis to understand. TAU is a robust, powerful, state-of-the-art toolset for performance investigation that has been applied across many scalable parallel computing paradigms and environments. TAU works efficiently on hundreds of thousands of threads and processes with codes written in Fortran, C/C++, Python, UPC, and Chapel, utilizing MPI, SHMEM, and DMAPP for communication, and pthreads and OpenMP for multi-threading.

Shown in Figure 1, TAU consists of three layers: instrumentation, measurement, and analysis. Each layer uses multiple modules that may be configured in a flexible manner under user control. TAU implements a multi-level instrumentation framework that includes source, runtime, and compiler-based instrumentation to expand the scope of performance instrumentation. This design makes it possible for TAU to easily provide alternative instrumentation techniques that target a common measurement API. The role of the instrumentation layer is to insert code (a.k.a. probes) to make performance events visible to the measurement layer. Performance events can be defined and instrumentation inserted in a program at several levels of the program transformation process. A complete performance view may require contribution of event information across code levels. To support this, TAU's instrumentation mechanisms are based on the code type and transformation level: source (manual, preprocessor), object (compiler-based instrumentation), library interposition (pre-wrapped libraries), static linker (redirecting and substituting calls to an alternate routine), runtime linker (runtime interposition of libraries), binary (pre-execution at runtime), re-writing (dynamic instrumentation), interpreter (language runtime), virtual

Listing 1.1. OpenSHMEM Minimum Spanning Tree

```
1   start_pes (0);
2   if (shmem_my_pe() == 0) {
3     // Read graph size (number of nodes) from file
4     // Broadcast graph size to all other PEs
5   }
6
7   // All PEs receive graph size
8   shmem_barrier_all();
9
10  // Calculate work division
11  nNodes = graphSize / n_pes;
12
13  // Allocate shmem for graph
14  graph = (int *)shmalloc(graphSize*nNodes*sizeof(int));
15  span = (int *)shmalloc(graphSize*nNodes*sizeof(int));
16  memset(span, 0, graphSize*nNodes*sizeof(int));
17
18  int * buffer = NULL;
19  if (my_pe == 0) {
20    buffer = malloc(graphSize*nNodes*sizeof(int));
21    for (i=0; i<n_pes; ++i) {
22      for (j=0; j<graphSize*nNodes; ++j) {
23        // Read edge weight from file into buffer[j]
24      }
25      shmem_int_put(graph, buffer, nNodes*graphSize, i);
26    }
27  }
28
29  // All PEs receive graph
30  shmem_barrier_all();
31  free(buffer);
32
33  // All PEs pick their lowest edges (Kruskal's algorithm)
34  for (j=0; j<nNodes; ++j) {
35    minWeight = INT_MAX;
36    minNode = 0;
37    for (i=0; i<graphSize; ++i) {
38      weight = graph[j*graphSize+i];
39      if (weight && (weight < minWeight)) {
40        minWeight = weight;
41        minNode = i;
42      }
43    }
44    span[j*graphSize+minNode] = minWeight;
45  }
46
47  shmem_barrier_all();
48  // span now contains the minimum spanning tree
```

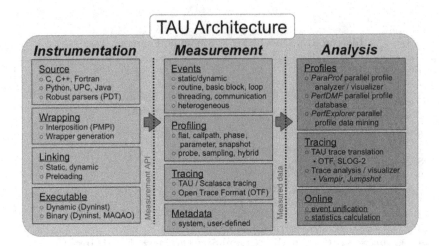

Fig. 1. The TAU framework architecture

machine (byte-code instrumentation), and operating system (kernel-level instrumentation). This broad coverage across instrumentation levels provides flexibility in exploring performance artifacts at any level of program transformation. TAU is open source and all instrumentation, measurement, and analysis tools are distributed under a BSD-like license.

The core of TAU is its scalable measurement infrastructure which provides rich parallel profiling and tracing support. Performance information containing execution time and hardware counter data can be captured for instrumented events for all threads of execution. Communication events additionally record message-related data that track process interactions. TAU can also associate metadata with performance experiments.

SHMEM application analysis is achieved with TAU via source code instrumentation, library interposition, compiler instrumentation, and sampling. TAU can track memory allocations – both in a PE's local memory and in the symmetric heap – and network I/O caused by transfers to and from symmetric memory. In statically linked binaries (e.g. for Cray systems), memory tracking is achieved by wrapping all allocation and deallocation routines at link time. Dynamically linked applications may use *tau_exec* to preload a memory tracking runtime library.

To track OpenSHMEM API calls and monitor communication between PEs, TAU provides a single wrapper library applicable to all OpenSHMEM implementations. In past, SHMEM wrapper library development was determined by the specific SHMEM library used by the system. This necessitated the production and maintenance of several library variants and complicated the goal of portable performance observation for the SHMEM runtime layer. However, the portability of the OpenSHMEM standard enables TAU to maintain only a single implementation of a single OpenSHMEM wrapper library. This approach provides performance measurements at the language and the runtime level to achieve complete coverage of the OpenSHMEM application source and runtime libraries.

2.2   Minimum Spanning Tree Algorithm

We use the symmetric hierarchical memory defined by OpenSHMEM to calculate
the MST as shown in Listing 1.1. The basic idea is to divide the graph among
the OpenSHMEM processing elements (PEs) by writing the edge weights to
symmetric memory (the *graph* variable in Listing 1.1). Each PE examines the
nodes it has been sent and writes the minimum edge weight to another region of
symmetric memory (*span* in Listing 1.1). This effectively distributes Kruskal's
greedy algorithm across all PEs. By selecting the minimum edge connected to
all nodes, we ensure the resultant graph will be the minimum spanning tree.

3   Related Work

OpenSHMEM [3,7] has emerged as an effort to join the disparate SHMEM imple-
mentations into a common, portable and high performance standard. Bader and
Cong have demonstrated fast data structures for distributed shared memory [1].
Pophale et. al defined the performance bounds of OpenSHMEM [14].

NNA benchmarks are emerging to evaluate HPC system at scale. The Graph
500 is one such benchmark [12]. The problem of finding a minimum spanning
tree (MST) can be formally stated as: given an undirected, weighted graph
$G = (V, E)$, a minimum spanning tree is the set of edges T in E that connect all vertices in V at a minimum cost. Figure 2 illustrates the MST for a
fully connected graph with random edge weights and eight vertices. Both Prim's
and Kruskal's algorithms are considered "greedy" since they make the locally
optimal choice at each iteration, i.e. they choose an edge with minimum weight
that does not create a cycle [15,10].

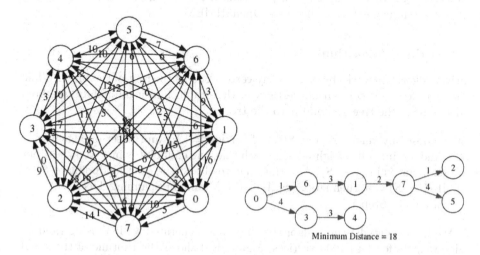

Fig. 2. Fully connected eight node graph with minimum spanning tree

3.1   Performance Analysis

Both profiling and tracing are relevant to better understanding the performance characteristics of an application. While profiling shows summary statistics, tracing can reveal the temporal variation in application performance. Among tools that use the direct measurement approach, the VampirTrace [9] package provides a wrapper interposition library that can capture the traces of I/O operations using the library preloading scheme used in `tau_exec`. Scalasca [4] is a portable and scalable profiling and tracing system that can automate the detection of performance bottlenecks in message passing and shared memory programs. Like many other tools, it uses library wrapping for MPI. TAU may be configured to use Scalasca or VampirTrace internally. TAU, VampirTrace, and Scalasca use the PAPI [2] library to access hardware performance counters present on most modern processors. However, only the `tau_exec` scheme provides the level of integration of all sources of performance information – MPI, I/O, and memory – of interest to us, with the rich context provided by TAU. With this support, we can utilize the VampirServer [8] parallel trace visualization system to show the performance data through scalable timeline displays. Profile performance data can also be easily stored in the PerfDMF database [6]. TAU's profile browser, Para-Prof, and its cross-experiment analysis and data-mining tool PerfExplorer [5] can interface with the performance database to help evaluate the scalability of an application.

4   Analysis of Prim's and Kruskal's MST Algorithms

This section provides time and space complexity analysis for a serial implementation of two MST algorithms in preparation for the discussion of a Kruskal's algorithm implementation that uses OpenSHMEM.

4.1   Prim's Algorithm

Prim's algorithm works by picking any vertex X to be the root of the MST. While the tree does not contain all vertices in the graph, find a minimally weighted edge leaving the tree and add it to the tree.

1. Choose any vertex X. Let S(set of vertices)=$\{X\}$ and A(set of edges)=$\emptyset$.
2. Find a minimally weighted edge such that one endpoint is in S and the other endpoint is in $(V - S)$. Add this edge to A and the other endpoint to S.
3. If $(V - S) = \emptyset$, then stop. $\{S, A\}$ is the Minimum Spanning Tree.
4. Else go to Step 1.

We implemented Prim's algorithm in C and generated a MST using random edge weights for 1 to 1000 vertices. Figure 3(a) shows the runtime of the serial Prim's implementation using both directed and undirected graphs. Only the number of vertices vary by case. These were run on an eight processor Intel Nehalem node that was not dedicated, thus others were using the system. We expect this is the cause of the fluctuation in times between the directed and undirected curves. The $O(n^2)$ time complexity of the algorithm is apparent, as shown by the blue line which was fit to the undirected data. We see that the directed graphs had the same $O(n^2)$ trend but ran slower overall by a constant.

The space complexity of Prim's Algorithm is shown in Figure 3(b). The data was fit to an $O(n^2)$ curve and we can see the actual space usage is between linear and quadratic, but not quite as low as $O(n \times log_2(n))$. The results for space usage for the directed and undirected graph experiments were identical so only the directed results are presented here.

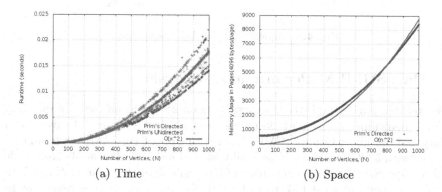

(a) Time   (b) Space

Fig. 3. Complexity of Prim's algorithm

4.2 Kruskal's Algorithm

Kruskal's algorithm is similar to Prim's but with a different search order:

1. Place every vertex in its own set.
2. Select edges in order of increasing weight.
3. As each edge is selected, determine if the vertices connected by that edge are in different sets. If so then insert the edge into the set that is the MST and take the union of sets containing each vertex.
4. Repeat steps 1-3 until all edges have been explored.

Figure 4(a) shows the Kruskal's algorithm runtime for an undirected graph under experimental conditions similar to those in the Prim's experiments. The graph representation is an adjacency matrix, so edge weights can be compared in constant time. At each iteration, the minimum edge can be located in $O(log_2(E))$ time, which is $O(log_2(V))$, since the graph is simple. The total running time is $O((V + E) \times log_2(V))$, which is $O(E \times log_2(V))$ since the graph is simple and connected. The data show a very tight $O(n \times log_2(n))$ fit, which was the theoretical expectation. The space complexity of Kruskal's algorithm is shown in Figure 4(b). The data fits almost perfectly to the theoretical $O(n^2)$ expectation.

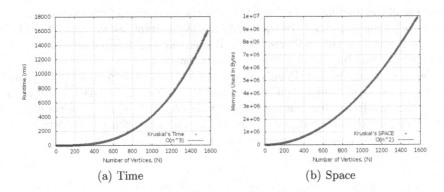

(a) Time   (b) Space

Fig. 4. Complexity of Kruskal's algorithm

5   OpenSHMEM Performance Analysis

We executed our OpenSHMEM experiments on 256 nodes of the "Titan" Cray
XK7 supercomputer and on a 48 core shared memory system at University of
Maryland Baltimore County (UMBC), consisting of 8, 6 core AMD Opteron processors with 530GB of globally accessible shared memory. The application code
was an OpenSHMEM implementation of Kruskal's algorithm as in Listing 1.1. In
each experiment, we used TAU to gather data for time spent in code regions of interest (e.g. `broadcast_graph` and `calc_spanning_tree`), heap memory allocated
and deallocated by routines like `malloc` and `free`, total bytes of memory used in
all routines, network I/O events initiated by routines like `shmem_int_put`), and
time spent waiting in barrier routines. We also enabled callpath profiling in TAU
so that the full execution path to all events was recorded. We used source based
instrumentation and the TAU compiler wrapper scripts to automatically introduce measurement hooks into the OpenSHMEM application code at compile
time.

TAU uses the PSHMEM interface to support measurement of OpenSHMEM
routines. For every routine in the OpenSHMEM standard, PSHMEM provides
an analogous routine with a slightly different name. This allows profiling tools
to intercept and measure OpenSHMEM calls made by a user's application by
defining routines with the same function signatures as OpenSHMEM routines
– "wrapper" functions – which call the appropriate PSHMEM routines. TAU
provides an OpenSHMEM wrapper library which can be linked to any OpenSH-
MEM application to acquire runtime measurements of OpenSHMEM routines.
The library can be used statically- or dynamically-linked applications. In our experiments the application was statically linked since statically linked executables
are preferred on Titan.

Our fully instrumented application was approximately 4% slower than the unin-
strumented application. If only time in code regions of interest were measured (no
memory or I/O measurements are taken) then overhead was approximately 1.5%.
Regardless of which events are recorded, TAU's overhead is approximately O(1) in

the number of application processes, i.e. as the number of PEs increases the overhead incurred by TAU remains relatively constant. Large applications can benefit from reducing instrumentation to only regions of interest by use of a TAU select file. We used a TAU select file to insert timers at specific source lines in the OpenSHMEM application rather than fully instrument every routine.

Figure 5 shows exclusive time spent by PE 0 in regions of the code. The vast majority of the time (64.987 seconds) is spent in reading the graph from file and broadcasting the edge weights to the other PEs. The time spent calculating the minimum spanning tree is minimal, only 0.008 seconds. Figure 6 is the counterpart to Figure 5. It shows exclusive time spent by PE 1 in regions of the code. The profile on all PEs except for PE 0 is nearly identical. The majority of time is spent receiving data from PE 0, followed by a brief calculation to construct the MST.

If we exclude the file I/O data we see only those routines directly involved in the MST calculation. Figure 7 shows inclusive mean time spent by all PEs in routines that do not perform file I/O or wait for PE 0 to complete its file I/O operations. This figure shows that the initial broadcast of the graph weights via shmem_int_put is the most expensive step in the MST calculation.

Figures 5-7 show data taken from *interval events*, which have a defined start and stop point. Interval events are used to measure time spent in a code region. Events such as memory allocations are recorded as atomic events, which record a quantity (e.g. bytes allocated) when they are triggered. Figure 8 shows the mean of atomic events gathered during the 512 PE experiment on Titan. Memory allocation events and network sends and receives are visible. For example, across all 512 PEs there was an average of thirteen heap memory allocations in the shmem_int_put call in the broadcast_graph section of the application. TAU has also flagged two potential memory leaks caused by not explicitly deallocating memory before the program exists. These leaks are of no concern since the operating system will deallocate all heap memory on program exit. However, if this application were converted to a library then these leaks would need to be addressed.

Communication atomic events record the number of bytes sent or received between PEs. TAU can display this information as a communication heat map as in Figure 9. The communications matrix of the Titan supercomputer and the 48-node shared memory appliance are markedly different. In both cases, there is virtually no communication between PEs after PE 0 has distributed the graph data. On both systems, peak communication volume is visible in red in the zeroth row of the array and we see that no nonzero PE communicates with itself. However, each PE on the 48-core appliance sends eight bytes to every other PE while on Titan only PE 0 communicates with other PEs. From our callpath data we determined that these sends on the 48-core appliance were initiated by the shmem_barrier_all routine. This demonstrates TAU's ability to highlight implementation differences between libraries and explain unexpected communication patterns.

Metric: TIME
Value: Exclusive
Units: seconds

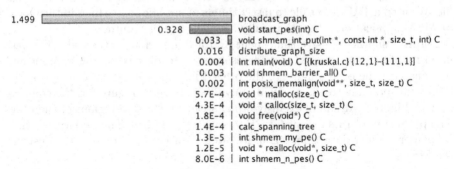

Fig. 5. Exclusive time on PE 0 of 512 on Titan, showing time spent reading the graph from file and broadcasting it to the other PEs

Metric: TIME
Value: Exclusive
Units: seconds

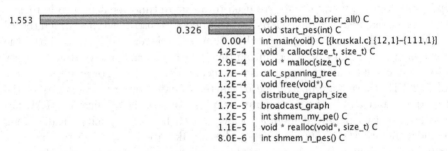

Fig. 6. Exclusive time on PE 1 of 512 on Titan, showing time spent waiting to receive the graph data from PE 0 and then calculating the MST

Metric: TIME
Value: Exclusive
Units: seconds

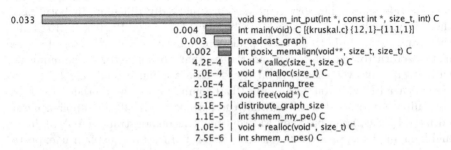

Fig. 7. Exclusive mean time on all 512 PEs on Titan in routines called while calculating the MST after the graph has been broadcast

Name ▽	Total	NumSamples	MaxValue	MinValue	MeanValue	Std. Dev.
▼ int main(void) C [{kruskal.c} {12,1}–{111,1}]						
▶ void start_pes(int) C						
▼ distribute_graph_size						
Heap Allocate	1,136	2	568	568	568	0
Heap Free	568	1	568	568	568	0
MEMORY LEAK! Heap Allocate	568	1	568	568	568	0
▶ void shmem_int_put(int *, const int *, size_t, int) C						
▼ broadcast_graph						
Heap Allocate	8,192	1	8,192	8,192	8,192	0
Heap Free	8,192	1	8,192	8,192	8,192	0
▶ void shmem_barrier_all() C						
▼ void shmem_int_put(int *, const int *, size_t, int) C						
Heap Allocate	3,204	13	1,728	8	246.462	468.864
Heap Free	1,136	2	568	568	568	0
MEMORY LEAK! Heap Allocate	2,068	11	1,728	8	188	487.43
Message size sent to node 0	8,192	1	8,192	8,192	8,192	0
Message size sent to node 1	8,192	1	8,192	8,192	8,192	0
Message size sent to node 10	8,192	1	8,192	8,192	8,192	0
Message size sent to node 100	8,192	1	8,192	8,192	8,192	0
Message size sent to node 101	8,192	1	8,192	8,192	8,192	0
Message size sent to node 103	8,192	1	8,192	8,192	8,192	0
Message size sent to node 102	8,192	1	8,192	8,192	8,192	0
Message size sent to node 104	8,192	1	8,192	8,192	8,192	0
Message size sent to node 105	8,192	1	8,192	8,192	8,192	0
Message size sent to node 107	8,192	1	8,192	8,192	8,192	0
Message size sent to node 106	8,192	1	8,192	8,192	8,192	0
Message size sent to node 108	8,192	1	8,192	8,192	8,192	0
Message size sent to node 109	8,192	1	8,192	8,192	8,192	0
Message size sent to node 111	8,192	1	8,192	8,192	8,192	0
Message size sent to node 11	8,192	1	8,192	8,192	8,192	0
Message size sent to node 110	8,192	1	8,192	8,192	8,192	0

Fig. 8. The mean of context events observed in the OpenSHMEM implementation of Kruskal's algorithm on 512 PEs on Titan

TAU can construct a complete application callgraph from the callpath data as shown in Figure 10. Boxes are colored according to their exclusive time: more time is spent in red boxes than blue boxes. We note that three different memory allocation routines were used in this application, though heap memory allocation was only explicitly performed via `malloc` and `shmalloc`.

TAU can also perform application scaling studies. To demonstrate this on Titan, we varied the number of PEs as a power of two ranging from four to 512. Afer each run, we used TAU's profile browser (ParaProf) to package the application data as a packed profile file and then imported the packed profile into a TAUdb database [6]. We then used TAU's cross-experiment analysis and data-mining tool PerfExplorer [5] to explore the application scalability.

Figure 11 shows the runtime breakdown for varying PE counts on Titan. `shmem_barrier_all` is the most expensive routine, accounting for approximately 80% of the application runtime in all cases. The relative cost of broadcasting the graph decreases as the number of cores increases. The cost of computing the MST is small in all cases and is included in the "other" category accounting for approximately 3% of the application runtime.

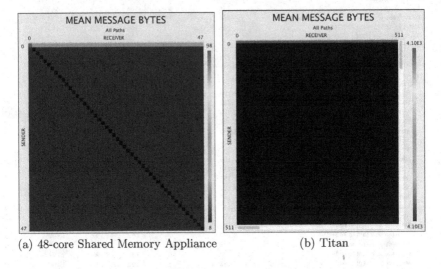

(a) 48-core Shared Memory Appliance   (b) Titan

Fig. 9. Communication heat maps showing differences in the OpenSHMEM implementations on the 48-core appliance and Titan

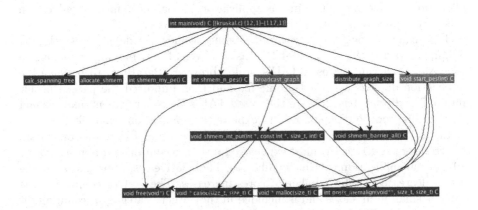

Fig. 10. Kruskal's OpenSHMEM callgraph. Box color corresponds to exclusive time. Blue boxes are close to minimum and red boxes are close to maximum.

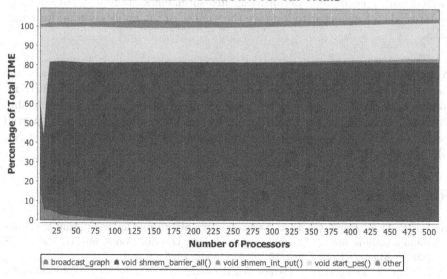

Fig. 11. Kruskal's OpenSHMEM callgraph. Box color corresponds to exclusive time. Blue boxes are close to minimum and red boxes are close to maximum.

6 Conclusions and Future Work

We have provided a performance analysis of both serial and parallel implementations of the standard minimum spanning tree (MST) algorithms from Prim and Kruskal. We have developed an efficient OpenSHMEM implementation of Kruskal's MST algorithm and provided a profile of that implementation on two HPC systems. We have demonstrated the portability of applications that use OpenSHMEM and the portability of the profiling features of the TAU Performance System. Our results suggest that OpenSHMEM is a flexible and powerful API for PGAS programming that can be applied effectively to non-numeric algorithms with a low FLOPS/byte ratio.

Profiling tools like TAU would benefit from further standardization and support for the PSHMEM interface. Unlike the PMPI interface which is fairly mature, complete, and widely available, the PSHMEM interface has not been completely established and in some implementations of OpenSHMEM is only partially implemented. This necessitates special checks when TAU compiles its OpenSHMEM wrapper library. TAU's maintainers will continue to improve TAU's resilience to variations in the PSHMEM interface until the interface is finalized.

TAU could also benefit from an interface which exposes synchronization of the symmetric heap. At present, TAU intercepts the underlying system allocation and deallocation calls and OpenSHMEM library calls to mark operations on the symmetric heap. However, it is difficult to observe in a trace when an update to the symmetric heap becomes visible to other PEs. TAU could make use of a mechanism for notifying a performance measurement system of symmetric heap updates when they occur to improve the quality of the application performance data.

Acknowledgments. Authors would like to thank The University of Oregon NeuroInformatics Center and the NSF Center for Hybrid Multicore Productivity Research at UMBC. This research used resources of the Oak Ridge Leadership Computing Facility at the Oak Ridge National Laboratory, which is supported by the Office of Science of the U.S. Department of Energy under Contract No. DE-AC05-00OR22725.

References

1. Bader, D.A., Cong, G.: Fast shared-memory algorithms for computing the minimum spanning forest of sparse graphs. J. Par. Distrib. Comp. 66(11), 1366–1378 (2006), http://dx.doi.org/10.1016/j.jpdc.2006.06.001
2. Browne, S., Dongarra, J., Garner, N., Ho, G., Mucci, P.: A portable programming interface for performance evaluation on modern processors. International Journal of High Performance Computing Applications 3(14), 189–204 (2000)
3. Chapman, B., Curtis, T., Pophale, S., Poole, S., Kuehn, J., Koelbel, C., Smith, L.: Introducing OpenSHMEM: SHMEM for the PGAS community. In: Proceedings of the Fourth Conference on Partitioned Global Address Space Programming Model, PGAS 2010, pp. 2:1–2:3. ACM, New York (2010), http://doi.acm.org/10.1145/2020373.2020375
4. Geimer, M., Wolf, F., Wylie, B.J.N., Mohr, B.: Scalable parallel trace-based performance analysis. In: Mohr, B., Träff, J.L., Worringen, J., Dongarra, J. (eds.) PVM/MPI 2006. LNCS, vol. 4192, pp. 303–312. Springer, Heidelberg (2006)
5. Huck, K., Malony, A.: PerfExplorer: A performance data mining framework for large-scale parallel computing. In: Proceedings of the ACM/IEEE Conference on Supercomputing, SC 2005 (2005)
6. Huck, K., Malony, A., Bell, R., Li, L., Morris, A.: PerfDMF: Design and implementation of a parallel performance data management framework. In: Proceedings of the International Conference on Parallel Processing. IEEE (2005)
7. Jose, J., Kandalla, K., Luo, M., Panda, D.: Supporting hybrid MPI and OpenSHMEM over InfiniBand: Design and performance evaluation. In: The 41st International Conference on Parallel Processing (ICPP), pp. 219–228 (2012)
8. Knüpfer, A., Brendel, R., Brunst, H., Mix, H., Nagel, W.E.: Introducing the open trace format (OTF). In: Alexandrov, V.N., van Albada, G.D., Sloot, P.M.A., Dongarra, J. (eds.) ICCS 2006. LNCS, vol. 3992, pp. 526–533. Springer, Heidelberg (2006)
9. Knupfer, A., Brunst, H., Nagel, W.: High performance event trace visualization. In: Proceedings of Parallel and Distributed Processing (PDP). IEEE (2005)
10. Kruskal, J.B.: On the shortest spanning subtree of a graph and the traveling salesman problem. Proceedings of the American Mathematical Society 7 (1956)
11. Meuer, H., Strohmaier, E., Dongara, J., Simon, H.: TOP 500 Supercomputer Sites (2013), http://www.top500.org

12. Murphy, R.C., Wheeler, K.B., Barrett, B.W., Ang, J.A.: Introducing the Graph 500 (May 2010)
13. Papadimitriou, C.H.: The Euclidean traveling salesman problem is NP-complete. Theoretical Computer Science 4(3), 237–244 (1977)
14. Pophale, S., Nanjegowda, R., Curtis, T., Chapman, B., Jin, H., Poole, S., Kuehn, J.: OpenSHMEM performance and potential: A NPB experimental study. In: The 6th Conference on Partitioned Global Address Space Programming Models, PGAS 2012 (2012)
15. Prim, R.C.: Shortest connection networks and some generalizations. Bell System Technical Journal 36, 1389–1401 (1957)
16. Shende, S.S., Malony, A.D.: The TAU Parallel Performance System. Int. J. High Perform. Comput. Appl. 20(2), 287–311 (2006), http://dx.doi.org/10.1177/1094342006064482

A Global View Programming Abstraction for Transitioning MPI Codes to PGAS Languages

Tiffany M. Mintz, Oscar Hernandez, and David E. Bernholdt

Oak Ridge National Laboratory
1 Bethel Valley Rd
Oak Ridge TN, USA
{mintztm,oscar,bernholdtde}@ornl.gov

Abstract. The multicore generation of scientific high performance computing has provided a platform for the realization of Exascale computing, and has also underscored the need for new paradigms in coding parallel applications. The current standard for writing parallel applications requires programmers to use languages designed for sequential execution. These languages have abstractions that only allow programmers to operate on the process centric local view of data. To provide suitable languages for parallel execution, many research efforts have designed languages based on the Partitioned Global Address Space (PGAS) programming model. Chapel is one of the more recent languages to be developed using this model. Chapel supports multithreaded execution with high-level abstractions for parallelism. With Chapel in mind, we have developed a set of directives that serve as intermediate expressions for transitioning scientific applications from languages designed for sequential execution to PGAS languages like Chapel that are being developed with parallelism in mind.

1 Introduction

The prevalence of multicore architectures for scientific computing has ushered in a new era in high performance computing. The multicore era has been marked by Peta-scale supercomputing machines with distributed shared memory architectures that exploit the advantages of both the data and message passing parallel paradigms[1]. The distributed shared memory architecture, known as the Non-Uniform Memory Access (NUMA) architecture [2, 3], is composed of a distributed yet globally accessible address space that allows all processors to have direct access to all memory. The address space is distributed such that each processor has a direct connection to a portion of memory, and is provided a mapping which allows direct access to memory connected to other processors. This global mapping enables a fast, direct reference of data stored in memory partitions connected to other processors (remote data), and even faster access to data in the processor's own memory partition (local data). Since the NUMA architecture is implemented on multicore devices [4–6], several processors are placed on a chip to form a single compute node with a direct connection to the

S. Poole, O. Hernandez, and P. Shamis (Eds.): OpenSHMEM 2014, LNCS 8356, pp. 120–133, 2014.
© Springer International Publishing Switzerland 2014

same memory partition. Each node is effectively a Symmetric Multiprocessor (SMP) with very fast, uniform access to memory from each processor.

While the multicore, NUMA architecture provides fast data movement and the potential for easy programmability, the current standard for programming scientific applications for parallel execution does not truly exploit these advantages. A sufficient programming model would need to provide mechanisms for managing data locality as well as take advantage of the global view of data provided by the architecture. Over the years, there has been much attention given to the need for programming models and languages that provide high level constructs that map well to scientific applications and provide opportunities for optimal use of the underlying architecture[7]. A programming model that has been the basis for much of the research and development of new languages is Partitioned Global Address Space (PGAS) [8–10]. There has been consistent research and development of PGAS languages from HPF in the early 90s to Chapel which debuted about a decade later with new features and functionality continually being added.

Although PGAS languages have yet to be fully adopted by the general HPC community, we are encouraged by the continued progress being made in the development of Chapel [11, 12] and the lessons learned from previous languages like HPF [13], X10[14] and ZPL[15]. So with a focus on aiding the adoption of PGAS languages by computational scientists in the HPC community, we have developed a directives based approach to expressing the global view of local data distributions and data movement in SPMD codes. This set of directives will serve as an intermediate step for incrementally transforming scientific codes from sequential, local view languages to parallel, global view languages.

The directives provide representations for high-level expressions of data distributions, parallel data movement, processor arrangements and processor groups. These assertions provide high-level constructs for describing the global nature of an application without programmers having to manage low-level details. The directives also correlate to high-level structures in Chapel, such as locales, parallel loops and domain maps so that replacing the directives with Chapel code is easy and straightforward. In addition to using the directives for describing the global state, a handle to the global domain is also created with every data distribution to allow parallel loops and interprocessor communication to be expressed from the global view using directives. For assertions of interprocessor data movement, the directives are translated to OpenSHMEM message passing operations, which provide consistent performance gains over MPI.

In this paper we continue our discussion of PGAS languages in Section 2. Section 3 gives more specific details about the directives and how they can be used to create explicit expressions of an application's global view. Section 4 provides a case study of the directives in stencil and matrix multiply codes. Section 5 concludes this paper with a summary of our approach.

2   Implementations of the PGAS Model

Parallel programming models designed for partitioned global address space (PGAS) languages UPC [16], Global Arrays (GA) [17], Co-Array Fortran (CAF) [18] Fortran 2008, and Titanium [19], target large distributed memory systems at different levels of abstraction. The PGAS languages provide a means for expressing local and global views of data and do not expect the programmer to provide all the details of data exchange, thus improving productivity. To achieve high performance, these models may be adapted to operate on a "local", or fragmented, view of data, which entails major code reorganization. These languages are good for single-sided communication of small to medium size messages since they are optimized for low message latencies. They map well to data decomposition parallel schemes. However, their adoption has been limited as they have limited support for hybrid programming models and incremental parallelism.

The DARPA-funded "HPCS" programming languages Fortress [20], Chapel [21], and X10 [22] were designed to support highly productive programming for ultra scale HPC systems and merge the concepts of global views of data, tasks and locality. They provide a wealth of new ideas related to correctness, locality, efficiency and productivity. These languages offer different levels of expressivity and abstraction, giving them distinct flavors from the application developer's perspective. Yet they have much in common, including the assumption of a hierarchically parallel architecture and a global address space. They allow users to control the placement of work and data (tasks and data distributions), exploit ideas from object-oriented programming, and provide efficient synchronization via transactions. These new languages imply a high learning curve for the user and may not be intuitive enough for widespread adoption. Many proposed features have yet to be tested in real petascale-level applications. Nevertheless, much can be learned from these efforts and in the longer term, one or more of them may be adopted.

3   Enabling a Global Perspective

In order to help programmers transition their applications from source code written with a sequential language and parallelism enabled through the use of MPI, we have developed a set of directives that are representative of some of the principal concepts that are expressible using PGAS languages. A few of the key features of most PGAS languages is the expression of data from a global view, expressing data distribution patterns, and processor affinity for data movement. To achieve our goal of providing high-level programming abstractions that map to PGAS language constructs, we developed directives that provide high-level descriptions of data distributions, parallel computation and interprocessor data movement, as well as high level expressions for arranging and grouping processors. With these directives, the programmer is able to identify the regions of their application that map well to the high level constructs provided by PGAS languages, and incrementally transition their source code to these languages.

The remainder of this section, gives a description of each directive and how they may be used in scientific applications.

3.1 Data Distributions

One of the major differences between PGAS languages and sequential languages is the view of data. Sequential languages provide abstractions for a processor centric, local view of data; while PGAS languages primarily provide abstractions for a global view of data. Since the current standard for programming parallel applications uses sequential languages coupled with message passing library calls, programmers currently have to write their programs so that their data sets are pre-distributed, and all subsequent computation and communication is expressed relative to the distributed local data. In this programming model, there is no native abstraction for expressing the global view and using this expression to program applications.

To enable the expression of a global view of data in scientific applications, we use the data_map directive to describe the distribution of data across processors. This directive allows the definition of BLOCK, CYCLIC and BLOCK_CYCLIC distributions, and provides a handle to a global domain that can be used to access data and perform specific operations from the global view. The clauses associated with data_map are local_data, global_domain, distribution and expand. The notation used to describe local and global data is:

$$buf{<}size1,...,sizeN{>}:[low1\_idx..high1\_idx,...,lowN\_idx..highN\_idx],$$

where buf is the name of a pointer or array, N is the number of dimensions in buf, size1,...,sizeN is a list of the size of allocated memory for each dimension (optional for global_domain clause), and low1_idx..high1_idx,...,lowN_idx..highN_idx is a list of the range of indices for each dimension. The distribution clause allows the programmer to specify a distribution that corresponds to each dimension, or specify the distributions in list form to explicitly indicate the distribution of each dimension (i.e. distribution(NONE, BLOCK) would indicate that the first dimension is not distributed and the second dimension has a BLOCK distribution). The expand clause is most applicable for data mappings that require a "scratch" space in the local data region. This region can be used to store regularly accessed data that is resident on another processor but should be mirrored on the current processor. Halo regions or ghost cells are common implementations of a scratch space in a data region. Section 4 provides examples of how data_map is used to describe distributions that are frequently used in scientific applications.

3.2 Processor Groups and Arrangements

Features such as processor groups and common processor arrangements provide a basis for which more complex expressions can be built. Our group and arrange_processors directives establish this foundation using succinct expressions that describe how the processors are assembled and ordered.

To create a processor group, a programmer would provide a group name and use triplet notation to indicate which processors would be in the group. A simple example of how the group directive could be used is provided in Fig. 1. The group that is created serves as a unique identifier for subsequent directive assertions. Once the group is created it can be mapped to an arrangement, data distribution, and some expression of computation or interprocessor data movement. If a group is not created or instanced by a directive, we assume the group to be all processors.

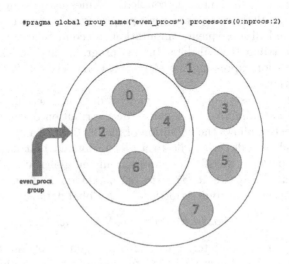

Fig. 1. Example using group directive to create the group 'even_proc'

Arranging processors has an equally simple expression which uses a combination of keywords and intuitively named clauses to describe the processors' disposition. This directive supports several arrangements, including **Master-Worker**, **Grid**, **Tree**, **Ring**, and **List**. Each of these arrangements have their own set of associated clauses for creating the corresponding formations. Table 1 gives a list of the arrangements and their clauses.

Each arrangement also has a unique set of relationships that can be assigned based on the values passed to the directive. See Table 1. These relationships help to describe data movement more concisely and with terminology that is familiar to the user. Using this directive also relieves the programmer from having to compute and manage, in some form, the process ids that correspond to these relationships.

3.3 Data Movement

Once the programmer has defined how the processors will be grouped and how they will be arranged within the group, expressing data movement using the

Table 1. Arrangements, associated clauses and the defined relationships within each formation

Arrangement	Clauses	Relationships in Arrangement
GRID <1D|2D|3D>	size_x_axis size_y_axis size_z_axis	North Neighbor South Neighbor East Neighbor West Neighbor
MASTER-WORKER	master_processor*	Master Worker Master_Worker
TREE	root* order*	Parent Sibling Children Root Leaves Depth (tree and positional)
RING	direction*	Previous Next
LIST	direction*	Previous Next Head Tail

*indicates optional clauses that have some default behavior defined when not in use

global domain is very straightforward. Configuring the data mapping relative to the processor arrangement enables a simplified expression of communication and computation from the global view. To express data movement across processors, programmers need only assert the **update** directive. The clauses associated with this directive are **update_domain**, **update_mirror**, and **on**. The **on** clause is used to specify the destination of the update.

When specifying a destination, the programmer can leverage the relationships among processors in the arrangement declared for the group. For example, if the processors are arranged in a list configuration, the programmer can simply indicate **HEAD**, **TAIL**, **NEXT**, or **PREVIOUS** as the destination for the update. To further support the PGAS programming model, this directive is translated to an appropriate communication pattern using the OpenSHMEM message passing library.

As previously stated, the expression of computation is also simplified when using the global view of data. Defining a global domain allows the expression of a parallel loop in the form of a **forall** directive. This directive has the clauses **index_var, domain** and **expression**. The **domain** clause is used to define the iteration space of the parallel forall loop. A user can specify the global domain created by the data distribution or express the domain as a range of indices. If an explicit range is specified, each processor's iteration space is determined by evenly distributing the indices in the range according to the number of the processors in the group. The **index_var** clause accepts a list if variables used to iterate over the domain. If the global domain handle is specified in the **domain** clause, then the variables' position in the list corresponds to that dimension in the global domain. If index ranges are specified in the **domain** clause, then the variables' position in **index_var** corresponds to the range in the same position of the **domain** clause.

The computation in the **expression** clause is then concurrently executed on each processor in the group.

4 Preliminary Experiments

As an initial step to demonstrating the simplicity of programming with our global view directives to incrementally transition applications to a PGAS programming paradigm, we have chosen two algorithms that are commonly implemented in scientific applications. The first algorithm is Jacobi's iterative method for solving a system of linear equations, and the second algorithm is a dense matrix-matrix multiplication. We compare C+MPI versions of these algorithms to selective portions of the algorithms programmed using the directives. These experiments were executed on a Cray XK7 system with 83 compute nodes. Each node has a 16-core AMD Opteron 6274 processor running at 2.2 GHz with 32 gigabytes of DDR3 memory, and Cray's high performance Gemini network.

4.1 2D Jacobi Iterative Solver

The 2D Jacobi iterative solver implements a common data distribution pattern where the problem space is mapped onto a two dimensional grid and partitioned across processors typically in block fashion. Points in the grid are updated iteratively, but an update may require data in neighboring cells that reside in a partition stored on another processor. This requires frequent remote data accesses to processors that "own" the neighboring data. So parallel implementations not only represent the program space as a 2D grid, but the processor formation is also conceptualized as a 2D grid. While this is a very common distribution and data access pattern, there are no native programming abstractions in sequential languages that embody the concept. PGAS languages like Chapel have native representations of this data distribution, but because of the global view of data, have no need for explicit point-to-point communication when accessing remote data.

Using our directives, we were able to explicitly express this distribution of data while preserving the global view in the program for very simple, unobtrusive assertions of communication. First we show, in Fig. 2, the difference in how the 2D Grid arrangement is constructed in the two versions of the algorithm. As you can see, we have been able to greatly reduce lines of code and programming effort for constructing a 2D Grid. Next, Fig. 3 shows how the **data_map** directive was used to express the block data distribution and create a handle to the global domain. In this assertion, we specify **mat** as the local partition of data with **plines** rows and **pcols** columns. The "scratch" space which will be used to store remote data is defined as an expansion of one row and one column (in every direction) of the local partition **mat**, and this data is to be mirrored in the distribution. The global domain is defined as a 2D matrix with **plines*proc_y** rows and **pcols*proc_x** columns, and is accessible through the handle **Global_Matrix**. **Global_Matrix** is then used to assert an update of

Directive Assertion of 2D Grid Processor Arrangement

```
#pragma global arrange_processors arrangement(GRID:2D) \
        size_x_axis(proc_x)   size_y_axis(proc_y)
```

C code to mimic 2D Processor Grid

```
x = myid % proc_x;
y = myid / proc_x;

if( y == 0 )
   north = BORDER;
else
   north = x + (y - 1) * proc_x;
if( y == proc_y - 1 )
   south = BORDER;
else
   south = x + (y + 1) * proc_x;
if( x == 0 )
   west = BORDER;
else
   west = myid - 1;
if( x == proc_x - 1 )
   east = BORDER;
else
   east = myid + 1;
```

Fig. 2. Comparison of C and directive versions of 2D Grid setup

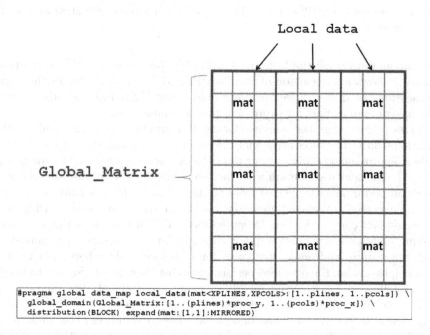

```
#pragma global data_map local_data(mat<XPLINES,XPCOLS>:[1..plines, 1..pcols]) \
   global_domain(Global_Matrix:[1..(plines)*proc_y, 1..(pcols)*proc_x]) \
   distribution(BLOCK)  expand(mat:[1,1]:MIRRORED)
```

Fig. 3. Depiction of the block distribution created with the directives in the Jacobi algorithm

Directive Assertion for Updating Neighbor Data

```
#pragma global update update_mirror(Global_Matrix) on(ALL_NEIGHBORS)
```

C+MPI Code to Exchange Data Across Neighboring Processors

```
if( west != BORDER ){
   for( i = 0; i < lines; i++ )
      *(awest + i) = MAT(i, 1);
   MPI_Send(awest,lines,MPI_DOUBLE,west,MSGTYPE,MPI_COMM_WORLD);
}

if( east != BORDER ){
   for( i = 0; i < lines; i++ )
      *(aeast + i) = MAT(i, cols - 2);
   MPI_Send(aeast,lines,MPI_DOUBLE,east,MSGTYPE,MPI_COMM_WORLD);
}

if( north != BORDER )
   MPI_Send(mat+cols,cols,MPI_DOUBLE,north,MSGTYPE,MPI_COMM_WORLD);

if( south != BORDER )
   MPI_Send(mat+(lines-2)*cols,cols,MPI_DOUBLE,south,MSGTYPE,MPI_COMM_WORLD);

if( west != BORDER ){
   MPI_Recv(awest,lines,MPI_DOUBLE,west,MSGTYPE,MPI_COMM_WORLD);
      for( i = 0; i < lines; i++ )
         MAT(i, 0) = *(awest + i);
}

if( east != BORDER ){
   MPI_Recv(aeast,lines,MPI_DOUBLE,east,MSGTYPE,MPI_COMM_WORLD);
      for( i = 0; i < lines; i++ )
         MAT(i, cols - 1) = *(aeast + i);
}

if( north != BORDER )
   MPI_Recv(mat,cols,MPI_DOUBLE,north,MSGTYPE,MPI_COMM_WORLD);

if( south != BORDER )
   MPI_Recv(mat+(lines-1)*cols,cols,MPI_DOUBLE,south,MSGTYPE,MPI_COMM_WORLD);
```

Fig. 4. Comparison of MPI code and directive assertion for communicating with neighboring processors

the remote data using the keyword ALL_NEIGHBORS to indicate the destination. Figure 4 shows a comparison of the C+MPI and directive version of this communication. As in Fig. 2 we are again able to greatly reduce the lines of code and programming effort for expressing this communication.

As for performance, the overhead for creating and managing a 2D grid and the additional data structures needed for the neighbor communication in the C+MPI code is approximately 3.7x greater than the overhead to create and manage the 2D grid and block distribution with the directives. This significant difference in overhead performance is primarily due to the need for additional data structures to send and receive non-contiguous data in the matrix columns when using MPI point-to-point communication. Because OpenSHMEM provides strided message passing operations for point-to-point communication, the directive translation does not require additional structures for transferring data between east and west neighbors. So, the overhead performance cost for constructing the topology and distribution for a Jacobi algorithm using these global view directives is $O(1)$ since the number of computations and memory accesses needed to assign neighbors and compute and maintain global offsets and indices in the underlying translation of the directives is constant on each process even as the number of processes increase.

Moreover, translating the communication between neighboring processes using OpenSHMEM put operations provided additional performance improvements over the original C+MPI code which implements MPI_Send and MPI_Recv operations. The OpenSHMEM translation of the directives provided a 2x average speedup over the MPI implementation of the neighbor communication. The performance results for the overhead and communication are plotted in Fig. 5 and Fig. 6, respectively.

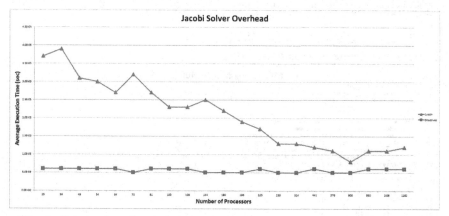

Fig. 5. Graph of overhead in C+MPI and directive version of the Jacobi solver

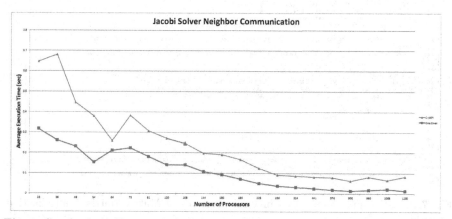

Fig. 6. Graph of neighbor communication time in C+MPI and directive version translated to OpenSHMEM of the Jacobi solver

4.2 Matrix-Matrix Multiply

The matrix-matrix multiply algorithm has a similar data distribution as the Jacobi algorithm. This distribution is also a block distribution, but only the first dimension of the 2D space is distributed. The processor arrangement for this algorithm is a MASTER-WORKER formation where the master also shares the computational workload. Because of its computational characteristics, we were able

Global View Matrix-Matrix Multiply with Directives

```
1  #pragma global arrange_processors arrangement(MASTER_WORKER, MASTER_SHARES_WORK)
2
3  #pragma global data_map local_data(a<nrows,NCA>:[0..nrows-1,0..NCA-1]) \
4      global_domain(global_a:[0..NRA-1,0..NCA-1]) distribution(BLOCK, NONE)
5
6  #pragma global data_map local_data(c<nrows, NCB>:[0..nrows-1,0..NCB-1]) \
7      global_domain(global_c:[0..NRA-1,0..NCB-1]) distribution(BLOCK, NONE)
8
9  #pragma global  forall index_var(i, j)  domain(global_a) \
10      expression(global_a[i][j] = i+j)
11
12 #pragma global forall index_var(i, j)  domain(global_c) \
13      expression(global_c[i][j] = 0.0)
14
15 for(k=0; k<NCB; k++)
16     #pragma global forall index_var( i, j) domain( global_a) \
17         expression(global_c[i][k] = global_c[i][k] + global_a[i][j] * b[j][k])
18
19 #pragma global update update_domain(global_c) on(MASTER)
```

C + MPI Matrix-Matrix Multiply

```
1  if (taskid == MASTER) {
2      for (i=0; i<NRA; i++)
3          for (j=0; j<NCA; j++)
4              a[i][j]= i+j;
5
6      offset = (extra > 0) ? averow+1 : averow;
7      for (dest=1; dest<numworkers; dest++) {
8          rows = (dest <= extra) ? averow+1 : averow;
9          MPI_Send(&offset, 1, MPI_INT, dest, FROM_MASTER, MPI_COMM_WORLD);
10         MPI_Send(&rows, 1, MPI_INT, dest, FROM_MASTER, MPI_COMM_WORLD);
11         MPI_Send(&a[offset][0], rows*NCA, MPI_DOUBLE, dest, FROM_MASTER, MPI_COMM_WORLD);
12         offset = offset + rows;
13     }
14     rows = (extra > 0) ? averow+1 : averow;
15
16     for (k=0; k<NCB; k++)
17         for (i=0; i<rows; i++) {
18             c[i][k] = 0.0;
19             for (j=0; j<NCA; j++)
20                 c[i][k] = c[i][k] + a[i][j] * b[j][k];
21         }
22     if(extra > 0) {
23         list_offsets[0] = 0;
24         row_cnts[0] = (averow+1)*NCB;
25         for (dest=1; dest<numworkers; dest++) {
26             rows = (dest <= extra) ? averow+1 : averow;
27             row_cnts[dest] = rows*NCB;
28             list_offsets[dest] = list_offsets[dest-1]+row_cnts[dest-1];
29         }
30         MPI_Gatherv(MPI_IN_PLACE,0,MPI_DATATYPE_NULL,&c,row_cnts,list_offsets,MPI_DOUBLE,MASTER,MPI_COMM_WORLD);
31     }else
32         MPI_Gather(MPI_IN_PLACE,0,MPI_DATATYPE_NULL,&c,rows*NCB,MPI_DOUBLE,MASTER,MPI_COMM_WORLD);
33 }
34
35 if (taskid > MASTER) {
36     MPI_Recv(&offset, 1, MPI_INT, MASTER, FROM_MASTER, MPI_COMM_WORLD, &status);
37     MPI_Recv(&rows, 1, MPI_INT, MASTER, FROM_MASTER, MPI_COMM_WORLD, &status);
38     MPI_Recv(&a, rows*NCA, MPI_DOUBLE, FROM_MASTER, mtype, MPI_COMM_WORLD, &status);
39
40     for (k=0; k<NCB; k++)
41         for (i=0; i<rows; i++) {
42             c[i][k] = 0.0;
43             for (j=0; j<NCA; j++)
44                 c[i][k] = c[i][k] + a[i][j] * b[j][k];
45         }
46     if(extra > 0)
47         MPI_Gatherv(&c,rows*NCB,MPI_DOUBLE,&c,row_cnts,list_offsets,MPI_DOUBLE,MASTER,MPI_COMM_WORLD);
48     else
49         MPI_Gather(&c,rows*NCB,MPI_DOUBLE,&c,rows*NCB,MPI_DOUBLE,MASTER,MPI_COMM_WORLD);
50 }
```

Fig. 7. C+MPI and global view directives versions of Matrix-Matrix Multiplication algorithm

to almost completely program this algorithm using our global view directives. Figure 7 shows a comparison of the C+MPI version and the version using our global view directives. The most obvious difference is the substantial reduction in the lines of code. Another significant difference is the use of the data's global view to express loop computation. We were able to execute each loop using the forall directive.

Since in the C+MPI code the master processor is responsible for computing then distributing initial data, there is a considerable difference in the overhead.

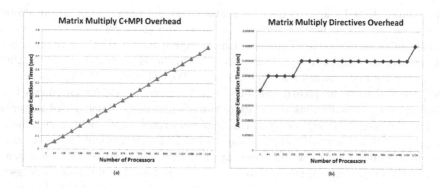

Fig. 8. Graph of matrix-matrix multiply overhead for (a)C+MPI version and (b)Directive version

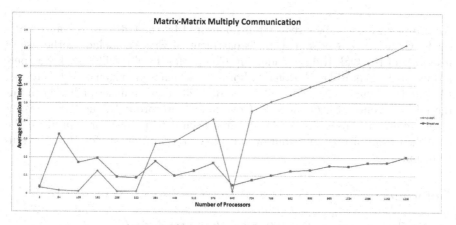

Fig. 9. Graph of average execution time for communication needed to transfer the matrix-matrix multiply solution to the master process

The directive code uses the `forall` directive to initialize data which does not require any message passing communication. Figure 8 provides the graphs plotting the overhead.

As for the communication needed to update the matrix-matrix multiply solution on the master processor, the update directive is translated to OpenSHMEM put operations on all the processors except the master with a barrier synchronization. Even with a notoriously costly collective synchronization, the OpenSHMEM translation of the directive provides a 2.5x average speedup over MPI. Figure 9 shows the average execution time for the matrix-matrix multiply communication.

5   Conclusion

Supercomputing architectures are steadily pushing the performance envelope in order to reach the next levels of computing capabilities. While our computer and computational scientists have been able to steadily evolve their applications to run on these advanced architectures, more and more effort is being spent transforming source code. This is a definite signal to the HPC community for a new programming paradigm that provides high- level abstractions for parallel programming and enables good performance. We believe the PGAS model has the potential to be or greatly influence a new paradigm. PGAS languages like Chapel are continually making progress toward providing a rich set of features for parallel programming and good run-time performance. We believe incrementally transitioning scientific applications to PGAS languages will facilitate their adoption. Our global view directives are a fitting approach to this incremental transition. By providing directive assertions for data distributions, processor groups and arrangements, and global data movement, we enable global expressions that are analogous to the expressions found in Chapel codes in applications with an otherwise local, processor centric view of data.

Acknowledgment. This research is sponsored by the Office of Advanced Scientific Computing Research; U.S. Department of Energy, including the use of resources of the Oak Ridge Leadership Computing Facility. The work was performed at the Oak Ridge National Laboratory, which is managed by UT-Battelle, LLC under Contract No. DE-AC05-00OR22725. This manuscript has been authored by a contractor of the U.S. Government. Accordingly, the U.S. Government retains a non-exclusive, royalty-free license to publish or reproduce the published form of this contribution, or allow others to do so, for U.S. Government purposes.

References

1. Top 500 supercomputers (2013), http://www.top500.org/
2. Bolosky, W., Fitzgerald, R., Scott, M.: Simple but effective techniques for numa memory management. In: Proceedings of the Twelfth ACM Symposium on Operating Systems Principles, SOSP 1989, pp. 19–31. ACM, New York (1989)
3. Black, D., Gupta, A., Weber, W.D.: Competitive management of distributed shared memory. In: COMPCON Spring 1989. Thirty-Fourth IEEE Computer Society International Conference: Intellectual Leverage, Digest of Papers, pp. 184–190 (1989)
4. Blagodurov, S., Zhuravlev, S., Fedorova, A., Kamali, A.: A case for numa-aware contention management on multicore systems. In: Proceedings of the 19th International Conference on Parallel Architectures and Compilation Techniques, PACT 2010, pp. 557–558. ACM, New York (2010)
5. Rabenseifner, R., Hager, G., Jost, G.: Hybrid mpi/openmp parallel programming on clusters of multi-core smp nodes. In: 2009 17th Euromicro International Conference on Parallel, Distributed and Network-based Processing, pp. 427–436 (2009)
6. Jin, H., Jespersen, D., Mehrotra, P., Biswas, R., Huang, L., Chapman, B.: High performance computing using mpi and openmp on multi-core parallel systems. Parallel Comput. 37(9), 562–575 (2011)
7. Kasim, H., March, V., Zhang, R., See, S.: Survey on parallel programming model. In: Cao, J., Li, M., Wu, M.-Y., Chen, J. (eds.) NPC 2008. LNCS, vol. 5245, pp. 266–275. Springer, Heidelberg (2008)

8. Yelick, K., Bonachea, D., Chen, W.Y., Colella, P., Datta, K., Duell, J., Graham, S.L., Hargrove, P., Hilfinger, P., Husbands, P., Iancu, C., Kamil, A., Nishtala, R., Su, J., Welcome, M., Wen, T.: Productivity and performance using partitioned global address space languages. In: Proceedings of the 2007 International Workshop on Parallel Symbolic Computation, PASCO 2007, pp. 24–32. ACM, New York (2007)

9. Bonachea, D., Hargrove, P., Welcome, M., Yelick, K.: Porting gasnet to portals: Partitioned global address space (pgas) language support for the cray xt. Cray User Group, CUG 2009 (2009)

10. Barrett, R.F., Alam, S.R., d Almeida, V.F., Bernholdt, D.E., Elwasif, W.R., Kuehn, J.A., Poole, S.W., Shet, A.G.: Exploring hpcs languages in scientific computing. Journal of Physics: Conference Series 125(1), 012034 (2008)

11. Dun, N., Taura, K.: An empirical performance study of chapel programming language. In: 2012 IEEE 26th International Parallel and Distributed Processing Symposium Workshops PhD Forum (IPDPSW), pp. 497–506. IEEE Computer Society, Los Alamitos (2012)

12. Chamberlain, B., Callahan, D., Zima, H.: Parallel programmability and the chapel language. Int. J. High Perform. Comput. Appl. 21(3), 291–312 (2007)

13. Kennedy, K., Koelbel, C., Zima, H.: The rise and fall of high performance fortran: an historical object lesson. In: Proceedings of the Third ACM SIGPLAN Conference on History of Programming Languages, HOPL III, pp. 7-1-7-22. ACM, New York (2007)

14. Charles, P., Grothoff, C., Saraswat, V., Donawa, C., Kielstra, A., Ebcioglu, K., von Praun, C., Sarkar, V.: X10: an object-oriented approach to non-uniform cluster computing. In: Proceedings of the 20th Annual ACM SIGPLAN Conference on Object-oriented Programming, Systems, Languages, and Applications, OOPSLA 2005, pp. 519–538. ACM, New York (2005)

15. Chamberlain, B.L., Choi, S.E., Deitz, S.J., Snyder, L.: The high-level parallel language zpl improves productivity and performance. In: Proceedings of the First Workshop on Productivity and Performance in High-End Computing (PPHEC 2004), pp. 66–75. Citeseer (2004)

16. Carlson, W.W., Draper, J.M., Culler, D.E., Yelick, K., Brooks, E., Warren, K.: Introduction to UPC and language specification. Technical report, Center for Computing Sciences (May 1999)

17. Nieplocha, J., Krishnan, M., Tipparaju, V., Palmer, B.: Global Arrays User Manual

18. Numrich, R.W., Reid, J.K.: Co-Array Fortran for parallel programming. ACM Fortran Forum 17(2), 1–31 (1998)

19. Yelick, K., Semenzato, L., Pike, G., Miyamoto, C., Liblit, B., Krishnamurthy, A., Hilfinger, P., Graham, S., Gay, D., Colella, P., Aiken, A.: Titanium: A high performance Java dialect. Concurrency: Practice and Experience 10, 825–836 (1998)

20. Allen, E., Chase, D., Luchangco, V., Maessen, J.W., Ryu, S., Steele Jr., G., Tobin-Hochstadt, S.: The Fortress language specification, version 0.785 (2005)

21. Cray Inc.: Chapel specification 0.4 (2005), http://chapel.cs.washington.edu/specification.pdf

22. Charles, P., Donawa, C., Ebicioğlu, K., Grothoff, C., Kielstra, A., Saraswat, V., Sarkar, V., Praun, C.V.: X10: An object-oriented approach to non-uniform cluster computing. In: Proceedings of the 20th ACM SIGPLAN Conference on Object-Oriented Programing, Systems, Languages, and Applications, ACM SIGPLAN, pp. 519–538 (2005)

Extending the OpenSHMEM Analyzer to Perform Synchronization and Multi-valued Analysis

Swaroop Pophale[1], Oscar Hernandez[2],
Stephen Poole[2], and Barbara M. Chapman[1]

[1] University of Houston, Houston, Texas 77004, USA
{spophale,chapman}@cs.uh.edu
[2] Oak Ridge National Laboratory, Oak Ridge, Tennessee, 37840, USA
{oscar,spoole}@ornl.gov

Abstract. OpenSHMEM Analyzer (OSA) is a compiler-based tool that provides static analysis for OpenSHMEM programs. It was developed with the intention of providing feedback to the users about semantics errors due to incorrect use of the OpenSHMEM API in their programs, thus making development of OpenSHMEM applications an easier task for beginners as well as experienced programmers. In this paper we discuss the improvements to the OSA tool to perform parallel analysis to detect collective synchronization structure of a program. Synchronization is a critical aspect of all programming models and in OpenSHMEM it is the responsibility of the programmer to introduce synchronization calls to ensure the completion of communication among processing elements (PEs) to prevent use of old/incorrect data, avoid deadlocks and ensure data race free execution keeping in mind the semantics of OpenSHMEM library specification. Our analysis yields three tangible outputs: a detailed control flow graph (CFG) making all the OpenSHMEM calls used, a *system dependence* graph and a *barrier tree*. The barrier tree represents the synchronization structure of the program presented in a simplistic manner that enables visualization of the program's synchronization keeping in mind the concurrent nature of SPMD applications that use OpenSHMEM library calls. This provides a graphical representation of the synchronization calls in the order in which they appear at execution time and how the different PEs in OpenSHMEM may encounter them based upon the different execution paths available in the program. Our results include the summarization of the analysis conducted within the middle-end of a compiler and the improvements we have done to the existing analysis to make it aware of the parallelism in the OpenSHMEM program.

1 Introduction

OpenSHMEM is a PGAS library that may be used with C, C++ or Fortran SPMD programs to achieve potentially low-latency communication via its *one-sided* remote direct memory access (RDMA) calls on shared as well as distributed systems that have the required hardware capability. Compilers are not aware of the parallel semantics of the OpenSHMEM library and they treat it like a

S. Poole, O. Hernandez, and P. Shamis (Eds.): OpenSHMEM 2014, LNCS 8356, pp. 134–148, 2014.

black box, thus hindering optimizations. OpenSHMEM analyzer (OSA) [1] is the first effort to develop a compiler-base tool aware of the parallel semantics of an OpenSHMEM library. OSA is built on top of the OpenUH compiler, that provides information about the structure of the OpenSHMEM code and semantic checks to ensure the correct use of the symmetric data in OpenSHMEM calls.

This paper describes how we built on top of the existing OSA framework to provide an in-depth synchronization analysis based on the control flow of the OpenSHMEM program that can be used to match collective synchronization calls, which are the building blocks for detecting the possible concurrent execution paths of an application. Our framework uses the concepts of multivalued seeds and multivalued expressions to build a multi-valued system dependence graph in the context of OpenSHMEM, which later is used to build a *barrier-tree* representation. Concurrency in an SPMD application results from distinct paths of execution which are effected by providing conditions that evaluate to different values on different PEs. Such expressions within the conditionals are called *multi-valued expressions* [2–5] and the particular variable used within the expression that causes this phenomenon is the *multi-valued seed*. Here we **implement** the critical parts of the framework proposed in [6] and provide insights into the the practical aspects of detection of *multi-valued* expressions by identification and tracing of *multi-valued* seeds.

Within the OpenUH compiler the source code is converted into an intermediate representation (IR) called WHIRL. Each phase within the OpenUH compiler performs *lowering* of WHIRL (starting from Very High WHIRL) to finally get the executable in machine instructions. We do our analysis within the interprocedural analysis phase (IPA) using the High WHIRL to help us build interprocedural control flow and data flow graphs while preserving the high level constructs of a program, such as DO_LOOP, DO_WHILE, and IF, which are critical for multi-valued analysis. We merge information available from different phases of the compiler and present the results of our analysis in the form of two graphs: a system dependence graph at the statement level clearly marking the control and data dependences across statements in the program, while the second graph structure is the *barrier- tree* where the leaves of tree are OpenSHMEM collective synchronization calls (*shmem_barrier* and *shmem_barrier_all*) and the nodes are operators (discussed in Section 4) that represent the possible concurrent control flow within the program. This visual aid provides the programmer with necessary information to verify if there is congruence in the intent of the program with its actual execution structure.

This paper is organized as follows. We describe our motivation for extending the analysis capability of OSA in Section 2 and provide better understanding of OpenSHMEM's memory model and synchronization semantics in Section 3. We discuss the changes to the infrastructure and implementation details in Section 4 and present our results with the help of the Matrix Multiplication application in Section 5. Section 6 describes different static analysis techniques that have been explored for concurrency and synchronization detection in parallel programming models. In Section 7 we summarize our contributions and our aspirations for the future of the OSA tool.

2 Motivation

The main characteristics of a program are captured by the control flow and data
flow within the program. Especially in parallel programming it is often benefi-
cial to be able to visualize the interaction of the different program components.
PEs executing in parallel may take different paths depending on the explicit or
implicit requirements set by the programmer. These are often expressed as conditions over variables that evaluate to different values on different PEs. Capturing
this information in a simplistic visual manner can aid the users understand the
concurrency in their applications. Figure 1 show a control flow graph (CFG) of
an OpenSHMEM program described in Listing 1.1. Here each basic block has
a single entry point and a single point of exit, and may contain OpenSHMEM
calls. Using this CFG alone cannot convey the different paths that are possible within the program. To be able to distinguish these different paths we need
to identify multi-value conditionals we need to essentially follow the propaga-
tion of the multi-value seeds through the program and mark the conditionals
that are affected directly or indirectly by them [7]. To build such multi-valued
CFG, we need to identify multi-valued seeds, determine the control flow and
capture the effect of such seeds by analyzing the data flow. This results in a
system dependence graph that can be used to do logical program slicing based
on multi-valued conditions. This can later used to build a barrier tree to perform
our synchronization analysis.

Listing 1.1. An OpenSHMEM program example with unaligned barriers

```
 1   int main(int argc, char *argv[]){
 2      int me,npes;
 3      int i,old;

 5      start_pes(0);
 6      me = _my_pe();
 7      npes = _num_pes();
 8      y = me*2;
 9      x=me;
10      if(me==0){
11         shmem_barrier_all();
12         int temp = x+y;
13         shmem_barrier_all();
14      }
15      else {
16       if(me==1){
17            shmem_barrier_all();
18            old = shmem_int_finc (&y, 0);
19            shmem_int_sum_to_all(&y,&x,1,1,0,npes-1,pWrk,pSync);
20            x= x+10;
21            shmem_int_get(&y,&y,1,0);
22            shmem_barrier_all();
23          }
24       else{
25            shmem_barrier_all();
26            shmem_int_sum_to_all(&y,&x,1,1,0,npes-1,pWrk,pSync);
27            x=y*0.23
28            shmem_barrier_all();
29          }
30      }
31      return 0;
32   }
```

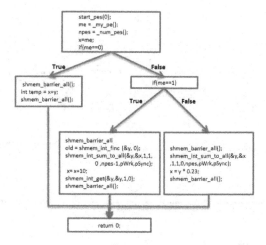

Fig. 1. Control Flow Graph of the OpenSHMEM program from Listing 1.1

The CFG is represented as a sequence of *basic blocks* which shows the possible alternatives within the program but does not provide explicit information on what or how the control is determined and what data dependence may affect the concurrency relationship between different parallel paths of execution. This is better depicted by the system dependence graph [8] as shown in Figure 2. To determine the exact execution path or slice we look at the combination of the data flow and control flow information generated by the compiler. The *system dependence graph* is expressed in terms of statements and based on the CFG and the outcome of the conditional statements each control edge is either marked *true* (T) or *false* (F). In Figure 2 if we were to take a forward slice of the sample program based on the *multi-valued* PE number *me* at A2, then we get either A2-A3-A4-A5-A6-B1-B2-B3-C or A2-A3-A4-A5-A6-C-D1-D2-D3-D4-D5-D6 or A2-A3-A4-A5-A6-C-E1-E2-E3-E4 depending on the value of *me*. These slices help us identify the *multi-valued* conditionals in the program by finding the points at with the execution paths diverge. Synchronization analysis is another important aspect to understand the relationship between code regions. A *code phases* [9] can be defined as a valid (synchronization free) path enclosed within two global synchronization statements. Since OpenSHMEM has unaligned global synchronization, the first step is to identify these statements across different execution paths. This helps in the identification of potentially concurrent code or errors due to unmatched barriers. Our work in this paper addresses the challenges of extracting information from the compiler and merging it with rules based off OpenSHMEM library semantics and presenting it to the user in a condensed meaningful format for visual inspection which can be used to detect synchronization mismatch, incorrect conditionals etc.

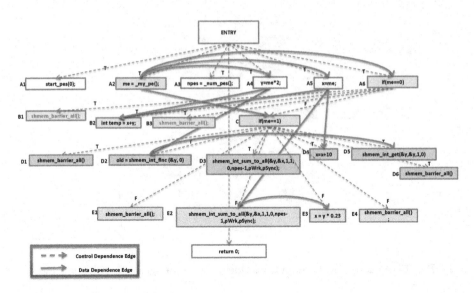

Fig. 2. System Dependence Graph of OpenSHMEM example (Listing 1.1) showing the control and data dependencies at statement level

3   OpenSHMEM Library

As mentioned before OpenSHMEM is a PGAS library that provides routines for programmers using the SPMD programming paradigm. The OpenSHMEM Specification [10] provides the definition, functionality and expected behavior of these library calls. OpenSHMEM communication calls are *one-sided*, i.e. they do not require the involvement of the target PE for completion and when the underlying hardware allows RDMA, it can provide excellent opportunities for hiding communication latency by overlapping communication with computation.

OpenSHMEM introduces the concept of *symmetric variables*. By definition, *symmetric* data consists of variables that are allocated by an OpenSHMEM library (using special memory allocation calls) or defined as *global* or *static* in C/C++ or in *common* or *save* blocks in Fortran [10]. These variables have the same name, size, type, storage allocation, and offset address on all PEs. The library calls *shmalloc* (C/C++) and *shpalloc* (Fortran) allocate and manage *symmetric* variables on the *symmetric heap*, which is remotely accessible from every other PE. Symmetric data allocation is a *collective* process and Open-SHMEM Specification requires that it appear at the same point in the code with identical *size* value [10]. This data is local to the PE and is not visible or directly accessible to a remote PE. Some OpenSHMEM library routines like *shmem put* and *shmem get* may use local variables as the *source* and *target* respectively. Hence for analysis for *multi-valued* seeds we must consider both types of data in conjunction with the OpenSHMEM calls they are used with.

3.1 Synchronization Semantics

Collective synchronization is provided by *shmem_barrier* and *shmem_barrier_all* (over a subset of PEs and all PEs respectively) in OpenSHMEM. A barrier call guarantees synchronization as well as completion of all pending remote and local OpenSHMEM data transfer operations and leaves the memory in a consistent state. A *shmem barrier* is defined over an **active set**. An active set is a logical grouping of PEs based on the triplet, namely, **PE_start**, **logPE_pe**, and the **PE_size** [10]. OpenSHMEM allows for unaligned barriers, both the code listings, Listing 1.2 and 1.3, are equivalent and valid as per OpenSHMEM Specification 1.0. This makes it easy to miss synchronization errors and may lead to unintended execution patterns or worse, dead-lock.

Listing 1.2. C code with unaligned barriers

```
1  if(_my_pe() % 2 == 0){
2     ...
3     shmem_barrier_all();
4  } else{
5     ...
6     shmem_barrier_all();
7  }
```

Listing 1.3. C code with aligned barrier

```
1  f(_my_pe() % 2 == 0){
2     ...
3  } else{
4     ...
5  }
6  shmem_barrier_all();
```

By providing information at compile time the programmer can analyze the program structure **before** execution, thus preventing resource wastage.

4 Methodology

As discussed above, the two main concepts to consider for concurrency analysis of OpenSHMEM program are *multi-valued expressions* and *unaligned barriers*. In this section, we discuss the structure of the OSA and the additional analysis added to it to be able to do the *multi-valued* analysis and evaluate the system dependence graph and the barrier-tree for the entire program.

4.1 OSA Infrastructure

Figure 3 shows the different stages within the compiler and the shaded region are the phases where OSA tool does most of its analysis. Since we need the data flow information, alias analysis and the control flow information for each individual procedure we build our analysis at the local inter-procedural phase. At this phase all analyses is performed on the High WHIRL IR where variables and control flow statements are preserved and can be easily mapped to the source code and the control flow is fixed [11]. We used the DU-manager, Alias Manager and control flow analysis data structures to build our system dependence graph to perform multi-valued analysis.

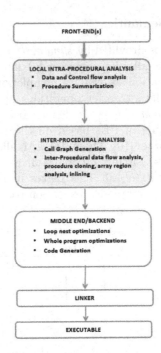

Fig. 3. Shaded blocks indicate OSA analysis within the OpenUH compiler

4.1.1   Identification of Multivalued Seeds

As defined in Section 2 *multi-valued* expressions evaluate to different results on different PEs. The outcome of a multi-valued expression depends on a *multi-valued* seed. [5] states certain generic rules governing the multi-calued property of programming variables. For example, uninitialized data structures are marked as multi-valued. We extend certain assumptions about the expressions that generate from a known single-valued or multi-valued seed based on the OpenSHMEM programming model. We modify the classification scheme for *multi-valued* seed in presence of OpenSHMEM calls and their treatment of different program variables.

For example, the return value for the OpenSHMEM call *_my_pe()* is unique for every PE and hence is multi-valued. In contrast *_num_pes()* returns the same value throughout the program for all PEs and hence the return value (and the variable associated with it) is considered single valued. Likewise, other Open-SHMEM library calls have an impact on the variable they modify. Generally, all PE-to-PE operations that modify data cause the variable to become *multi-valued*, while collective operations that modify *target* variables on **all** the PEs cause the target to be single-valued (else they result in *multi-valued target*). By analyzing the type of a variable and how it is modified (for example, if it is defined via a multi-valued OpenSHMEM call) we can then classify it as a *single* or *multi-valued* seed. A multi-valued seed may affect the value of other program variables or may only alter the control flow. The detection of resulting *multi-valued* variables is done by propagating the multi-valued seeds using the D-U

Table 1. Rules for building a barrier expression

Placement of barriers	Operator used	Result
b1 followed by b2	·	b1 · b2
if{ b1 } else { b2 };	|	b1 | b2
for(n times) b;	·	b1· b2 · ... bn

Chains generated. For every definition of a program variable there is a use-list associated with it and a set of statements that may directly or indirectly (via aliases) use the variable. We append this information with the control dependencies extracted from the control flow graph with the help of the *dominator frontier* information. Both of this combined gives the system dependence graph which the OSA generates for the user to inspect.

4.1.2 Generating Barrier Trees

[7] defines a *barrier expression* as being very similar to a path expression, with barriers connected by operators that best describe the control flow of the program. We extract the synchronization structure in a tree format by iterating over the IR generated by the compiler. By recording the barriers (both *shmem_barrier_all and shmem_barrier*) their relative position, and the control flow between them we generate a barrier tree for the entire program where the barriers are leaf nodes and the *operators* are the nodes of the tree. Like regular expressions, barrier trees use three types of operators: concatenation (·), alternation (|), and quantification (∗) [12]. Table 1 gives the rules that govern the barrier expression generation. It is important to note that if the result of a quantification operation can at times be statically non-deterministic and we may not be able to compute the barrier-expression in terms of the exact number of barriers encountered for such a program. Additionally we borrow the operator |[c] from [7] to indicate the operator *concurrent alternation*. This operator indicates that the different execution paths diverge from a *multi-valued* conditional.

Listing 1.4. OpenSHMEM example to explain concurrent alternate paths of execution

```
1   int main(){
2       if( ){
3         shmem_barrier_all();   //b1
4              ..
5         shmem_barrier_all();   //b2
6       }
7       else {
8         shmem_barrier_all();   //b3
9              ..
10      }
11          return 0;
12  }
```

We use the multi-value analysis saved in the system dependence graph to distinguish concurrent paths that may be present with a barrier tree. In our barrier tree representation the main function entry is indicated by the concatenation

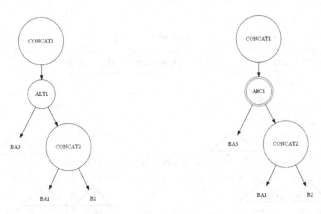

(a) Barrier-tree without multi-valued analysis

(b) Barrier-tree with multi-valued analysis

Fig. 4. Barrier trees generated by OSA for code Listing 1.4(where CONCAT=concatenation, ALT= alternation, AltC = alternate concurrent, B = shmem_barrier, and BA = shmem_barrier_all)

(CONCAT) as root. All operators are appended by a number which indicates their relative position of occurrence in the program's control flow. All barriers (barrier_all = BA, barrier=B) have independent numbering based on breadth first traversal ordering. This means that barriers in the *if-then* branch will have lower numeric labels than the *if-else* branch. Other operators are represented as follows: quantification (QUANT), alternation (ALT), and alternate concurrent (AltC). For example, the code in Listing 1.4 would evaluate to the barrier expression: (b1.b2) | b3 and would be represented by our compiler analysis (without multi-value information)by a barrier-tree in Figure 4a. Purely based on Figure 4a the programmer has no way of knowing the different paths of execution that may be possible. Consider two possible scenarios, if the first **if** conditional in line 2 resulted in the same value on all PEs then all PEs would either encounter barriers *b1-b2* **or** *b3*. But if the same conditional resulted in different values on different PEs then some PEs would encounter barriers *b1-b2* and others would encounter *b3*: which is a obvious stall situation caused by un-matched synchronization calls. This is indicated by AltC (alternate concurrent) label in Figure 4b. We augment the multi-value analysis to this providing a more meaningful representation of the program structure. Figure 4b depicts the barrier tree for the second scenario discussed above.

5   Results

We test our analysis framework on the Matrix Multiplication application which is part of the examples in the OpenSHMEM Validation and Verification Suite [13]. The application consists of three 2-D arrays A, B, and C, where C is used to store the product of two matrices A and B.

Listing 1.5. Matrix Multiplication application's main body

```
2    for (i = 0; i < rows; i++)
3    {
4      for (p = 1; p <= np; p++)
5      {
6        // compute the partial product of c[i][j]
7        ...
8        // send a block of matrix A to the adjacent PE
9        shmem_barrier_all ();
10       if (rank == np - 1){
11         shmem_double_put (&a_local[i][0], &a_local[i][0], blocksize, 0);
12         shmem_barrier_all ();
13       }
14       else{
15         shmem_double_put (&a_local[i][0], &a_local[i][0], blocksize,
16             rank + 1);
17         shmem_barrier_all ();
18       }
19       ...
20     shmem_barrier_all ();
```

This program performs matrix multiplication based on 1D block-column distribution where in every iteration, the PE calculates the partial result of matrix-matrix multiply and communicates the current portion of matrix A to its right neighbor and receives the next portion of matrix A from its left neighbor. The main body of the benchmark is as shown in the code Listing 1.5.

Figure 5 shows the control flow as captured by our analysis which clearly marks out the OpenSHMEM calls and their placement. From the control flow analysis of the compiler, we use the *dominator frontier* information to extract control dependencies at the statement level. We merge this information with the data flow analysis (captured by Def-Us chains as discussed in Section 4) and present it as a **system dependence** graph in Figure 6.

Here, the control dependencies are represented by light/dashed arrows while the data dependencies are represented by bold arrows. For conditionals branches are marked with either **T** or **F** indicating when the branch is taken. This makes understanding the control and data dependence easier for the programmer.

We present the result of our multi-valued analysis in Figure 7. When we perform a logical *slicing* on the system dependence graph based on the PE number (stored in variable *rank*). In a multi PE execution scenario the statements in shaded boxes are executed only by **PE 0**. The program synchronization structure along with the multi-valued analysis is captured by the barrier tree generated by OSA in Figure 8. The entry into main() is indicated by operator **CONCAT1**. We follow the representation discussed in Section 4. The alternate concurrent paths are indicated by the double-circles labeled **AltC4** and **AltC5** and the two nested *for-loops* are represented by **QUANT2** and **QUANT3**. Since all loops run for the same number of times for all PEs, all PEs will encounter either BA4 or BA5 equal number of times. Thus, just by glancing at the barrier tree generated by OSA it is evident that the all PEs will encounter the same number of barriers. This makes the process of debugging and verification a trivial task. This becomes more critical when applications become more complex with numerous branching statements involving multi-valued conditionals.

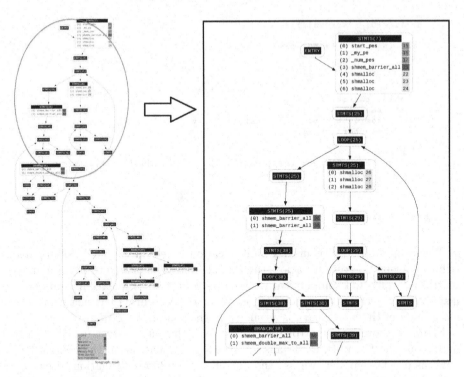

Fig. 5. Control flow representation with OpenSHMEM calls for Matrix Multiplication application

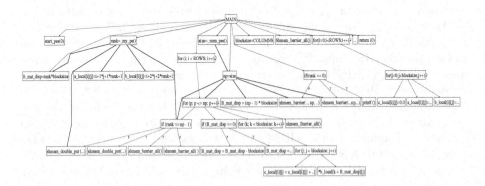

Fig. 6. System dependence graph as generated by OSA for Matrix Multiplication application

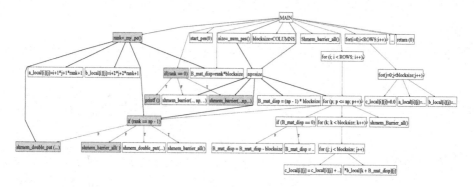

Fig. 7. Slicing of the System dependence graph on PE 0 indicating statements executed by PE 0 only

6   Related Work

Depending on the semantics of the parallel programming model, most applications rely on synchronization primitives to ensure updates or maintain ordering of different programming sub-tasks. Errors in synchronization could lead to incorrect or irreproducible execution characteristics. Hence research on synchronization and concurrency has always been an important aspect for the high performance programming community. One of the first research to verify program synchronization patterns and was done in [14] for Split-C. They analyze the effects of *single valued expression* on the control flow and concurrency characteristics of the program and define rules that govern the synchronization sequences. Like OpenSHMEM, Split-C has unaligned barriers and this work simplifies their identification with the use of keywords that are used for annotating the named barriers. [7] tries to identify and match unaligned barriers for MPI programs to uncover potential synchronization errors. They evaluate the different concurrent paths the processes in the MPI program may take by using multi-value conditional and barrier expression analysis and verify that each processes encounters an equal number of barriers. For other PGAS languages, like Titanium [15] is in identification of textually aligned barriers and was first proposed in [9]. They propose an inter-procedural algorithm that computes the set of all concurrent statements by first modifying the CFG and provide rules to perform a modified depth first search to ascertain pairs of concurrent expressions. Other parallel programming languages, such as X10 [16,17], Ada [18,19], and Java [20,21] have also explored analysis based on synchronization structure of a program.

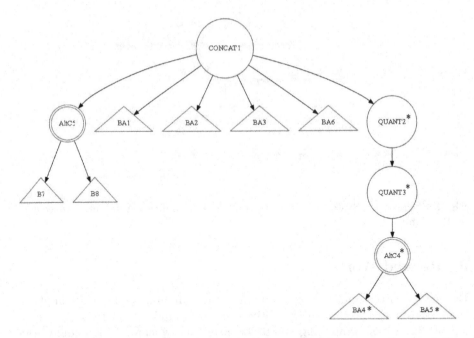

Fig. 8. Barrier tree as generated by OSA for Matrix Multiplication application (where CONCAT=concatenation, ALT= alternation, AltC = alternate concurrent, QUANT = quantification, B = shmem_barrier, and BA = shmem_barrier_all). * Indicates operators and barriers in code Listing 1.5.

7   Conclusions and Future Work

The main contribution of our work is to provide an enhanced OSA that presents more complex analysis in an easy to understand visual manner to an Open-SHMEM programmer. We provide CFG explicit with the OpenSHMEM calls, for providing detailed information about the usage and placement of OpenSHMEM calls, and a system dependence graph that clearly indicates the control and data dependencies prevalent in the application. The barrier tree provides a simplistic representation of the synchronization pattern along with information on concurrent execution paths available which makes discovering potential errors due to mis-aligned or missing synchronization easier for the OpenSHMEM programmer. We also pave the way for more complex analysis towards suggesting optimizations, which needs information like the system dependence graph along with the multivalued analysis and the synchronization analysis.

During the development of this analysis framework tracking and evaluating *active-sets* was challenging and we hope that the future library specification of OpenSHMEM will address this by providing implicit *active-sets* with handles. This will simplify the analysis considerably resulting in better accuracy of predicting which PEs may take a particular concurrent path making it possible to provide specialized optimization feedback based on a particular PE or a group of

PEs. Our current implementation considers OpenSHMEM barrier and barrier all synchronization calls but can be easily extended to account for other collective calls with implicit synchronization semantics. As future work we would like to integrate support for implicit synchronization and provide useful optimization hints to the user based on OpenSHMEM semantics. For example, if an application has no updates between two consecutive barriers on the same execution path we would want to indicate that there is no requirement for the extra synchronization to the application programmer/user at compile time thus helping achieve better performance.

Acknowledgments. This work is supported by the United States Department of Defense and used resources of the Extreme Scale Systems Center located at the Oak Ridge National Laboratory.

References

1. Oscar, H., Siddhartha, J., Pophale, S., Stephen, P., Kuehn, J., Barbara, C.: The OpenSHMEM Analyzer. In: Proceedings of the Sixth Conference on Partitioned Global Address Space Programming Model, PGAS 2012 (2012)
2. Taylor, R.N.: A general-purpose algorithm for analyzing concurrent programs. Commun. ACM 26, 361–376 (1983)
3. Lin, Y.: Static nonconcurrency analysis of openMP programs. In: Mueller, M.S., Chapman, B.M., de Supinski, B.R., Malony, A.D., Voss, M. (eds.) IWOMP 2005/2006. LNCS, vol. 4315, pp. 36–50. Springer, Heidelberg (2008)
4. Masticola, S.P., Ryder, B.G.: Non-concurrency analysis. In: Proceedings of the Fourth ACM SIGPLAN Symposium on Principles and Practice of Parallel Programming, PPOPP 1993, pp. 129–138. ACM, New York (1993)
5. Auslander, J., Philipose, M., Chambers, C., Eggers, S.J., Bershad, B.N.: Fast, effective dynamic compilation. In: Proceedings of the ACM SIGPLAN 1996 Conference on Programming Language Design and Implementation, PLDI 1996, pp. 149–159. ACM, New York (1996)
6. Swaroop, P., Oscar, H., Stephen, P., Barbara, C.: Static analyses for unaligned collective synchronization matching for OpenSHMEM. In: Proceedings of the Seventh Conference on Partitioned Global Address Space Programming Model, PGAS 2013 (2013)
7. Zhang, Y., Duesterwald, E.: Barrier matching for programs with textually unaligned barriers. In: Proceedings of the 12th ACM SIGPLAN Symposium on Principles and Practice of Parallel Programming, PPoPP 2007, pp. 194–204. ACM, New York (2007)
8. Horwitz, S., Reps, T., Binkley, D.: Interprocedural slicing using dependence graphs. In: Proceedings of the ACM SIGPLAN 1988 Conference on Programming Language Design and Implementation, PLDI 1988, pp. 35–46. ACM, New York (1988)
9. Kamil, A.A., Yelick, K.A.: Concurrency analysis for parallel programs with textually aligned barriers. Technical Report UCB/EECS-2006-41, EECS Department, University of California, Berkeley (2006)
10. OpenSHMEM.org: OpenSHMEM specification 1.0 (2011)
11. Chakrabarti, G., Chow, F.: Structure layout optimizations in the open64 compiler: Design, implementation and measurements (2008)

12. Kleene, S.C.: Representation of events in nerve nets and finite automata. Automata Studies (1956)
13. Swaroop, P., Oscar, H., Stephen, P., Barbara, C.: Poster: Validation and verification suite for OpenSHMEM. In: Proceedings of the Seventh Conference on Partitioned Global Address Space Programming Model, PGAS 2013 (2013)
14. Aiken, A., Gay, D.: Barrier inference. In: Proceedings of the 25th ACM SIGPLAN-SIGACT Symposium on Principles of Programming Languages, POPL 1998, pp. 342–354. ACM, New York (1998)
15. Luigi, K.Y., Semenzato, L., Pike, G., Miyamoto, C., Liblit, B., Krishnamurthy, A., Hilfinger, P., Graham, S., Gay, D., Colella, P., Aiken, A.: Titanium: A high-performance java dialect, pp. 10–11. ACM (1998)
16. Markstrum, S.A., Fuhrer, R.M., Millstein, T.D.: Towards concurrency refactoring for x10. In: Proceedings of the 14th ACM SIGPLAN Symposium on Principles and Practice of Parallel Programming, PPoPP 2009, pp. 303–304. ACM, New York (2009)
17. Muller, S., Chong, S.: Towards a practical secure concurrent language. In: Proceedings of the ACM International Conference on Object Oriented Programming Systems Languages and Applications, OOPSLA 2012, pp. 57–74. ACM, New York (2012)
18. Kaiser, C., Pajault, C., Pradat-Peyre, J.-F.: Modelling remote concurrency with ada. In: Abdennadher, N., Kordon, F. (eds.) Ada-Europe 2007. LNCS, vol. 4498, pp. 192–207. Springer, Heidelberg (2007)
19. Burns, A., Wellings, A.: Concurrency in Ada. Cambridge University Press, New York (1995)
20. Vakilian, M., Negara, S., Tasharofi, S., Johnson, R.E.: Keshmesh: a tool for detecting and fixing java concurrency bug patterns. In: Proceedings of the ACM International Conference Companion on Object Oriented Programming Systems Languages and Applications Companion, SPLASH 2011, pp. 39–40. ACM, New York (2011)
21. Magee, J., Kramer, J.: Concurrency: state models & Java programs. John Wiley & Sons, Inc., New York (1999)

OpenSHMEM Extensions and a Vision for Its Future Direction

Stephen Poole[1], Pavel Shamis[1], Aaron Welch[2],
Swaroop Pophale[2], Manjunath Gorentla Venkata[1], Oscar Hernandez[1],
Gregory Koenig[1], Tony Curtis[2], and Chung-Hsing Hsu[1]

[1] Extreme Scale Systems Center
Oak Ridge National Laboratory
{spoole,shamisp,manjugv,oscar,koenig,hsuc}@ornl.gov
[2] Computer Science Department
University of Houston
{dawelch,swaroop,arcurtis}@uh.edu

Abstract. The Extreme Scale Systems Center (ESSC) at Oak Ridge
National Laboratory (ORNL), together with the University of Houston,
led the effort to standardize the SHMEM API with input from the vendors and user community. In 2012, OpenSHMEM specification 1.0 was
finalized and released to the OpenSHMEM community for comments. As
we move to future HPC systems, there are several shortcomings in the
current specification that we need to address to ensure scalability, higher
degrees of concurrency, locality, thread safety, fault-tolerance, parallel
I/O capabilities, etc. In this paper we discuss an immediate set of extensions that we propose to the current API and our vision for a future
API, OpenSHMEM Next-Generation (NG), that targets future Exascale
systems. We also explain our rational for the proposed extensions and
highlight the lessons learned from other PGAS languages and communication libraries.

1 Introduction

OpenSHMEM [1] [2] [3], an API for the Partitioned Global Address Space
(PGAS) programming model, is a derivative of SGI's SHMEM API, which was
originally developed by Cray. The SHMEM API is widely used in parallel applications [4] and has been adopted by multiple system vendors including IBM,
Quadrics, Hewlett Packard, QLogic, and Mellanox Technologies. Although these
implementations are similar in functionality and semantics, they have minor differences that inhibit portability. The *OpenSHMEM* API is the result of an open
source community effort to standardize the SHMEM API used by the scientific
community and hardware vendors, jointly led by the ESSC at ORNL, and the
University of Houston.

The *OpenSHMEM* API provides a complete set of concise and powerful library calls to satisfy the communication needs of parallel applications. These
include collective communication operations, remote memory access (RMA),

S. Poole, O. Hernandez, and P. Shamis (Eds.): OpenSHMEM 2014, LNCS 8356, pp. 149–162, 2014.
© Springer International Publishing Switzerland 2014

atomic memory operations, synchronization operations, distributed lock operations, and operations to check process and data accessibility. A complete set of operations, and semantics of the operations are detailed in [1].

Although the *OpenSHMEM* API provides an adequate and complete set of operations for implementing communication libraries for the time it was developed, it requires additional functionality for the exascale era. Particularly, as the needs of exascale applications change, so does system architecture - nodes have multiple CPU sockets and computing cores with varying instruction sets and power calibrating interfaces, network interfaces provide low-latency and high bandwidth communication, native support for RMA operations, collective operation functionality, etc. To better accommodate these technological shifts, the API needs to incorporate other useful concepts either born out of *OpenSHMEM* user experience or lessons from the evolution of other parallel programming languages and communication libraries (e.g. CAF 2.0, Titanium, UPC, Chapel, MPI 3.0).

The most important changes that are critical for *OpenSHMEM* are the following:

– Non-blocking Operations: The invocation of a library call returns before the operation is complete, providing the application with the opportunity to hide the latency of the operation with additional computation.
– Fault Tolerance: The API should enable implementation of fault-tolerant and fault-aware communication. In addition, it should provide adequate support for building fault resilient applications.
– Hybrid Programming: The API should support, or at least not prohibit, interoperability with other programming models. This provides the application an opportunity to use multiple programming models simultaneously to better suit architectural needs, including heteregenous systems.
– Isolation: This provides private communication contexts for groups of PEs. This is an important attribute for enabling the construction of libraries, so as to separate communication performed within an *OpenSHMEM* application with communication performed by libraries that application may call.
– Locality: This will help to define processing elements (PEs) and symmetric memory areas that are "next" to each other and that can be mapped to multiple devices/accelerators within a node or to nodes close to each other.

In this paper, we propose a series of extensions to the *OpenSHMEM* API that work toward adding some of the above functionality. Our work in this paper can be classified into two different categories:

1. A series of extensions that strive to maintain backward compatibility with the current *OpenSHMEM* API, while aiming to improve programmer productivity and the performance and scalability of *OpenSHMEM* applications. The extensions include 1) Explicit active sets 2) Non-blocking operations 3) Library shutdown, and 4) Multi-threading support.
2. We make a case for a series of extensions that is far-reaching and geared more towards the needs of exascale era applications and hardware. The extensions

in this category include 1) Isolation 2) Locality 3) Error model, and 4) Parallel I/O.

The rest of the paper is organized as follows: In Section 2, we describe the motivation behind adding the proposed incremental extensions to *OpenSHMEM* and the potential benefit that can be gained by adding these useful features. In Section 3, we describe in detail the different extensions and their semantics with concrete examples and prototypes. We also provide a broader view of the different aspects that may greatly impact *OpenSHMEM* in the march towards Exascale and discuss a few nascent concepts for *OpenSHMEM-NG* in Section 4. Section 5 throws light on the different features that were found lacking and then added into other parallel programming languages and libraries (namely Chapel, UPC, Co-array Fortran, Titanium, and MPI-3). We conclude in Section 6 by summarizing our work and highlighting the key contributions.

2   Motivation for the Incremental Extensions

In *OpenSHMEM* 1.0, collective operations are performed on implicitly defined active sets, which represent a subset of participating PEs for the collective call. These must be defined using a strided pattern that is restricted to powers of two. These operations are expected to be called by all members of the defined set of PEs, but for any PEs that are not in the set, calling the same operation results in undefined behavior. There are a number of limitations to this approach, including the inability to specify an arbitrary stride or to select participating PEs through other methods. It can also become cumbersome and redundant to provide the full details of the active set with each successive call, and could lend itself to error and inconsistencies. Furthermore, active sets are currently designed to exist only during the life of a particular collective call. Allowing the user to explicitly define an active set provides opportunity for reuse, which will increase programmer productivity. This is possible while still maintaining backward compability with *OpenSHMEM* 1.0 since active sets may be reused throughout the entire application without significantly changing the memory, execution, and synchronization models of OpenSHMEM 1.0.

Overlapping computation with communication allows for better concurrency and utilization of resources when using hardware that supports the operations. There are very tangible benefits that may be realized by making collectives, atomics, and RMA communication calls non-blocking. The time spent waiting on the results of a computation or a RMA operation may be better utilized by doing other useful work. Non-blocking calls expose potential completion latency that may be utilized by the application to execute other units of work or by hybrid programming models (i.e. *OpenSHMEM* plus multithreading and tasking).

For verifying the potential for overlap in the context of *OpenSHMEM*, we developed a working prototype for a non-blocking version of the atomic call *shmem_longlong_fadd()* called *shmem_longlong_fadd_nb()*. The prototype was implemented using the *OpenSHMEM* reference implementation [5] with the Universal Common Communication Substrate communication middleware (UCCS)

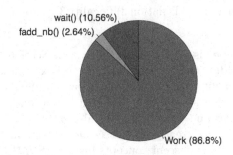

Fig. 1. Potential Overlap using Non-blocking Fetch-and-Add

[6] [7]. UCCS is a high-performance communication middleware that provides a broad range of semantics useful for the PGAS programming model. This prototype was put to the test using a custom version of the Communication Offload MPI-based Benchmark (COMB) [8], modified to work using *OpenSHMEM* instead of MPI code. This test first times the execution of *shmem_longlong_fadd _nb()* immediately followed by a wait call on the operation (effectively making it a blocking atomic operation). Next, it times the execution of the non-blocking atomic followed by increasingly large amounts of work before waiting on the operation. When the total time spent starts to exceed the "blocking" time, all the latency that can be exploited for additional computation has been used, so it records the time breakdown for the point at which it crossed the latency boundary.

Using this benchmark, we show that for atomic memory updates, 86% of the total time taken by the call can be employed doing other useful work (see Figure 1). This is significant and insightful especially since atomics are low latency calls - the overlap opportunity afforded by other non-blocking calls like collective operations and data transfer will be much greater. Additionally, the non-blocking call was shown to not add any noticeable overhead, so there is no disadvantage to using the non-blocking calls over their blocking counterparts.

3   Proposed Extensions

In this section, we describe and present our proposed set of extensions to *Open-SHMEM* 1.0. These incremental extensions are aimed at addressing some of the scalability bottlenecks of *OpenSHMEM* interfaces, and providing communication interfaces that enable overlapping communication with computation in applications.

Our set of extensions consist of:

- *Explicit active sets*, which allow the *OpenSHMEM* users to define the criterion for creation of the active set as well as the lifetime of the active set.
- *Non-blocking collective* operations include a method for invoking the collective operation, and a method for learning the progress of the call. It enables the *OpenSHMEM* users to overlap collective communication with computation.

- *Non-blocking put, get, and atomic operations*, like the non-blocking collective operations extension, have a method for invoking the call, and a method for learning the progress of the call.
- *Abort and exit support* allows *OpenSHMEM* programs to terminate at any point during their execution. It enables applications to free the resources before exiting, or facilitate sanity checks before exiting the *OpenSHMEM* environment.

3.1 Explicit Active Sets

Our proposed extension to active sets will help the programmer define and reuse active sets explicitly via a proposed API. The active set construct will help the user group sets of processes and reuse active sets across collective operations using the *OpenSHMEM* API. Our proposed active set extension is an incremental extension to the active sets in *OpenSHMEM* 1.0, where it implicitly created sets of processes used for executing collective operations. A set of API calls will be used to define a set of PEs that comprise an active set, each using a different selection strategy, and will return an opaque handle that can be used thereafter to identify this set of PEs. This handle will only be guaranteed to be usable within collectives for PEs within the set, though the associated creation function may be called by any superset of the PEs contained in the set. Whether a particular calling PE is in the active set defined by the handle may be checked by calling the *shmem_in_aset()* function, which will return a non-zero value if it is in the set, or zero if it is not. The size of a particular set can be queried through the *shmem_aset_size()* function, and the *shmem_aset_delete()* function destroys the active set object. The full list of supported call signatures for active sets is included below in Table 1.

In the case of concurrent collective operations that involve overlapping active sets the user has to ensure that they do not work on the same pSync or pWrk arrays. With these new extensions, the user will be able to create active sets using one of the four active set creation calls that can be used to select the member PEs of the active set. These calls allow the user to create active sets using strided sets based on both powers of two and arbitrary strides, generic arrays of participating PE ids, and via user-defined functions. For the latter case, a user may define an active set with a function that when called on a set of size n, will produce the i_{th} PE id in the set for $0 \leq i < n$. All PE ids generated by the function must be both valid and unique in the set, and the id generated for a particular input must always be the same regardless of how many times it is called. The user can pass an arbitrary amount of data as actual parameters to the function specified at creation time of the active set. After being passed to the creation function, these parameters should remain constant for the lifetime of the active set. As an example, a custom function may be thought of as being very similar to a mathematical function such as $f(i) = i^2 + \text{PE\_start}$, for $0 \leq i < n$, for which $n = 4$ and PE_start = 2 would produce the set $\{2, 3, 6, 11\}$.

In addition, we will use explicit active sets as arguments to create the proposed non-blocking collective calls as described in Section 3.2.1. This is to

Table 1. Examples of Proposed active set operations and their APIs

Create a strided active set.	shmem_aset *shmem_create_strided_aset(int PE_start, int PE_stride, int PE_size)
Create a log-strided active set.	shmem_aset *shmem_create_log_strided_aset(int PE_start, int PE_log_stride, int PE_size, int stride_base)
Create a user-defined active set.	shmem_aset *shmem_create_custom_aset(int PE_start, shmem_offset_fn offset, int PE_size, void *const_params)
Create a generic active set.	shmem_aset *shmem_create_generic_aset(int *PE_list, int PE_size)
Check if a PE is in an active set.	int shmem_in_aset(shmem_aset *aset)
Query the size of an active set.	int shmem_aset_size(shmem_aset *aset)
Delete an active set.	void shmem_delete_aset(shmem_aset *aset);

encourage the use of explicit active sets, together with non-blocking collective operations, while minimizing changes to the existing *OpenSHMEM* 1.0 API. The behavior for the original collective operations will remain the same, including shmem_barrier_all(), which will always require the participation of all PEs in the system.

An example is shown below demonstrating the process of creating and using a strided active set:

```
1   int main(int argc, char **argv) {
2       shmem_aset *aset;
3       ...
4       /* creates an active set containing PEs 0, 3, 6, 9, ... */
5       aset = shmem_create_strided_aset(0, 3, npes / 3);
6       /* equivalent to the OpenSHMEM 1.0-style (me % 3 == 0) */
7       if (shmem_in_aset(aset)) {
8           shmem_barrier_aset(aset, pSync);
9       }
10  }
```

Similarly, creating a custom function for selecting the PEs in an active set involves little more than creating the custom function itself:

```
1   int my_custom_index_fn(int PE_index, int PE_start, int PE_size, void
        *const_params) {
2       return PE_index * PE_index + PE_start;
3   }
4   int main(int argc, char **argv) {
5       shmem_aset *aset;
6       ...
7       /* creates an active set containing PEs 2, 3, 6, 11 */
8       aset = shmem_create_custom_aset(2, &my_custom_index_fn, 4, NULL);
9       if (shmem_in_aset(aset)) {
10          shmem_barrier_aset(aset, pSync);
11      }
12  }
```

The placement and use of the *shmem_create_custom_aset()* and *shmem_in_aset()* functions here may seem unusual for some *OpenSHMEM* application developers. Being placed outside of the conditional means that the create function can be called by PEs that are not in the defined active set. This is due to the updated syntax for active set creation, and will still result in valid code.

The performance of each of the four methods is compared using barrier operations to that of the implicitly defined active sets from *OpenSHMEM* 1.0 in Figure 2. All the tests were performed using the same *OpenSHMEM* reference implemention modified to use UCCS as described in Section 2. Each of the results represents the time spent performing a barrier on four PEs, using either an implicitly defined logarithmically strided active set or one of the four methods for creating explicit active sets as previously described. It can be seen that not only is there no additional overhead for defining active sets explicitly compared to the original implicit definitions, but there is also no performance penalty dependent on which method for defining an explicit active set is chosen.

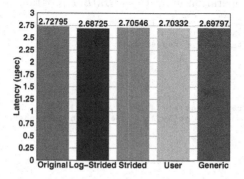

Fig. 2. Performance of Barriers on Active Sets

3.2 Non-blocking Operations

All proposed non-blocking operations require a mechanism to check for completion of the request. For this purpose we introduce an opaque request object of type *shmem_request_handle_t* and two query functions defined on this request object, namely, *shmem_wait_request()* and *shmem_test_request()*. Each non-blocking operation will produce exactly one such handle, which will be unique to that particular outstanding operation. All calls to non-blocking operations return immediately and all participating PEs must check for completion by using a *wait* or a *test* before reusing any resources involved in the operation. A call to *wait* will return only once the operation is completed, while *test* returns immediately with information on the status of the request, regardless of whether or not it has completed. There are no specific requirements in terms of the progress model for these operations and an *OpenSHMEM* library implementation is free to choose when and how the operations progress.

3.2.1 Non-blocking Collective Operations
We extend the *OpenSHMEM* API for collective operations such as collection, reduction, barrier and broadcast by adding their non-blocking variants. With the

new non-blocking collective operations a single collective call is replaced by a call to the non-blocking collective (which would return a request handle) followed by a call to *shmem_wait_request()* which accepts the handle as a parameter and returns when the collective call has completed on the calling PE. All non-blocking collective operations are defined on explicit active set handles as discussed in Section 3.1, instead of the triplet *PE_start, logPE_stride* and *PE_size*. Worth noting is that pSync remains a required part of the function call. This is due to the fact that the active set handles themselves do not have any dedicated memory assigned to them, separating the handling of memory from the selection of PEs for any particular active set definition. This allows a developer to maintain the same high degree of control over lower level management of the program and its associated memory as has been traditionally possible, while still receiving the benefits of the new active set definitions. A complete example showing a non-blocking collective operation in an *OpenSHMEM* program is illustrated below:

```
1    int main(int argc, char *argv[]){
2        shmem_aset *aset1;
3        shmem_request_handle_t request1;
4        ...
5        start_pes(0);
6        ...
7        if(me%2 == 0){
8            // aset1 contains 0,2,4,6
9            aset1 = create_aset_strided(0,2,4,&err);
10           shmem_broadcast32_nb(&y,&x,1,aset1,pSync, &request1);
11           ...
12           //some useful work
13           ...
14           shmem_wait_request(request1);
15       }
16       ...
17       return 0;
18   }
```

The non-blocking collective semantics allow multiple outstanding collective operations to be in progress on a given active set at any particular point in time. Each outstanding non-blocking and blocking collective requires its own symmetric array. A high quality implementation would not require a call to *shmem_test_request()* to progress the outstanding collective operation. However, a semantically correct implementation can progress asynchronously, or during a call to the *OpenSHMEM* library.

3.2.2   Non-blocking Atomic Operations

In the same manner, we introduce non-blocking variants for the *OpenSHMEM* atomic library calls (swap, compare-and-swap, increment, fetch-and-increment, add, and fetch-and-add). A call to a non-blocking atomic returns a handle which can be passed as a parameter to *shmem_wait_request()*. The *wait* returns when the atomic operation has completed on all the local as well as target PE. An example of non-blocking atomic operation in an *OpenSHMEM* program is illustrated below:

```
1   int main(int argc, char *argv[]){
2      shmem_request_handle_t request1;
3      ...
4      start_pes(0);
5      ...
6      shmem_longlong_fadd_nb(target, 10, 1, &oldval, &request1);
7      ...
8      //some useful work
9      ...
10     shmem_wait_request(request1);
11     ...
12     return 0;
13  }
```

3.2.3 Non-blocking Data Transfer Operations

According to *OpenSHMEM* Specification 1.0, a *put* operation returns only after the local buffer is available for reuse. As a non-blocking extension to the *put* operation, the call will return immediately and the local buffer will not be available for reuse until the operation has achieved local completion. These non-blocking semantics can be especially advantageous for communication patterns that involve communicating parts of an array to different PEs without immediate reuse. The *get* operation returns only after the value is updated at the local PE. For programs that do not need the value updated by the *get* call immediately, waiting for local completion is an unnecessary burden. The non-blocking *get* operation will allow the local PE to execute other calls and operations while waiting for the remote data to be communicated. An example of a non-blocking *get* operation in an *OpenSHMEM* program is illustrated below:

```
1   int main(int argc, char *argv[]){
2      shmem_request_handle_t request1;
3      ...
4      start_pes(0);
5      ...
6      shmem_int_get_nb(target, source, 1, me+1, &request1);
7      //some useful work
8      //call wait before the value is required by local PE
9      shmem_wait_request(request1);
10     x = target + 0.25 * y;
11     ...
12     return 0;
13  }
```

Non-blocking data transfer is not a novel concept and SHMEM implementations like Quadrics [9] have included it in their library APIs. We differ in our approach as we define the non-blocking operations on explicit active set handles. By creating an explicit active set we not only simplify the API but make *OpenSHMEM* programs more suitable for analysis via compiler based tools.

3.3 Thread Safety

In *OpenSHMEM* 1.0 there is no support for thread safety nor guarantees for what one might expect when trying to execute an *OpenSHMEM* program in a multi-threaded environment. Providing basic thread safety support may promote interoperability between *OpenSHMEM* and other programming models and allow data transfers to be broken down into smaller units to facilitate communication latency hiding via overlap. Since a PE maps to a process in a multi threaded environment, as the current specification stands, multiple threads executing *OpenSHMEM* calls such as *start_pes()*, *shmem_finalize()*, *shmalloc()*, *shfree()*, and *shrealloc()* can lead to unpredictable execution patterns and results. Collective operations are a major *OpenSHMEM* functionality group that may be executed by only one thread per PE. Since the concept of an active set is a purely logical one in *OpenSHMEM* Specification 1.0 there is no way to define operations on it. With explicit active set handles there is a programmable object on which we can now define thread-safe operations and constraints. Although prototypes to these functions are beyond the scope of this paper, four hierarchical execution model modes for threading support proposed by Cray (*thread single*, *thread funneled*, *thread serialized* and *thread multiple*) [10] could be well suited for providing thread safety semantics with the new extensions. Each of the four levels of threading support specifies the number of threads per PE that may participate, and this is set through a thread safety initialization call *shmem_init_thread()* which accepts one of the four modes as an argument.

3.4 Abort and Exit Support

The *OpenSHMEM* Specification 1.0 does not have any support for an abort or exit call. As an extension to *OpenSHMEM* Specification 1.0, we propose a *shmem_finalize()* function to shut down the library, and *shmem_abort()* to signal the abortion of the *OpenSHMEM* program. The primary difference in the semantics of *shmem_finalize()* and *shmem_abort()* is that *shmem_finalize()* indicates normal completion of the program and the *OpenSHMEM* environment can be re-initialized after *finalize* by calling *start_pes()*. *shmem_abort()*, however, signals the run-time that *OpenSHMEM* library operations cannot continue after the call returns. Semantics for both the calls are as follows:

1. *shmem_finalize()*
   (a) It is the last *OpenSHMEM* call by any PE.
   (b) All pending *OpenSHMEM* operations will have completed when the call returns.
   (c) The *OpenSHMEM* environment can be re-initialized by calling *start_pes()* after *finalize*.
   (d) Any *OpenSHMEM* calls after *shmem_finalize* and before the *start_pes()* will lead to undefined behavior.
2. *shmem_abort()*
   (a) Any PE can call *shmem_abort()* to the program execution. After any PE calls the *shmem_abort()* call, the behavior of the program is undefined.
   (b) Any *OpenSHMEM* operation after any PE calls *shmem_abort()* will lead to undefined behavior.
   (c) After exiting the *OpenSHMEM* environment, a process may or may not terminate depending on the library implementation.

4   A Vision for OpenSHMEM's Future

OpenSHMEM-NG is a vision for the next big leap in the evolution of *Open-SHMEM*. Here we propose new ideas: changes are not incremental, and not necessarily backward compatible with *OpenSHMEM* 1.0. In order to address the need for backward compatibility, we plan to develop source-to-source translation tools that will help to update legacy applications to a new standard.

4.1   Adding Memory Context to Active Sets

In the current *OpenSHMEM* Specification 1.0, all symmetric memory allocations have to be made across all the PEs in an application. However, with the introduction of explicit active sets (Section 3), the active set opaque handle may be reused for multiple collective operations. This provides more control and flexibility to the user when decomposing the work within an *OpenSHMEM* application. Adding a memory context to the active set, where memory context is a symmetric memory space available only to the members of the active set, is the next logical step. The memory context will provide an efficient medium for memory management without incurring the cost of memory allocation across all PEs. Moreover, this will also help address the issue of isolation, where applications and multiple libraries using *OpenSHMEM* can safely co-exist independently of each other. Introducing memory context to active sets can also address the issue of *locality*, where logical sets of PEs and memory spaces can be used to define locality and be mapped to cores and memory that are close to each other.

4.2   Error Model

In *OpenSHMEM-NG*, error reporting will be an important aspect. As the complexity of the hardware and programming environment increases, it becomes increasingly important to be able to identify errors and provide meaningful information to the programmer. This also paves the path towards fault tolerance and resilience. Other than programming errors there exist a plethora of error conditions related to memory, network, and communication failures. Extending the *OpenSHMEM* API with error handlers and defined error states will enable proper error handling on the application level.

4.3   OpenSHMEM I/O

The *OpenSHMEM* I/O extensions will be aimed at providing interfaces with parallel I/O capabilities for *OpenSHMEM* applications. The interfaces will be geared towards facilitating and co-ordinating concurrent I/O access among the *OpenSHMEM* PEs, and abstracting the semantics provided by parallel file systems to match the needs of applications.

5   Related Work

Process groups is a concept that has been around in programming models such as MPI. It has also been proposed as an extension to existing PGAS languages such as CAF 2.0 and Titanium. The concept of *locales* in Chapel and *places* in X10 is tied to process affinity and locality, where the programmer can map computations or data to specific *locales* or *places*. The concept of groups has been used to define communication contexts that can be used in coupled applications that perform communication and computation in subsets and independently from each other, such as an application and library using the same communication library independently of each other.

Co-array Fortran 2.0 introduced the concept of teams [11], ordered sequences of process images that represent a subset of an existing team. All process images start as members of a global team known as team_world. New teams can be created from existing teams by splitting based on a common "color" or merging two teams to produce the union of them. Additionally, a topology can also be applied to a team to abstract the layout and access patterns of the processes involved in an operation. Titanium also uses a similar concept where teams of threads are defined as objects that have methods to split into sub teams.

Similarly, communicators in MPI are arbitrary sets of processes used for performing communication on them selectively as independent functional units. Initially, all processes are part of a single global communicator, after which sub-communicators may be created from it either by splitting or by specifying a subset of parent processes to either include or exclude [12]. While this approach can provide a lot of flexibility, the communicator creation process imposes implicit synchronization, which might be undesirable for other programming models.

The incremental change to *OpenSHMEM* Specification 1.0 will include explicit handles to active sets. At this juncture, however, there is no communication context associated with it. This is due to the desired separation between active set definitions and memory spaces and handling, as described in Section 3.2.1. For *OpenSHMEM-NG*, having a concept similar to communicators in MPI with isolated communication contexts may be useful.

CAF 2.0 incorporated asynchronous point-to-point and collective operations [13] and detailed the benefits that such operations could provide by providing a higher degree of communication to computation overlap. Hiding the latency of communication has been employed in other places before CAF 2.0. For example, MPI showed that adding non-blocking collectives to MPI-2 allowed them to provide a 99% overlap between communication and computation along with an approximate performance gain between 13 to 15% (depending on the underlying network) for the 3D-FFT application [14]. Even before that, asynchronous collective operations like broadcast in MPI [15] [16] and barrier [17] have been studied to enable hiding of communication latency and barrier duration of barrier regions. Other PGAS languages like X10 support asynchronous activities via the *async* statement, and use *phaser accumulators* for increasing communication-computation overlap for reduction operations [18]. Both UPC [19] and MPI have varying degrees of support for a global exit of all threads and processes respectively. This allows for the executing process elements to do a collective exit when some explicit execution requirement is not met (*abort*) or do a clean exit at the end of the program (release resources and do other sanity checks). The obvious benefit of these concepts has prompted these proposed extensions to *OpenSHMEM* 1.0.

6 Conclusions

In this paper, we described a series of extensions to the *OpenSHMEM* API that strive to maintain backward compatibility with the current *OpenSHMEM* API, and aim to improve programmer productivity as well as the performance and scalability of *OpenSHMEM* applications. The extensions include 1) Explicit active sets 2) Non-blocking operations 3) Library shutdown, and 4) Multi-threading support.

We made a case for a series of extensions that is far-reaching and geared more towards the needs of exascale era applications and hardware. The extensions in this category include 1) Isolation 2) Locality 3) Error model, and 4) Parallel I/O.

Acknowledgments. This work is supported by the United States Department of Defense and used resources of the Extreme Scale Systems Center located at the Oak Ridge National Laboratory.

References

1. OpenSHMEM Org.: OpenSHMEM specification (2011)
2. Chapman, B., Curtis, T., Pophale, S., Poole, S., Kuehn, J., Koelbel, C., Smith, L.: Introducing OpenSHMEM: SHMEM for the PGAS community. In: Proceedings of the Fourth Conference on Partitioned Global Address Space Programming Model, PGAS 2010, New York, NY, USA (2010)
3. Poole, S.W., Hernandez, O., Kuehn, J.A., Shipman, G.M., Curtis, A., Feind, K.: OpenSHMEM - Toward a Unified RMA Model. In: Encyclopedia of Parallel Computing, pp. 1379–1391 (2011)
4. Pophale, S., Nanjegowda, R., Curtis, T., Chapman, B., Jin, H., Poole, S., Kuehn, J.: Openshmem performance and potential: A npb experimental study (2012)
5. Pophale, S.S.: SRC: OpenSHMEM library development. In: Lowenthal, D.K., de Supinski, B.R., McKee, S.A. (eds.) ICS, p. 374. ACM (2011)
6. Shamis, P., Venkata, M.G., Kuehn, J.A., Poole, S.W., Graham, R.L.: Universal common communication substrate (uccs) specification. version 0.1. Tech Report ORNL/TM-2012/339, Oak Ridge National Laboratory, ORNL (2012)
7. Graham, R.L., Shamis, P., Kuehn, J.A., Poole, S.W.: Communication middleware overview. Tech Report ORNL/TM-2012/120, Oak Ridge National Laboratory, ORNL (2012)
8. Lawry, W., Wilson, C., Maccabe, A.B., Brightwell, R.: Comb: A portable benchmark suite for assessing mpi overlap. In: IEEE Cluster, pp. 23–26 (2002)
9. Quadrics Supercomputers World Ltd.: SHMEM Programming Manual (2001)

10. CRAY: Thread-safe shmem extensions (2012)
11. Mellor-Crummey, J., Adhianto, L., Scherer III, W.N., Jin, G.: A new vision for coarray fortran. In: Proceedings of the Third Conference on Partitioned Global Address Space Programing Models, PGAS 2009, pp. 5:1–5:9. ACM, New York (2009)
12. Walker, D.W., Dongarra, J.J.: Mpi: A standard message passing interface. Supercomputer 12, 56–68 (1996)
13. Scherer III, W.N., Adhianto, L., Jin, G., Mellor-Crummey, J., Yang, C.: Hiding latency in coarray fortran 2.0. In: Proceedings of the Fourth Conference on Partitioned Global Address Space Programming Model, PGAS 2010, pp. 14:1–14:9. ACM, New York (2010)
14. Hoefler, T., Kambadur, P., Graham, R.L., Shipman, G., Lumsdaine, A.: A case for standard non-blocking collective operations. In: Cappello, F., Herault, T., Dongarra, J. (eds.) EuroPVM/MPI 2007. LNCS, vol. 4757, pp. 125–134. Springer, Heidelberg (2007)
15. Almási, G., Heidelberger, P., Archer, C.J., Martorell, X., Erway, C.C., Moreira, J.E., Steinmacher-Burow, B., Zheng, Y.: Optimization of mpi collective communication on bluegene/l systems. In: Proceedings of the 19th Annual International Conference on Supercomputing, ICS 2005, pp. 253–262. ACM, New York (2005)
16. Cachin, C., Kursawe, K., Petzold, F., Shoup, V.: Secure and efficient asynchronous broadcast protocols. In: Kilian, J. (ed.) CRYPTO 2001. LNCS, vol. 2139, pp. 524–541. Springer, Heidelberg (2001)
17. Gupta, R.: The fuzzy barrier: a mechanism for high speed synchronization of processors. In: Proceedings of the Third International Conference on Architectural Support for Programming Languages and Operating Systems, ASPLOS III, pp. 54–63. ACM, New York (1989)
18. Shirako, J., Peixotto, D.M., Sarkar, V., Scherer, W.: Phaser accumulators: A new reduction construct for dynamic parallelism. In: IEEE International Symposium on Parallel Distributed Processing, IPDPS 2009, pp. 1–12 (2009)
19. UPC Consortium: Upc language specifications, v1.2. Tech Report LBNL-59208, Lawrence Berkeley National Lab (2005)

Reducing Synchronization Overhead Through Bundled Communication

James Dinan, Clement Cole, Gabriele Jost, Stan Smith, Keith Underwood, and Robert W. Wisniewski

Intel Corp.
{james.dinan,clement.t.cole,gabriele.jost,stan.smith,
keith.d.underwood,robert.w.wisniewski}@intel.com

Abstract. OpenSHMEM provides a one-sided communication interface that allows for asynchronous, one-sided communication operations on data stored in a partitioned global address space. While communication in this model is efficient, synchronizations must currently be achieved through collective barriers or one-sided updates of sentinel locations in the global address space. These synchronization mechanisms can over-synchronize, or require additional communication operations, respectively, leading to high overheads. We propose a SHMEM extension that utilizes capabilities present in most high performance interconnects (e.g. communication events) to bundle synchronization information together with communication operations. Using this approach, we improve ping-pong latency for small messages by a factor of two, and demonstrate significant improvement to synchronization-heavy communication patterns, including all-to-all and pipelined parallel stencil communication.

SHMEM is a popular partitioned global address space (PGAS) parallel programming model, and it has been in use for over two decades [4]. Recently, the SHMEM library has been codified as an open, community standard in the OpenSHMEM 1.0 specification [19]. SHMEM provides a global address space that spans the memory of the system and allows the programmer to create symmetric objects, which are present at all processing elements (PEs). These objects can be read and updated using one-sided get and put operations.

While SHMEM provides high-performance one-sided data movement operations, it includes few primitives for synchronizing between PEs. In the current Open SHMEM standard, synchronization can be achieved using a collective barrier, or by polling or waiting on a flag that will be remotely updated using a one-sided operation. While these synchronization primitives are sufficient for achieving point-to-point and global synchronization, they are not able to fully utilize capabilities provided by modern high performance interconnects. In particular, barrier synchronization can generate more synchronization than is needed by the algorithm, and its performance can be negatively impacted by system noise and imbalance. In addition, point-to-point synchronization using counting or boolean flag locations in the global address space requires additional communication when updating the flag.

S. Poole, O. Hernandez, and P. Shamis (Eds.): OpenSHMEM 2014, LNCS 8356, pp. 163–177, 2014.

Modern networks used in high performance computing systems provide a variety of mechanisms that can be used to bundle synchronization and communication. One such example is communication events, which notify the recipient that a one-sided communication operation has arrived and is complete.

We present a new synchronization extension to OpenSHMEM, called counting puts, that utilizes network-level events to provide efficient point-to-point synchronization. Counting puts can utilize communication completion events to inform a PE that it has been the target of a one-sided communication operation, and that the data written is available to read. Counting puts effectively enables receiver-side synchronization. In contrast, existing point-to-point synchronization in SHMEM is sender-side, and requires additional communication to update flag locations at the target PE.

We describe the counting puts interface and its implementation in an open source SHMEM implementation for the low-level Portals networking API [6]. We demonstrate that bundling communication for a Portals network reduces communication latency by half for small messages, and that it significantly improves the bandwidth achieved to the synchronization-heavy all-to-all communication algorithm. We further demonstrate the performance impact of counting puts on a pipelined parallel stencil computation, that relies heavily on point-to-point synchronization. While our evaluation focuses on a Portals implementation, we describe several methods for creating efficient receiver-side implementations of counting puts that can achieve the demonstrated performance improvements on a variety of networks.

1   Overview

The SHMEM parallel programming model provides a global address space, shown in Figure 1, where the memory of each processing element (PE), or SHMEM process, is partitioned into private and shared segments. Data in the private segment is accessible locally, while data in the shared segment is accessible both locally and remotely, through SHMEM library routines. The shared segment contains both a shared heap, for dynamically allocated shared objects, and a shared data segment, which allows statically declared objects to be accessed by remote PEs.

Objects in a shared segment are symmetric, meaning that an instance of the object is accessible at every PE, and that the object can be accessed using the address of the corresponding symmetric object in the local PE's address space. Thus, when accessing data in the global address space, the target address is the pair containing the destination PE rank and the symmetric address. Remote accesses are performed using one-sided *get* and *put* data copy operations, that transfer data between local and remote buffers. In addition SHMEM provides a variety of collective and atomic, one-sided communication routines.

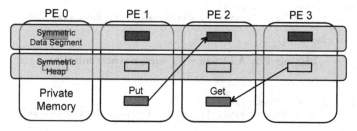

Fig. 1. SHMEM communication model, showing shared and private memory areas, and one-sided get and put communication operations

1.1 Portals

In this work, we demonstrate the counting puts interface using the open source OpenSHMEM implementation for the low-level Portals networking API [1,5]. The Portals interface exposes sections of a process' address space for one-sided remote access using read, write, and atomic operations. Accesses to exposed memory regions can be guarded through matching criteria that are used when implementing matched, or two-sided, communication operations. For one-sided communication, a non-matching interface is provided that allows all operations targeting the process to access the given memory region.

The ordering of operations is an important component in synchronization for one-sided communication models. Portals presents the programmer with an unordered network model, where data is not guaranteed to arrive at the target in the order in which it was sent. This delivery model enables dynamic message routing, and also ensures reliable delivery. As data arrives at the target, acknowledgement messages are returned to the sender. Thus, when a process waits for communication operations to complete, it waits for acknowledgement messages from the target.

1.2 Synchronization in OpenSHMEM

The OpenSHMEM standard provides both collective and point-to-point synchronization primitives. SHMEM barriers are collective synchronization operations that can include all PEs, or a regular subset that includes PEs whose ranks are a multiple of a power of two. In addition to synchronizing the involved PEs, before returning, SHMEM barriers also ensure that all preceding writes to symmetric objects have completed.

Point-to-point synchronization is achieved through symmetric flag variables that are acted upon using one-sided operations. These flags can be updated using one-sided writes, when a single PE updates the flag, or atomic operations, when multiple PEs update the flag. A PE can wait for the value of the flag to satisfy a certain condition by using one of the waiting routines provided in the OpenSHMEM API. In addition, some applications also poll flag locations directly, which can require the use of additional system-specific memory fences to ensure data consistency.

```
1  for (pe = 0; pe < NPES; pe++)
       shmem_putmem(&data_recv[pe], &data_send[pe], data_size, pe);
3
   shmem_barrier_all();
```

Listing 1.1. All-to-all with barrier synchronization

```
   for (pe = 0; pe < NPES; pe++)
2      shmem_putmem(&data_recv[pe], &data_send[pe], data_size, pe);

4  shmem_fence();

6  for (pe = 0; pe < NPES; pe++)
       shmem_int_add(&flag, -1, pe);
8
   shmem_int_wait_until(&flag, SHMEM_CMP_EQ, 0);
```

Listing 1.2. All-to-all with point-to-point synchronization

For point-to-point synchronization, data consistency is achieved using either *fence* or *quiet* operations. A SHMEM fence operation provides ordering, by ensuring that any operations performed by the calling PE to a particular remote PE will be completed before any subsequent operations issued by the calling PE to the same remote PE. A SHMEM quiet operation provides a stronger ordering semantic, and ensures that all put operations performed by the calling PE will be remotely completed and visible to all PEs when the call to quiet returns

We illustrate these two synchronization mechanisms with a simple all-to-all communication example, similar to the type of communication that is performed in a fast Fourier transform or parallel sort. In this data exchange, each PE must wait until all data has arrived before proceeding with the next phase of the computation. Listing 1.1 shows this communication pattern when a barrier synchronization is used, and Listing 1.2 shows this communication pattern when point-to-point synchronization is used.

In comparison with barrier synchronization, point-to-point synchronization can be performed more efficiently, because a PE does not need to wait for all other PEs to receive data. However, the flag update operation requires an additional communication and, depending on the underlying network, a fence or quiet operation can require additional communication to ensure ordering or remote completion, respectively. Overhead from these operations can outweigh the benefits from relaxed synchronization. For example, on ordered networks, a fence is a no-op, but a quiet operation requires sending a round-trip message to all other PEs that the calling PE has communicated with, to flush the ordered communication channels. In comparison, on unordered networks, both fence and quiet operations require waiting for point-to-point remote completion with each other PE. In the case of a fence, the calling PE must only wait before performing additional communication operations, whereas a quiet requires waiting for communication with all other PEs to complete before returning. When using the Portals communication API, communication operations are completed by

```
1   void shmem_ct_create(shmem_ct_t *ct);
    void shmem_ct_free(shmem_ct_t *ct);
3   long shmem_ct_get(shmem_ct_t ct);
    void shmem_ct_set(shmem_ct_t ct, long value);
5   void shmem_ct_wait(shmem_ct_t ct, long wait_for);
    void shmem_putmem_ct(shmem_ct_t ct, void *trg, void *src, size_t bytes, int pe);
```

Listing 1.3. Counting puts API extension

waiting for acknowledgement messages to be returned from the target PE to the source PE for each operation.

2   Bundling Communication and Synchronization

We propose an extension to OpenSHMEM that bundles communication and synchronization. A variety of bundled communication interfaces are possible, based on the operations that will be bundled and the interface that will be used to access notification information. For example, the ARMCI one-sided communication library [18] provides the ARMCI_Put_flag operation that bundles two put operations, where a notification flag in the target process' address space is updated after the main data payload has been delivered. While it is easy to use, this interface requires distinct flags for each PE that will perform a put-and-notify operation. For all-to-all communication, this can result in $O(\text{NPEs})$ flags at every PE.

Our proposed interface is shown in Listing 1.3. This interface bundles an atomic increment operation with the communication operation, allowing the flag to be shared by multiple communicate-and-notify operations. We use an opaque shmem_ct_t representation for the counter, to enable a broader variety of efficient implementations. When network events are used to signal completions, the SHMEM implementation or networking layer can locally increment the counter as operations are performed, rather than requiring the remote PE to perform the update. Our discussion of this interface focuses on providing support for a put-and-notify operation; however, the proposed interface and implementation can also be utilized to provide a get-and-notify operation to support producer-consumer computational patterns.

The proposed interface provides functions that can be used to create and free an event counter (CT); get and set the counter's value; and wait for the counter to reach a particular value [20]. New communication functions are also provided that add a CT parameter that should be updated when the operation has completed. An example all-to-all communication using the new interface is shown in Listing 1.4. In comparison with Listing 1.1, this example achieves point-to-point synchronization, and in comparison with Listing 1.2, this example can eliminate overheads associated with the fence operation and flag updates.

```
  shmem_ct_create(&ct);
2
  for (pe = 0; pe < NPES; pe++)
4     shmem_putmem_ct(ct, &data_recv[pe], &data_send[pe], data_size, pe);

6 shmem_ct_wait(ct, NPES);
```

Listing 1.4. All-to-all with counting puts synchronization

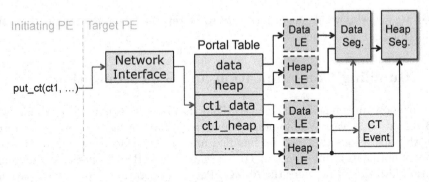

Fig. 2. Portals implementation of the counting puts interface

2.1   Implementation of the Counting Puts Interface

A variety of implementation strategies are possible for the counting puts interface; we chose an opaque representation of the CT object to provide more flexibility in the implementation. For example, in addition to enabling implementations that use low-level network counting events, the opaque CT object enables an implementation on top of the existing SHMEM interface. In such an implementation, a symmetric counter location is allocated at each PE during CT creation, and counted put operations perform a put, fence, and atomic increment using the functions provided in the SHMEM API.

Most networks provide mechanisms that can be utilized to implement these operations more efficiently by bundling communication and synchronization. On networks that are programmable, or on-load communication to the processor (e.g. sockets or PSM), CT information can be embedded in message headers enabling a receiver-side implementation to perform bookkeeping. Many networks report low-level communication events when one-sided operations complete in a given PE's memory. As these events are consumed in the SHMEM runtime system, the corresponding counter can be incremented.

We implement the CT interface in the open source Portals 4 [6] implementation of SHMEM [5]. We utilize Portals 4 counting communication events to achieve an efficient receiver-side implementation of counting puts. A high-level schematic of our implementation is shown in Figure 2. This example shows the Portals objects that are components in the implementation of the CT interface, and the flow of control when processing a counted put operation.

As shown in Figure 2 our implementation utilizes Portals lightweight counting events, that are incremented when each counted operation is completed at the target PE. Full events utilizing an event queue that can be attached to each portal table entry (not shown in Figure 2, for clarity) can also be used, resulting in an implementation similar to one that uses InfiniBand event queues. In such an implementation, CT query and wait routines would need to search this queue for operations affecting the counter. Counting events provide a more efficient implementation vehicle, as they use a fixed amount of memory and do not incur queue processing overheads.

Individual event counters are distinguished using distinct portal table entries that act as separate communication contexts. Communication operations in Portals specify the target network interface, portal table entry, and offset relative to the beginning of the memory portal. When the system can provide identical segment base addresses, a single portal table entry can be used to expose memory for one-sided access. On most clusters, separate portal table entries must be created for the static data and dynamic heap segments, because these segments can be disjoint in memory and located at different starting addresses across PEs. Prior to performing communication, the corresponding portal table entry is identified by comparing the symmetric address with the local addresses of the heap and data segments. The symmetric address is then converted to an offset relative to the beginning of the corresponding memory segment, and the offset and portal table entry are passed to the desired communication routine. Distinct heap and data segment portal table entries are created for each counter, allowing the implementation to identify which counter should be incremented when a counted put arrives. Non-matching list entries that describe the complete heap and data memory segments are attached to the respective portal table entries, and a counting event is registered with each list entry.

We note that the proposed interface does not guarantee any ordering or consistency beyond the completion of the counted communication operation. This targeted completion rule allows for greater concurrency and performance potential. Thus, we do not enforce any additional ordering in our implementation. If the algorithm requires ordering of non-counted operations, or ordering across different counted operations targeting the same PE, existing OpenSHMEM synchronization operations must be used.

3   Experimental Evaluation

We extended the Portals OpenSHMEM implementation [5] with the counting puts interface, and utilize the Portals 4 InfiniBand reference implementation [2] to provide Portals support. While this is not a native implementation of the Portals interface, it utilizes InfiniBand network events to implement Portals counting events, which allows us to demonstrate the relative performance improvement of the receiver-side counting puts protocol. This protocol eliminates additional messages that are generated when synchronizing through shared flag variables.

We utilize a 15-node cluster with a Mellanox QDR InfiniBand interconnect for experimentation. Each node in this cluster is configured with 24GB of memory and two Intel Xeon X5680 processors, for a total of 12 cores per node, each supporting two hyperthreads, for a total of 24 hardware threads per node. We demonstrate the impact of the proposed CT interface on communication efficiency using ping-pong and all-to-all microbenchmarks. In addition, we demonstrate significant performance improvement for a pipelined parallel stencil computation, that relies heavily on point-to-point synchronization.

3.1 Ping-Pong Latency

We measured ping-pong latency using a simple benchmark with two PEs. In each iteration of the benchmark, one PE is the sender and one is the receiver. After each iteration, sender and receiver roles are reversed. For the baseline implementation using the operations available in the current OpenSHMEM specification, the sender performs the following sequence of operations.

```
shmem_putmem(rcv_buf, snd_buf, msg_length, target);
shmem_fence();
shmem_int_inc(&flag, target);
```

The receiver performs the following sequence of operations.

```
shmem_int_wait(&flag, 0);
flag = 0;
```

For the CT implementation of the benchmark, the sender performs the following operation.

```
shmem_putmem_ct(ct, rcv_buf, snd_buf, msg_length, target);
```

The receiver performs the following sequence of operations.

```
shmem_ct_wait(ct, 1);
shmem_ct_set(ct, 0);
```

The half round-trip latency is shown in Figure 3 for baseline and CT implementations. From this data, we see that the latency is approximately halved for small messages. For larger message sizes, the cost associated with the fence and flag update operations is amortized over a larger message transfer and results in a decreasing speedup from the CT extension.

3.2 All-to-All Bandwidth

We measure the bandwidth achieved using a simple all-to-all communication benchmark, where every PE sends a message to every other PE and waits for messages to arrive. For the baseline version of this benchmark, each PE performs the sequence of operations shown in Listing 1.5. For the CT version of the benchmark, the fence is omitted, and flags are replaced with a CT object, using the same approach as in the ping-pong algorithm. For the CT and flags versions of the benchmark, a pair of synchronization constructs is created and alternated across loop iterations to eliminate the race that arises in resetting the value of the counter or flag. In addition, a barrier synchronization version was created that replaces the fence and all flag operations with a single call to

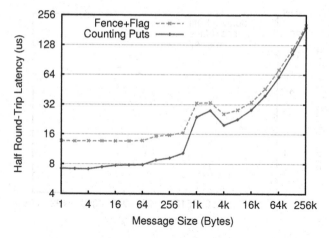

Fig. 3. Half round-trip latency for the ping-pong benchmark on the InfiniBand cluster

```
   /* Initially, flag = num_pes */
2
   pe = me;
4  do {
         shmem_putmem(&target_buf[me], &src_buf[pe], msg_size, pe);
6        pe = (pe + 1) % num_pes;
   } while (pe != me);
8
   shmem_fence();
10
   pe = me;
12 do {
         shmem_int_add(&flag, -1, pe);
14       pe = (pe + 1) % num_pes;
   } while (pe != me);
16
   shmem_int_wait_until(&flag, SHMEM_CMP_EQ, 0);
```

Listing 1.5. Baseline implementation of the all-to-all communication benchmark

shmem_barrier_all(), which synchronizes all processes and ensures that all communication has been completed. Communication operations are staggered across PEs to spread out communication. While more sophisticated algorithms for all-to-all exist [10,21], this algorithm captures the approach that would be taken in a loosely synchronized or pipelined application.

The bandwidth achieved per node, when one PE is run per core, for each version of the all-to-all benchmark is shown in Figure 4. The barrier implementation achieves the lowest bandwidth because of the overhead from global synchronization. The fence implementation provides increased network efficiency, but incurs overhead from $O(\text{NPEs})$ additional communications per PE that are required to update the flag variables. By eliminating these operations, the CT version of the benchmark provides the best performance. As was the case with ping-pong latency,

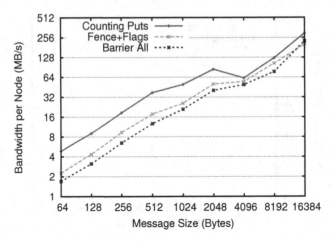

Fig. 4. All-to-all bandwidth achieved per node on the InfiniBand cluster

the cost of the additional synchronization communications is amortized over long transfer times, and the relative impact of increased communication is reduced.

The bandwidth we report in Figure 4 is significantly lower than the theoretical peak of 40 Gb/sec for our QDR InfiniBand network. This is caused by overhead incurred in simulating Portals communication on top of InfiniBand. However, these results still capture the performance improvement from eliminating additional messages needed to update flag locations at every PE.

3.3   Pipelined Parallel Stencil Kernel

Next, we investigate the performance impact of counting puts on a fine-grain pipelined parallel stencil computation. This type of computation has strong data dependencies across units of work, requiring frequent point-to-point synchronization. Pipelined parallel stencils are encountered in a variety of numerical methods, including the Lower-Upper Symmetric Gauss-Seidel (LU) NAS Parallel Benchmark [23] and wavefront-parallel algorithms. We utilize the Synch_p2p kernel, provided in the Intel Parallel Research Kernels (PRK) [16] to investigate the performance impact on this class of algorithms. The PRK suite consists of a set of common low level operations, and it has recently been released as open source [16]. PRK provides serial, OpenMP, and MPI implementations; for the purpose of this study we ported the MPI version of the Synch_p2p kernel to the OpenSHMEM programming model.

Synch_p2p implements a one-dimensional software pipeline. A two-dimensional array A of size $n \times m$ is distributed in vertical strips among the PEs. The matrix elements are updated through the stencil operation, $A(i,j) = A(i-1,j) + A(i,j-1) - A(i-1,j-1)$. This operation carries dependences in each of the spatial dimensions and is, therefore, not parallelizable in a straightforward manner. Parallelism is achieved by setting up pipelined execution. The first PE computes one partial

```
1   /* Let vector be an array that holds the grid values. */
    /* We define the ARRAY macro to simplify indexing with halo elements. */
3   #define ARRAY(i, j) vector[i+1 + (j)*(segment_size+1)]

5   for (j = 1; j < n; j++) {
        /* I am not at the left boundary; wait for my left neighbor to send data */
7       if (PE > 0) {
            shmem_ct_wait(ct, j);
9           ARRAY(start[PE]-1, j) = dst[j];
        }

11

        for (i = start[PE]; i <= end[PE]; i++) {
13          ARRAY(i, j) = ARRAY(i-1, j) + ARRAY(i, j-1) - ARRAY(i-1, j-1);
        }

15

        /* I am not on the right boundary; send data to my right neighbor */
17      if (PE != NPES-1) {
            src[j] = ARRAY(end[PE], j);
19          shmem_putmem_ct(ct, &dst[j], &src[j], 1 * sizeof(double), PE+1);
    }
```

Listing 1.6. Pipelined parallel stencil kernel, using counting puts for point-to-point synchronization

row (fixed j) of updated elements. It then synchronizes with its right neighbor and proceeds to the second row. The neighboring process can now start with the update of its segment of the first row. Once the pipeline is filled, all PEs will be working in parallel. A code listing of the kernel using counting puts is shown in Listing 1.6.

In Figure 5, we show results from a strong scaling experiment, comparing the counting puts implementation with an implementation that uses explicit flags. For this experiment, we use a fixed matrix size of 12800×1280 and utilize 4 PEs per node to reduce noise generate by per-PE communication helper threads created by the Portals-on-InfiniBand runtime system. Threads are also pinned to cores to further reduce system noise. Results are reported in terms of the giga-FLOPs (floating point operations) per second achieved by the benchmark.

The total number of synchronizations required for each iteration of the Sync_p2p kernel increases with an increasing number of PEs while the computational work between synchronization points decreases. Because of this, synchronization cost is a significant factor in performance. From the results in Figure 5, we can see that the cost of synchronization when explicit flags are used is high, resulting in poor scaling. Counting puts eliminate the overhead of synchronization, significantly improving the parallel efficiency.

3.4   Impact of Problem Size on Performance Improvement

We now consider a fixed number of PEs and report the performance when the problem size is varied. To vary the problem size, we fix the length of the m dimension and vary the length of the n dimension. Figure 6 compares the performance for each problem size when counting puts and explicit flags are used. Experiments were run on 48 PEs, with 4 PEs per node. We note that the performance difference between the two implementations decreases with an increase in problem size. This is expected, as the number of synchronizations required per iteration depends only on the length of the second dimension. It is therefore the same for all sizes under consideration. The computational workload,

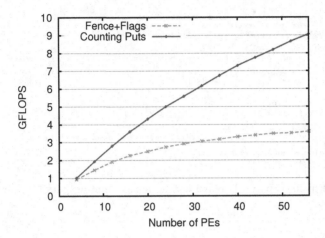

Fig. 5. Synch_p2p performance in GFLOPs/sec, for a strong scaling experiment with problem size of 12800×1280 and 4 PEs per node

however, increases, reducing the impact of synchronization cost. We note that the granularity of the algorithm could be increased by grouping rows together.

4 Related Work

Unified Parallel C (UPC) [22] is another PGAS parallel programming model, that provides capabilities similar to SHMEM. The current UPC language provides similar synchronization routines as SHMEM, with the addition of split-phase barriers and locks. A proposal to extend UPC with semaphores has been presented [9]. Semaphores would add a similar signaling capability to UPC put operations, and the authors demonstrated significant performance improvements across several platforms. An implementation of this extension is provided with Berkeley UPC [7]. UPC semaphores are implemented using carefully optimized active message and one-sided operations. The implementation approach we have presented utilizes receiver-side communication events to further reduce synchronization overheads.

Split-C [12] also provided signaling store operation through the :- assignment operation. A process that is the target of a signaling store operation can wait for a programmer defined number of bytes to arrive, but cannot distinguish among different update operations. Both the SHMEM counting puts and UPC semaphore extension allow this distinction by providing distinct synchronization objects. The Tera MTA [3], Cray XMT [14], and the Chapel programming language [11] also provide signaling store operations through full/empty bits that are associated with each word in memory, in the case of the MTA and XMT architectures, and distinct objects in the case of Chapel.

The ARMCI [18] one-sided communication library also provides a put-with-flag operation, that bundles a flag variable update with data movement.

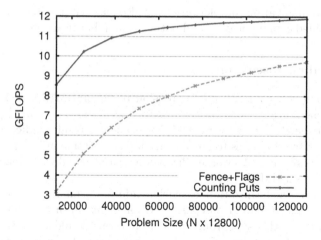

Fig. 6. Synch_p2p performance for various problem sizes with increasing first dimension N on 48 PEs, 4 PEs per node

Similarly, the GASPI [15] PGAS library provides a write-and-notify operation, that bundles an event notification with data movement. In both cases, the notification is performed by a write, rather than an atomic update. Thus, for algorithms that require many synchronizations, many flag and event variables would be needed. Depending on the number of variables needed, checking for completion can become costly and has the potential to negatively impact application data residency in the processor cache.

The Message Passing Interface (MPI) [17] provides both one-sided and two-sided messaging. Two-sided messaging effectively couples synchronization and data movement, since both sender and receiver participate in the communication operation. By bundling these two operations, two-sided messaging does not require additional operations for synchronization. However, in comparison with one-sided messaging, two-sided messaging incurs additional protocol overheads from the matching of send and receive operations. In addition, if the sender performs its send operation before the receiver performs its receive operation, the MPI library must buffer the unexpected message or delay data transmission. In contrast, PGAS programming models do not require message matching, buffering, or rendezvous protocols because remotely accessible memory in the global address space is necessarily posted before communication can occur and the sending process determines all communication parameters.

Active messages [8,13] provide a general-purpose mechanism for asynchronous operations that access memory at the target process. One-sided communication, can be implemented using active messages [8], and such an implementation can also notify the target process that the operation has been performed. Hardware support for RDMA has made it possible to implement one-sided operations directly in hardware without a target-side software agent. In this paper, we observe that hardware support for communication completion events also makes it possible to implement bundled one-sided communication and notification in hardware efficiently.

4.1 Concluding Discussion

We have presented a counting puts extension to OpenSHMEM, and discussed efficient implementations on a variety of networks, focusing on an implementation on top of the Portals network API. Experimental results indicate that the counting puts extension maps to an efficient implementation in Portals, and that it can offer a significant reduction in the overhead associated with point-to-point synchronization in SHMEM.

The proposed synchronization extension addresses an important need for SHMEM users, and it should be considered for inclusion in the OpenSHMEM standard. However, other synchronization mechanisms should also be considered, to provide a more flexible and efficient interface to users. Overlapping communication and computation is an important performance optimization, that can be used to hide communication costs. Counting puts can enable the user to achieve this overlap by periodically polling for data arrival. For some algorithms, global synchronization is needed. Non-blocking global synchronization is an increasingly popular primitive that is provided by several popular parallel programming models, including UPC [22] and MPI 3.0 [17]. The addition of a non-blocking, or split-phase barrier primitive could also help to address the synchronization needs of such applications.

Acknowledgements. We thank Tim Mattson and Rob van der Wijngaart of Intel Coporation, who developed the Parallel Research Kernels benchmark suite, and assisted us in porting the Sync_p2p benchmark to SHMEM.

References

1. OpenSHMEM implementation using portals 4. Website, http://code.google.com/p/portals-shmem/
2. Portals 4 open source implementation for InfiniBand. Website, http://code.google.com/p/portals4/
3. Alverson, R., Callahan, D., Cummings, D., Koblenz, B., Porterfield, A., Smith, B.: The Tera computer system. In: Proc. ACM Intl. Conf. on Supercomputing, ICS (June 1990)
4. Bariuso, R., Knies, A.: SHMEM user's guide. Tech. Rep. SN-2516, Cray Research, Inc. (1994)
5. Barrett, B.W., Brightwell, R., Hemmert, K.S., Pedretti, K.T., Wheeler, K.B., Underwood, K.D.: Enhanced support for OpenSHMEM communication in Portals. In: Hot Interconnects, pp. 61–69. IEEE (2011)
6. Barrett, B.W., Brightwell, R., Hemmert, S., Pedretti, K., Wheeler, K., Underwood, K., Riesen, R., Maccabe, A.B., Hudson, T.: The portals 4.0.1 network programming interface. Tech. Rep. SAND2013-3181, Sandia National Laboratories (April 2013)

7. Berkeley UPC: Berkeley UPC user's guide version 2.16.0. Tech. rep., U.C. Berkeley and LBNL (2013)

8. Bonachea, D.: GASNet specification, v1.1. Tech. Rep. UCB/CSD-02-1207, U.C. Berkeley (2002)

9. Bonachea, D., Nishtala, R., Hargrove, P., Yelick, K.: Efficient point-to-point synchronization in UPC. In: 2nd Conf. on Partitioned Global Address Space Programming Models, PGAS 2006 (October 2006)

10. Bruck, J., Ho, C.T., Upfal, E., Kipnis, S., Weathersby, D.: Efficient algorithms for all-to-all communications in multiport message-passing systems. IEEE Trans. Parallel Distrib. Syst. 8(11), 1143–1156 (1997)

11. Chamberlain, B., Callahan, D., Zima, H.: Parallel programmability and the Chapel language. Intl. J. High Performance Computing Applications (IJHPCA) 21(3), 291–312 (2007)

12. Culler, D., Dusseau, A., Goldstein, S., Krishnamurthy, A., Lumetta, S., von Eicken, T., Yelick, K.: Parallel programming in Split-C. In: Proc., Supercomputing 1993, pp. 262–273 (1993)

13. von Eicken, T., Culler, D.E., Goldstein, S.C., Schauser, K.E.: Active messages: a mechanism for integrated communication and computation. In: Proc. 19th Intl. Symp. on Computer Architecture, ISCA 1992, pp. 256–266 (1992)

14. Feo, J., Harper, D., Kahan, S., Konecny, P.: ELDORADO. In: Proc. 2nd Conf. on Computing Frontiers, CF 2005 (2005)

15. GASPI Consortium: GASPI: Global address space programming interface specification of a PGAS API for communication. Version 1.00 (June 2013)

16. Mattson, T., van der Wijngaart, R.: Parallel research kernels. Website (2013), https://github.com/ParRes/Kernels

17. MPI Forum: MPI: A message-passing interface standard version 3.0. Tech. rep., University of Tennessee, Knoxville (September 2012)

18. Nieplocha, J., Carpenter, B.: ARMCI: A portable remote memory copy library for distributed array libraries and compiler run-time systems. In: Rolim, J., et al. (eds.) IPPS-WS 1999 and SPDP-WS 1999. LNCS, vol. 1586, pp. 533–546. Springer, Heidelberg (1999)

19. OpenSHMEM Consortium: OpenSHMEM application programming interface, version 1.0 (January 2012)

20. Reed, D., Kanodia, R.: Synchronization with event counts and sequences. Communications of the ACM 22(2), 115–123 (1979)

21. Thakur, R., Rabenseifner, R., Gropp, W.: Optimization of collective communication operations in MPICH. International Journal of High Performance Computing Applications (IJHPCA) 19(1), 49–66 (2005)

22. UPC Consortium: UPC language specifications, v1.2. Tech. Rep. LBNL-59208, Lawrence Berkeley National Lab (2005)

23. Yarrow, M., van der Wijngaart, R.: Communication improvement for the LU NAS parallel benchmark: A model for efficient parallel relaxation schemes. Tech. Rep. NAS-97-032, NASA Ames Research Center (1997)

Thread-Safe SHMEM Extensions

Monika ten Bruggencate, Duncan Roweth, and Steve Oyanagi

Cray Inc.

Abstract. This paper is intended to serve as a proposal for thread safety extensions to the OpenSHMEM specification and at the same time describes planned support for thread-safety for Cray SHMEM on Cray XE and XC systems.

1 Introduction

The original impetus for implementing thread-safe Cray SHMEM and proposing thread safety extensions to OpenSHMEM were requests from SHMEM customers for thread safety support. Subsequent discussions with some SHMEM customers and review of the MPI specification [1] led to the proposal detailed in this paper. The paper describes basic thread safety support for Cray SHMEM. The thread safety support is basic in that it imposes policies on SHMEM applications and contains minimal extensions to the Cray SHMEM and OpenSHMEM APIs. However, it does enable processes to issue small Puts, small Gets, and AMOs at higher aggregate rates than is possible in a single-threaded environment, which can lead to better performance for certain multi-threaded applications. As much as possible, this proposal was guided by the thread safety extensions to the MPI standard and by customer input, in an effort to facilitate acceptance by the OpenSHMEM community. Note that what is known in a single-threaded environment as a processing element (PE) or rank corresponds to a process, not a thread, in a multi-threaded environment. The remainder of the paper will discuss the proposed thread safety extensions to OpenSHMEM, including assumptions and new functions.

2 Assumptions

As mentioned above, reviewing the MPI specification and discussions with some SHMEM customers led to this proposal, including several agreed-upon assumptions.

1. Initialization and finalization routines are restricted to being called by one thread per process. A new initialization routine, `shmem_init_thread()`, enables the user to specify that support for thread safety is desired.
2. Thread safety support is required for Put, Get and AMO operations so that an application with multiple threads per process can make one-sided SHMEM calls from multiple threads.

S. Poole, O. Hernandez, and P. Shamis (Eds.): OpenSHMEM 2014, LNCS 8356, pp. 178–185, 2014.

3. Not necessarily all threads make SHMEM calls. It may be that only a subset of the threads of a process make SHMEM calls.

4. The pool of threads that make SHMEM calls may be static or may be dynamic.

5. SHMEM collectives operate on sets of processes and the use of SHMEM collective calls with multiple threads per process can be problematic. For instance, in the OpenSHMEM specification 1.0 [2], in some cases collective operations are defined not only in terms of PE synchronization, but also memory consistency. The semantics of operations like shmem_barrier() would either need to be redefined for the proposed thread-safety extensions, or new SHMEM collective functions would need to be defined which would address these memory consistency issues. Either effort is beyond the scope of this initial proposal and should be coordinated with future proposals for modernizing the collective operations component of the SHMEM API. Thus, for the purpose of this paper, SHMEM collective calls are subject to the following restrictions:

   (a) A collective operation can be called from only one thread per process at a time and several threads per process cannot simultaneously participate in different collective operations.

   (b) Where an application makes SHMEM collective calls from multiple threads per process, it is the responsibility of the application to ensure that calls are made in the same order in each participating process.

6. The symmetric heap management functions shmalloc(), shfree(), and shrealloc(), and shfree() are all defined to call shmem_barrier_all() before they return and thus must be treated as collective operations.

7. The lock functions shmem_clear_lock(), shmem_set_lock(), and shmem_test_lock() are restricted such that multiple threads on the same process cannot access the same lock at the same time. Note that this restriction does permit two different threads on the same process to access two different locks at the same time.

8. Cray is proposing the thread safety extensions described in this paper to the OpenSHMEM committee for inclusion in the OpenSHMEM standard.

3 Precautions

Programmers using thread-safe SHMEM should be mindful of the following caveats.

1. It is the applications responsibility to ensure that collectives are called in the right order, no matter whether the application is single-threaded or multi-threaded. The SHMEM programming model does not recognize individual threads. Any SHMEM operation initiated by a thread is considered an action of the process as a whole. In particular, note that:

   (a) shmem_quiet() and shmem_fence() affect the entire process, not just the calling thread. While a thread is calling shmem_quiet() or shmem_fence(), no other thread should be able to make calls who's behavior is affected by shmem_quiet()/shmem_fence(). Further, a call to shmem_quiet() by one thread should affect all threads in that the call will wait for completion of all outstanding Puts and non-blocking Gets issued by the process. Similarly, a call to shmem_fence() by one thread should affect all threads.

(b) The symmetric heap is a per process resource. A thread making a shmalloc(), shrealloc(), or shfree() call affects the entire process. The existing requirement that the same symmetric heap operations must be executed by all processes in the same order also applies in a multi-threaded environment.

2. When using multiple threads and SHMEM, be mindful of the order of access and race conditions. For example, if one thread of a process is issuing Puts and another thread of the same process is calling shmem_quiet(), it is the programmer's responsibility to ensure the correct ordering of those operations.

3. Thread safety should not be activated unless needed. Activating thread safety causes additional overhead even if no additional threads are created or used.

4   SHMEM Thread Safety Extensions

Where appropriate, SHMEM thread safety extensions have been modeled after the existing MPI thread safety interface. The following naming convention applies: functions which relate to the level of thread safety activated are named shmem_ <action> _thread(). Functions which apply to a specific thread only are named shmem_thread_ <action>(). Return types of new functions are chosen to follow the OpenSHMEM model of being void or returning a result. This differs from the MPI model where functions return a success or failure code and results are passed via output parameters.

4.1   shmem_init_thread()

A new function, shmem_init_thread(), allows a user to indicate that thread safety support is desired. The function initializes SHMEM in the same way that shmem_init() or start_pes() does. In addition, it performs thread safety specific initialization. This function is used in place of shmem_init() either before additional threads are created or by only one thread per process. The thread which calls shmem_init_thread() is known as the main/primary thread. The syntax of the function is as follows:

```
int shmem_init_thread(int required, int max_num_threads)
```

Following the MPI standard, there could be four levels of threading support. Note that these levels are hierarchical. The higher levels should support any lower levels.

1. SHMEM_THREAD_SINGLE – no threading/one thread per process. SHMEM implementers can assume there is no threading.

2. SHMEM_THREAD_FUNNELED – processes may have multiple threads but only one of the threads can make SHMEM calls. (All functions are funneled through one thread.) It is the user's responsibility to make certain all SHMEM calls by a process are executed by the same thread.

   Cray does not provide support for this level. It is unclear whether this level should be included in the OpenSHMEM spec.

3. SHMEM_THREAD_SERIALIZED – processes may have multiple threads. Any thread may issue SHMEM calls, but only one SHMEM call per process can be active at any given time. Simultaneous calls from two threads belonging to the same process are not allowed. It is the user's responsibility to make certain that SHMEM calls by a process are not concurrent.

   Cray does not provide support for this level. It is unclear whether this level should be included in the OpenSHMEM spec.

4. SHMEM_THREAD_MULTIPLE – processes may have multiple threads. Any thread may issue a SHMEM call at any time, subject to the restrictions and policies described earlier.

To specify which level of threading support is desired, use the shmem_init_thread()'s required argument to pass in one of the above symbols, specifying which level of threading support is desired. The return value of the function is the level of threading support that the SHMEM library can provide. If possible, the function returns the required value. If that is not possible, the library returns the lowest threading support level that can be supported that is greater than required. If that is not possible, the function returns the highest threading support level SHMEM can provide. The user is responsible for checking the return value to make certain that the available thread-safety level is suitable for their program. All processes in a SHMEM application must request the same level of threading support.

   The input parameter max_num_threads allows a user to specify the maximum number of threads per process that will make SHMEM calls. If the maximum number is not known, a negative number (or appropriate macro) indicates that no upper limit exists. Knowing the maximum number allows lower level software to optimize use of hardware and minimize startup and teardown overhead.

   Additional input parameters may be added to shmem_init_thread() as our implementation progresses. Calls to the standard SHMEM initialization routines, shmem_init() and start_pes(), are considered to request the threading support level SHMEM_THREAD_SINGLE.

4.2 shmem_query_thread()

A new query function, shmem_query_thread(), enables SHMEM application developers to query the current level of thread safety support. When invoked, it returns the same thread safety level that was returned when shmem_init_thread() was called. The syntax is as follows:

```
int shmem_query_thread(void)
```

4.3   shmem_thread_register()

After `shmem_init_thread()` has been called by the primary thread, any other thread that wishes to make SHMEM calls must call `shmem_thread_register()` before making any other SHMEM calls. The primary thread which called `shmem_init_thread()` does not have to call `shmem_thread_register()`. Introducing a function which explicitly registers threads has several advantages.

- It allows optimized use of hardware, for instance by initializing thread safe storage to allow dedicated use of hardware components by a thread.
- It minimizes overhead of pt2pt operations since such operations don't have to check a thread-private registration variable and, if necessary, perform thread registration under the cover.
- It allows dynamic creation and destruction of threads throughout a program run while not wasting hardware resources. For instance, if a thread is destroyed in the middle of a program run and calls `shmem_thread_unregister()` prior to that event, the hardware resources which were dedicated to that thread can be reassigned to another thread which calls `shmem_thread_register()` later in the program run.

An error may be returned if the maximum level of concurrency is exceeded, i.e. if more threads are attempting to register than was specified via the `max_num_threads` input parameter to `shmem_init_thread()`. The syntax is as follows:

```
int shmem_thread_register(void)
```

4.4   shmem_thread_unregister()

Any thread that previously called `shmem_thread_register()` must call `shmem_thread_unregister()` before exiting. The thread that called `shmem_init_thread()` does not have to call `shmem_thread_unregister`. The syntax is as follows:

```
int shmem_thread_unregister(void)
```

The following pseudo code illustrates a sample call sequence of a multi-threaded SHMEM program.

```
if (primary) {                      if (non-primary)
shmem_init_thread()                 {
pthread create loop                 shmem_thread_register()
shmem calls                         shmem calls
pthread join loop                   shmem_thread_unregister()
shmem_finalize()                    }
}
```

4.5   shmem_thread_quiet()

This is the thread specific version of the shmem_quiet() function. It allows an individual thread to wait for completion of Puts and non-blocking Gets which it previously issued. There is no requirement on the implementation to only complete operations issued by the calling thread. The syntax is as follows:

```
void shmem_thread_quiet(void)
```

4.6   shmem_thread_fence()

This is the thread specific version of the shmem_fence() function. It allows an individual thread to ensure ordering of Puts and non-blocking Gets which it previously issued. There is no requirement on the implementation to only order operations issued by the calling thread. The syntax is as follows:

```
void shmem_thread_fence(void)
```

4.7   shmem_thread_barrier()

This function performs an efficient local barrier among the threads that have registered themselves by calling shmem_thread_register(). Decisions regarding return type and input/output parameters remain to be made. The syntax is as follows:

```
void shmem_thread_barrier(void)
```

4.8   shmem_thread_is_registered()

This function determines whether a thread can make SHMEM calls. It will return TRUE if the thread has previously called shmem_thread_register() or is the main thread. It will return FALSE otherwise. The syntax is as follows:

```
int shmem_thread_is_registered(void)
```

4.9   Sample Pseudo Code

The following pseudo code illustrates a possible code flow and usage of the new API functions. It is not related to any real world example.

```
#include <stdio.h>
#include <omp.h>
#include <mpp/shmem.h>

int
main (int argc, char *argv[])
{
    int nthreads, /* number of threads */
        tid,      /* thread id */
        rc;       /* return value */

    Initialization phase;

    rc = shmem_init_thread(SHMEM_THREAD_MULTIPLE, 8);

#pragma omp parallel private(tid) /* fork threads whith each having a private tid */
    {
        if (tid != 0)
            shmem_thread_register(); /* additional threads must register */

        shmem_int_get_nb(...); /* all threads transfer data */

        Computation phase by each thread;

        if (tid == 1)
            shmem_thread_quiet(); /* thread 1 waits for own transfer completion */

        Computation phase by each thread;

        if (tid == 0)
            shmem_quiet(); /* wait for transfers of all threads to complete */

        Computation phase by each thread;

        shmem_thread_barrier(); /* synchronize all threads of the rank */

        if (tid == 2)
            shmem_barrier(...); /* one thread participates in a collective */

        if (tid != 0)
            shmem_thread_unregister(); /* additional threads unregister */

    } /* all threads join master thread and terminate */

    shmem_finalize();
}
```

5   Performance Considerations

The original impetus for supporting thread-safe Cray SHMEM came from customer requests, where requests focused on point-to-point operations and on performance. Thus, one goal when implementing the described thread safety extensions
on Cray XE and XC systems is to increase the per process, aggregate issue rate for
Puts, Gets and AMOs. At the time of the publication of this paper, the implementation of the thread safety extensions in Cray SHMEM has not been completed and
we are not able to present performance data at the SHMEM level.

In our software stack, Cray SHMEM is implemented on top of DMAPP, a network library supporting one-sided program models. The majority of the work to support thread safety in a well-performing manner needed to occur in DMAPP and has been completed. DMAPP was modified to use NIC resources effectively in the presence of threads. Specifically, registering a thread with DMAPP allows the thread to use a dedicated NIC resource, thereby eliminating bottlenecks when accessing hardware resources. This approach also allowed us to eliminate the use of a global lock in DMAPP. We carried out preliminary performance experiments at the DMAPP level, comparing the older implementation where a thread did not use a dedicated NIC resource and which used a global lock, with the new, better-performing implementation. Preliminary performance data on XE shows an increase in per-process aggregate issue rate by a factor of 4 to 5 for non-blocking 8 byte Puts using 8 threads per process. More thorough performance analysis will be done at the DMAPP level and, once the work has been completed in Cray SHMEM, at the SHMEM level. We will then use the performance analysis to guide further improvements in our software stack.

6 Future Work

The proposed thread safety extensions are modeled after the MPI standard for thread safety, as it is hoped that by following a well-known and well-defined interface, the proposed extensions will be more readily accepted. The thread-safe SHMEM interface could be expanded beyond the minimum required should this be desired by SHMEM users. Some of the policies imposed on SHMEM applications may be lifted over time. In particular, we plan to work with the community to determine whether and how policies on the use of collective operations in a multi-threaded environment should be loosened over time.

References

1. Message Passing Interface Forum: MPI: A Message-Passing Standard Version 3.0 (2012)
2. OpenSHMEM: OpenSHMEM Specification v1.0 (2012)

Implementing Split-Mode Barriers in OpenSHMEM

Michael A. Raymond

Silicon Graphics International
mraymond@sgi.com

Abstract. Barriers synchronize the state of many processing elements working in parallel. No worker may leave a barrier before all the others have arrived. High performance applications hide latency by keeping a large number of operations in progress asynchronously. Since barriers synchronize all these operations, maximum performance requires that barriers have as little overhead as possible. When some workers arrive at a barrier much later than others, the early arrivers must sit idle waiting for them. Split-mode barriers provide barrier semantics while also allowing the early arrivers to make progress on other tasks. In this paper we describe the process and several challenges in developing split-mode barriers in the OpenSHMEM programming environment.

Keywords: OpenSHMEM, barrier, split-mode.

1   Introduction

Barriers are a common construct in parallel programming environments. They allow multiple processing elements (PEs) to synchronize their progress. When a PE arrives at a barrier it waits for all the other PEs to arrive before they can all leave. Barriers let PEs know that all the others have arrived at a known point in their execution. Barriers are an important part of the OpenSHMEM [1], MPI [2], and UPC [3] environments.

Like other collective operations, the performance of barriers may be critical to application performance. Barriers may involve many PEs operating on different nodes, and so they must be scalable. PEs waiting at a barrier for other PEs to arrive cannot make progress on any other tasks, and thus any time spent in a barrier can be considered overhead.

While several designs for barriers have been proposed in the past to increase scalability while minimizing time and space consumption [4], split-mode barriers address the issue of PEs arriving at different times. When a PE arrives at a synchronization point it signals to the barrier that it has arrived. This sends out a notification to the other PEs. The PE is then free to perform other work. From time to time it checks the status of the barrier to see if every other PE has arrived. When every PE has signaled arrival, the barrier can be considered complete and all PEs may move past the synchronization point. Split-mode barriers were added to MPI as part of version 3.0 [5].

The OpenSHMEM programming environment models symmetric memory across parallel PEs that perform memory puts, gets, and atomic memory operations (AMOs) to it. OpenSHMEM also includes collective operations such as reductions, gather

S. Poole, O. Hernandez, and P. Shamis (Eds.): OpenSHMEM 2014, LNCS 8356, pp. 186–190, 2014.

operations, and synchronous barriers. The OpenSHMEM 1.0 standard does not include split-mode barriers.

This paper describes the process of an experimental addition of split-mode barriers to the SGI implementation of OpenSHMEM. SGI SHMEM ships as part of the SGI MPI product [6] and both make use of the SGI MPT high performance communications middleware. We modified an existing synchronous barrier implementation in SGI SHMEM to operate as a split-mode barrier and then made numerous optimizations to improve performance.

2   Experimental Environment

2.1   Target Benchmark

The experimental environment was largely motivated by a paper by Hoefler, Siebert, and Lumsdaine on the dynamic sparse data exchange problem [7]. They describe a common communication pattern where PEs must periodically exchange data with a sparse and dynamic set of neighbors. Challenges include how to notify a changing set of neighbors that PEs have data for them, and how to efficiently verify that all the data has been exchanged. Hoefler et al. described a variety of implementation possibilities and a microbenchmark for studying just the communication phase of similar applications.

We propose a microbenchmark similar to that done by Hoefler et al. As in theirs, it performs 1000 loops where each PE randomly identifies a sparse set of neighbors, then randomly sends 1 to 1024 bytes of data to them. In its communication routine (see figure 1), the benchmark does a 20-byte `shmem_putmem()` to the identified neighbors to notify them that it has data for them, then starts a split-mode barrier. The PE then loops checking for notification of available incoming data, doing a `shmem_getmem()` to receive the data, and checking for completion of the split-mode barrier. The split-mode barrier lets each PE know that it has received all the incoming notices of data. When the split-mode barrier is complete, a synchronous barrier is performed to let each PE know that all the data has been read from its outgoing buffers and it is now safe to reuse them. We do not claim that this routine is optimal, only that it may represent one possible pattern used by real applications.

This research makes a number of assumptions about how the split-mode barrier interacts with other parts of the program. Since the microbenchmark involves all PEs in the application, the split-mode barrier is also assumed to be application-wide. An alternative approach would allow only designated subsets of the PEs to participate. This implementation also assumes that the split-mode barrier should force all preceding RMAs to complete when `barrier_start()` is called. An alternative approach might delay RMA completion until `barrier_check()` returned success. Intuitively, this alternative better fits the semantics of the barrier and allows more overlapping of work, but we feel that it would also add cost and complexity. We feel that most implementers would put the RMA flush in the `barrier_start()` anyway.

```
communicate(int num, msg_t * msgs)
{
  int done = 0;
  send_notices(num, msgs);
  barrier_start();
  do {
    msg_t msg;
    done = barrier_check();
    while (msg_probe(&msg)) {msg_receive(&msg);}
  } while (!done);
  shmem_barrier_all();
}
```

Fig. 1. Distributed Sparse Data Exchange using OpenSHMEM

2.2   Experimental Setup

All performance experiments were run on an SGI ICE-X cluster. Each cluster node had two 2.70 Ghz Intel IvyBridge sockets with 12 cores each. Each node had 96 GB of memory and a Mellanox ConnectX-3 InfiniBand HCA using a single InfiniBand plane operating at FDR speed. All runs were done with 764 SHMEM PEs split across 32 cluster nodes. Each PE sent data to log(#PEs) = 64 other PEs each iteration of the benchmark.

3   Split-Mode Barrier Design

One of the synchronous barrier implementations used in SGI SHMEM is based on dissemination barriers [4]. Over a series of steps, each PE signals and waits for a signal from a PE twice as far away from itself as in the previous step. There are log(# of PEs) steps. Additional similar code exists to support situations with a non-power-of-2 number of PEs. The SGI implementation uses AMOs on 32-bit integers. The primary benefit is that it only needs a tiny amount of space, log(# of PEs), and can safely handle the arrival of a PE back at the barrier while another PE is still in the process of leaving it.

We initially implemented the benchmark using the MPI 3.0 MPI_Ibarrier() split-mode barrier interface. This provided a control to compare OpenSHMEM implementations against. SGI MPT allows applications to use both MPI and OpenSHMEM safely at the safe time. Excluding application launch and shut down, the benchmark ran in 0.551 seconds.

We copied the SGI SHMEM dissemination barrier and turned it into a split-mode barrier. During the starting call the PE does its first signal operation and then immediately returns. Every later call to check on the barrier's status has the PE check the current step's local variable to see if it has been altered. If not, the PE returns indicating that the barrier is not complete. If it was altered, the PE advances to the next step of the barrier and signals the step's partner PE. When all the steps are completed, the

PE safely reinitializes the barrier and returns indicating that the barrier is complete. This initial OpenSHMEM trial ran in 1.463 seconds.

For the next evolution, we switched the barrier data structure from using 32-bit integers to 64-bit integers. AMOs done over Mellanox InfiniBand HCAs are not coherent with CPU memory operations. To preserve coherency during runs across multiple cluster nodes in SGI SHMEM, all AMOs are done through InfiniBand. This does not protect CPU loads and stores to the same 64-bit word that a 32-bit atomic variable resides in, and so the OpenSHMEM implementation must take extra steps. The end result is that 32-bit AMOs are slower than 64-bit AMOs. By switching to using 64-bit AMOs the run time dropped to 0.663 seconds.

We noticed that in the barrier code, the local PE does not require any result from AMOs to other PEs' memories. That is, for some AMOs like fetch-and-add and compare-and-swap, the AMO returns a value that was in the target PE's memory and the AMO caller uses the value for later computation. For the AMOs used in the barrier implementation, shmem_long_inc() and shmem_long_add(), the AMOs return void. In the SGI SHMEM implementation those interfaces were built upon the same code as AMOs with return values. Those interfaces waited for the return values from the lower code but did not return them to the caller. We modified the SHMEM implementation to allow those two AMOs to proceed asynchronously. This reduced the performance to 0.688 seconds.

Since the split-mode barrier implementation could do several AMOs in succession, we experimented with a modification to the SHMEM library that could keep multiple AMOs going at once. We verified that in the benchmark and the split-mode barrier implementation, the possibility of AMOs completing out of order would not affect correctness. Trials with allowing two and four AMOs at once resulted in 0.678 and 0.671 seconds respectively.

We reasoned that since changes to how AMOs were being used or implemented had stopped showing any further performance improvements, experimentation should be done on not using AMOs. The split-mode barrier code was modified to use only shmem_long_put(). For purposes of safely allowing one barrier synchronization to end while the next was starting, we doubled the size of the data structure involved. Synchronization points iterated between using different halves of the data structure to prevent interfering with each other. While this did slightly increase the amount of space used, it resulted in a drop in time to 0.485 seconds.

Finally, we observed that while the application was looping calling msg_probe() and msg_receive() to read in data, no progress was being made on the split-mode barrier. In the control implementation using MPI_Ibarrier(), SGI MPT's internal progress engine ensured regular updates of the barrier every time that a communication routine was called. Because the experimental spilt-mode barrier existed entirely inside the application, it was not seeing the same benefit. A high quality productization would include complete internal support for split-mode barriers, but for this research project we changed the application to visit the barrier_check() code more often. This resulted in an insignificant drop to 0.484 seconds. This suggests that the benchmark had already been checking barrier progress frequently enough.

Table 1. Summary of Results

Split-Mode Barrier Implementation	Run Time (seconds)
MPI_Ibarrier()	0.551
AMOs on 32-bit integers	1.463
AMOs on 64-bit integers	0.663
Non-blocking AMO	0.688
2 AMOs in progress	0.678
4 AMOs in progress	0.671
Puts to 64-bit integers	0.485
More frequent status checks	0.484

4   Conclusions

We showed that a split-mode barrier using OpenSHMEM primitives can be competitive with a tuned split-mode barrier using message passing. We explored the performance implications of using different operations and data type sizes in OpenSHMEM on an InfiniBand cluster. Future research will explore basing the barrier implementation on designs other than dissemination barriers, and on benchmarking their performance on other kinds of computing platforms, such as SGI's UV CC-NUMA machines. As the OpenSHMEM community explores releasing a revision to its standard, split-mode barriers have been shown to be feasible and useful to OpenSHMEM applications.

Acknowledgements. We thank SGI engineers James Custer and John Baron for their critiques of this paper.

References

1. OpenSHMEM, http://www.openshmem.org/
2. MPI Forum: MPI: A Message Passing Interface. In: Proceedings of Supercomputing (1993)
3. UPC Consortium, UPC Language Specifications, v1.2. Lawrence Berkeley National Lab, Tech. Rep. LBNL-59208 (2005)
4. Hengsen, D., Finkel, R., Manber, U.: Two Algorithms for Barrier Synchronization. International Journal of Parallel Programming 17, 1–17 (1988)
5. Message Passing Interface Forum: MPI: A Message-Passing Interface Standard Version 3.0 (2012)
6. SGI MPI, http://www.sgi.com/products/software/sps.html
7. Hoefler, T., Siebert, C., Lumsdaine, A.: Scalable Communication Protocols for Dynamic Sparse Data Exchange. In: Principles and Practice of Parallel Programming. ACM (2010)

Author Index